Philosophy and Archaic Experience

Duquesne Studies — Philosophical Series
Volume Thirty-Eight

ANDRÉ SCHUWER AND JOHN SALLIS, *editors*

Philosophy and Archaic Experience

Essays in Honor of Edward G. Ballard

Edited by

JOHN SALLIS

DUQUESNE UNIVERSITY PRESS
Pittsburgh

Published by Duquesne University Press, 600 Forbes Avenue, Pittsburgh, PA 15219.

Distributed by Humanities Press, Atlantic Highlands, New Jersey 07716.

First Edition

Library of Congress Cataloging in Publication Data
Main entry under title:

Philosophy and archaic experience.

   Bibliography: p.
   1. Ballard, Edward G.–Addresses, essays, lectures. 2. Experience–Addresses, essays, lectures. 3. Philosophy–Addresses, essays, lectures. I. Sallis, John, 1938-
B945.B254P47   191   81-17254
ISBN 0-8207-0152-1   AACR2

Contents

Introduction   vii

I. ARCHAIC EXPERIENCE IN PHILOSOPHY: HISTORICAL REFLECTIONS

1. DAVID FARRELL KRELL. *Descensional Reflection*   3
2. JOHN SALLIS. *Metaphysical Security and the Play of
   Imagination: An Archaic Reflection.*   13
3. ANDREW J. RECK. *Hodgson's Metaphysic of Experience.*   29

II. ARCHAIC EXPERIENCE IN MYTH AND ART: PHILOSOPHICAL SUPPLEMENTS

4. CHARLES E. SCOTT. *Freedom with Darkness and Light:
   A Study of a Myth.*   51
5. CAROL A. KATES. *Myth and Art: The Authentic Image.*   64
6. MICHAEL E. ZIMMERMAN. *Archetypes, Heroism and the
   Work of Art.*   81

III. ARCHAIC DIMENSIONS OF LIFE: PHILOSOPHICAL INTERPRETATIONS

7. EDWARD H.HENDERSON. *Archaic Experience and Philosophical
   Anthropology: The "Enuma Elish" and the Exodus.*   101
8. C. P. BIGGER & C. A. H. BIGGER. *Recognition in
   Biological Systems.*   122
9. HAROLD ALDERMAN. *The Text of Memory.*   150
10. LESTER EMBREE. *Phenomenological Speculations on
    Lived Marriageability.*   163

IV. ARCHAIC EXPERIENCE IN PHENOMENOLOGY: PHILOSOPHICAL ARCHAEOLOGY

11. JOHN SCANLON. *Empirio-Criticism, Descriptive Psychology, and the Experiential World.* 185
12. BERNARD P. DAUENHAUER. *Mere Things.* 199
13. ALEXANDER VON SCHOENBORN. *Heidegger's Articulation of Falling.* 210

BIBLIOGRAPHY OF EDWARD G. BALLARD 227
ABOUT THE CONTRIBUTORS 233

Introduction

Philosophy as the interpretation of archaic experience, then, is the art which seeks, in the light of a principle, to disengage the intelligible aspects of the compulsion which has precipitated the more radical transitions in human experience.

Edward G. Ballard
Philosophy at the Crossroads

Ballard's conception of philosophy as the interpretation of archaic experience was first broached in a paper published in 1958 under the title "The Subject-Matter of Philosophy."[1] This paper marks a beginning, not only in the sense of outlining a retrospective reading of much of Ballard's subsequent work, but also in the sense of delimiting a privileged *arche*, a kind of beginning to which one can most appropriately refer the statement: "To be advanced in philosophy is to be at this beginning, or near to it."[2] This beginning—archaic experience—constitutes the subject matter of philosophy.

The paper opens, characteristically, by posing a reflexive involvement:

> The expressions used so often to define philosophy,—e.g. philosophy is the study of reality; it is the attempt to understand the whole of our experience; it is the daughter of religion and the mother of the sciences—require a philosophy in order to interpret them sensibly (5).

Philosophy is and remains a problem for itself; it does not come to rest in a "complete system" capable of terminating all philosophical questioning (and especially self-questioning), either by supplying definitive answers or by banishing such questions to the nether world of the irrelevant or meaningless. To such reflexive involvement, to the continuous renewal that it demands of philosophy and of the philosopher,

---

1. In *Tulane Studies in Philosophy* 7 (1958) 5–26. Hereafter page-references to this paper will be cited in parentheses in the text.
2. *Philosophy at the Crossroads* (Baton Rouge: Louisiana State University Press, 1971), p. 6.

Ballard has forcefully testified in word: "The person who believes that he possesses the definitive solution to a philosophic problem is, doubtless, no less in error than the person who believes philosophic problems to be altogether irrelevant to his concern" (5 n.). Ballard has testified to it also in deed, quietly perhaps but no less forcefully—in those deeds accomplished precisely through the artful use of words: teaching and writing.

The paper of 1958 holds back from a radical engagement in the reflexivity it so succinctly poses. Or rather, it operates under a reduction, a deliberate deferral, in order that another definition—that of philosophy as the interpretation of archaic experience—might be inscribed between the dashes, displacing those illustrative definitions cited in the opening sentence. It is a matter of delimiting "the most nearly primary datum" (6) of philosophical interpretation, of bringing into focus the experience that, archaic in a temporal sense, provided the content for that history of interpretation that constitutes the Western philosophical tradition.

Of course that history is not merely a piling up of interpretations, one upon another; it is not merely reiteration, interpretation of interpretation, progressively more distant from a progressively more buried experience. On the contrary, philosophical interpretation holds the possibility not only of sedimentation but also of reactivation and deepening: "An interpretation may in turn render a more sophisticated experience possible which *might* then become the subject matter of finer and more fertile interpretation—and so on" (6).

But the paper holds back also from the full problem of that tradition—that is, it reduces history, its own history, the history through which one must pass on the way back to the beginning, the history whose opaqueness would eventually have to become a problem. It reduces history in order to delimit, almost immediately, the beginning, the archaic experience that *first* provided philosophy with a content to be interpreted, or rather, the experience that first called forth philosophical interpretation, the matter, as it were, from which philosophy was born. And yet the historical distance, though reduced, is unmistakably marked within Ballard's text—marked not *as* historical distance but in a way more appropriate to the Greek beginning itself. In the concluding summary it is declared that the "paper is intended to provide a likely story concerning the philosophic datum" (24)—that is, a *mythos* in the tradition of the *Timaeus*.

The likely story told is one of *psyche* and *thymos*, the water-soul and the blood-soul, or—reading back from the philosophical interpretations—intuitive reason and conscious thinking. It is a story of dual-

3. *Socratic Ignorance: An Essay on Platonic Self-Knowledge* (The Hague: Nijhoff, 1965).

natured man involved in the toils of fate and dependent upon them—a philosphical myth of the original myth in which archaic experience was expressed, if not constituted. And it is a story also of the philosophical supplement to the original myth—for example, the Platonic transformation of the ritual pattern embedded in archaic experience into a way of access not to the gods but to the intelligible *eide*. It is a philosophical myth of myth and philosophy.

Near the end of the paper the distance from the Greek beginning appears on the horizon, in the guise of the polysemy and the opaqueness of myth:

> For if the material of philosophy is to be recognized in myth and if myth is regarded as a likely story having indefinitely many interpretations, then the philosopher is apt to accept the obligation of remaining in touch with his origins and to preserve a healthful attitude of Socratic ignorance in his dealings with this oracular material (26).

Here especially are traced, for a retrospective reading, the principal themes of Ballard's later interpretation of Plato—the themes of self-knowledge, myth, ignorance—that would serve to organize *Socratic Ignorance*.[3] Beyond that, it was principally a matter of undoing the reduction of history, of taking up the conception of tradition that was from the outset integral to the conception of philosophy as the interpretation of archaic experience, of rigorously articulating it by means of the concept of crisis or radical transition. And the reflexivity too was to be broached again and again—perhaps nowhere more forcefully than in that epigram that Ballard took from Heidegger and placed at the beginning of *Philosophy at the Crossroads:* "Every moment the crossroad moves along with us."

One of Ballard's inestimable gifts to his friends and students has been to make us attentive to this movement, the incessant movement of the crossroad. Thereby he has exemplified for us, disclosed in deed, that openness of questioning that is so utterly essential to genuine teaching and to every original philosophical *agon*—that openness perhaps best expressed at the end of the 1958 paper:

> Evidently the primary obligation of the philosopher is to respect his subject-matter. It is not to take sides in contemporary controversy and defeat his opponent, nor to construct an elenchus-proof system within which he may take refuge. Rather he expresses respect for this subject-matter and enters effectively into the philosophic *agon* by keeping open the ways of interpretation and philosophic conversation and by this means continually exploring and illuminating the sources of conflict and resolution, of blindness and insight (26).

J.S.

PART ONE

Archaic Experience in Philosophy:
Historical Reflections

David Farrell Krell

1/*Descensional Reflection*

*Den Weg des Wassers, der immer nach unten geht, muss man wohl gehen,
wenn man den Schatz, das kostbare Erbe des Vaters, wieder heben will.*

C. G. Jung

Is anything more characteristic of the philosopher than his desire to go
up? To extend to the stars that arc man's upwardtending spine
describes? To visit the outermost spheres where gods and goddesses
dwell, dining on rarest essences, far from everything fallen, from
muck, offal, the corpse, all waste and ruin? Of Aristophanes' heroes
one flies to heaven on a dungbeetle while the other drifts among clouds
in a think tank. The second has proved the more emulable model.

Only the images of ascension into light in the *Phaedo, Republic* and
Timaeus have taken root in Occidental consciousness, so that those who
were compelled to think in a new way could liberate their thought
only by overturning Platonism. That inversion became Nietzsche's
passion; it consumed the part of his life that said no. The power of that
"no" can be measured only against the full weight of an entire tradition.
For whether in the *Enneiads*, the *Confessions* and the *Summa Theologiae*,
where humans participate in the divine comedy, or in the *Meditations*,
the *Theodicy* and the *Philosophy of Spirit*, where the divine comedy is
reproduced in more sober, secular guise, the persistent trajectory of
reflection is

inasmuch as the ground of things is not to be felt by the feet or in the
bowels, but within the head, modeled on the circles of the Same,
spinning crystalline threads of imperishable Ideas. In all cases the

essential strategy is to purify spirit of its mortal dross, to wean the soul from its corporeal integument,

which remains an unfortunate and wholly unaccountable accident, a vast practical joke, a matter for Ishmael's "desperado philosophy,"

catharsis by mortification, so that *mors* itself is drawn into the circle of reflection and hence circumscribed, circumvented: got around. For Hegel, death is precisely what the life of spirit withstands (*erträgt*): life preserves itself (*erhält sich*) in death. Philosophy is thus the enchantment (*Zauberkraft*) to charm the monstrous power of the negative, to cancel and surpass, to go up and up. Ascensional reflection is a matter of dying ahead of time, moving the hands of the clock ahead, beating the system.

In his book on the problem of truth in Nietzsche's philosophy, Jean Granier argues that the various senses of "truth" in Nietzsche's thought can be arranged in a sort of hierarchical structure, reflecting a dialectical progression from "lower" to "higher" levels. The characterization is helpful because it is exactly contrary to the Nietzschean effort: we do not ascend through the sundry senses of "truth" in Nietzsche's thought; we go down and under rather than up and over. The fierce resistance to ascensional reflection, the will to overcome two thousand years of centrifugal force—ascensional inertia—is felt everywhere. Zarathustra's high-flying eagle of good courage is bound by blood to the serpentine wisdom of the earth.

From beginning to end, Nietzsche's reflection is *descensional*, its trajectory decisively earthbound. His thought describes an epochal turn in the history of Western thought from Hegel to Heidegger, which I define provisionally as

the descent of reflection from thought on the Absolute to thought on the Absurd;

the descent of reflection from the death of God to the death of human beings—

the descent of reflection in both cases implying the demise of metaphysical *logos*.

No flight instructor is available for counsel in matters of descensional reflection. Daedalus taught the ways of ascent long ago, but because Icarus alone has made the return voyage—in a way peculiar to him—we lack instruction.

However, because the inversion of Platonism is basic to Nietzsche's descensional reflection, I look for clues in "the ladder of love" (*Symposium*, 210a ff.) and in "the divided line" (*Republic*, 509d ff.). Regarding the former I am satisfied to cite William Butler Yeats's "The Circus Animals' Desertion":

> Now that my ladder's gone,
> I must lie down where all the ladders start,
> In the foul rag-and-bone shop of the heart.

But let me introduce a word about ascent/descent up/down the divided line.

Socrates begins by pointing to simple reflections of the visible, the water-soaked strand of *eikasia*, and advances through *pistis*, true belief regarding plants, animals and human artifacts, through *dianoia*, corresponding to the geometer's imaging of the visible, clambering upward to a conclusion, to *noesis*, a thinking that makes use of no images but levitates over a presuppositionless source among systems of Ideas, hence, an ascent from *eidola* to *eide*, from idols to ideas,

although

he prefaces all this with the *image* of the sun and concludes it with the *image* (not to say idol) of the Cave, so that, at least in the philosopher's education, any movement *up* the line is rooted in a concealed *downward* movement toward the visible, rooted in a

reflection under way to *eikasia*, the images of the seastrand or lakeshore, the source of all eidoletic *eide*. To invert Platonism is to negotiate with Plato—to negotiate his texts without traditional supports.

But now to begin the search for the telling image for descensional reflection in our time.

Nectar-laden Zarathustra quits his mountain cave and goes down to humans. He sees a tightrope-walker plunge to the earth. Zarathustra learns that every moment in transition across the lifeline, across the boundary, is decisive for eternity, inasmuch as any fool can surpass another mortal and precipitate his death. Zarathustra's first task is to inter his predecessor; his first lesson is that to advance is to go down.

Not up.

Also begann Zarathustras Untergang.

Nietzsche himself descends even further after composing *Thus Spoke Zarathustra* and so fulfilling the yes-saying portion of his life. Yet in the genealogical critique of metaphysics and morals (*Beyond Good and Evil, Toward a Genealogy of Morals*) Nietzsche returns to his earliest haunts, grubbing beneath encrusted layers of illusion and life-negation in the

Occidental tradition, rooting underground, beneath all its sacred but no longer secure monuments, subverting old ruins. Once again he dons the baleful mask of suspicion; once again he performs the grimly gleeful spadework of Yorick's uncoverers. . . .

While still an undergraduate, I read in utter fascination these two books, which are the keystone of Nietzsche's genealogical critique. *This* dialectician seemed to undercut everything others had taught and then to advance a step and with a laugh undercut himself. An image formed—the first image of Nietzsche's thinking to possess me. It was not yet a subterranean image, but descensional nonetheless:

the reaper of truths cuts broad swaths in the tall grass of cant and sophistry, exposing the bitterest truths in their lairs.

But what kind of "truths" could these be? Upon what "grounds" were they founded? The image recoiled upon itself:

the scythe swings round, slicing into the reaper's ankles. The blow leaves him standing in the shadow of his own feet. He laughs. Again the scythe describes its arc, returns again.

Could a person keep it up eternally? The image became a thought or question. I tried to avoid it. There should have been easier ways to go down, but no other image came to my rescue. I had not yet met the mole.

But it is not beside himself, in pieces, that Nietzsche descends, so long as his thinking endures, but down into him/it/self, far below the eyebrow-line of the *cogito*, so that these bottomless truths, as he says, "are *my* truths." Because the descent excavates beneath the *cogito*, it is merely quaint to accuse genealogical critique of relativism or subjectivism or even Epimenidean contradiction. (Empedoclean would be another matter.) Nietzsche's thinking does not *speak* against itself but *acts* against itself: not contradiction but contraction is its *modus operandi*: recoil.

Contradiction, apparent groundlessness, is only genealogy's mask. Nietzsche needs it when he writes, as the tragedian needs it when he plays. Especially if he would play Oedipus at Colonus but still keep his eyes. Section 278 of *Beyond Good and Evil* pursues the excavation:

> Wanderer, who are you? I see you going your way without scorn or love and with relentless eyes. . . .What are you looking for down there? Rest yourself up here: this place is hospitable to everyone.
> Rest and recuperate!
> What would serve your recuperation? Only name it: what I have I offer you!
>
> "For my recuperation? Recuperation? O you curious fellow, what are you saying there . . .? But give me, I beg you. . . ."

What? What? Speak up, say it.

"One more mask! A second mask!"

What *is* Nietzsche looking for down there? *"Glissez, mortels, n'appuyez pas,"* warns Jean-Paul's grandmother. "Gently, mortals, be discreet." Still, we want to know: why is descensional reflection today a requirement? May we not let the dead bury their dead and proceed to equip ourselves with new values—transvalued ones, of course—and new beliefs founded on the bases of agnosticism and weariness? Or may we not proclaim again the old values, letting fanaticism cover a multitude of doubts? Why all that digging by folk who ought otherwise to be concerned with their health?

Act V, Scene 1: *A Churchyard. Enter two clowns with spades, etc.*

1st Clown:—Come, my spade. There is no ancient gentlemen but gardeners, ditchers, and grave-makers: they hold up Adam's profession.

The very discretion Mamie counsels—mortal discretion—demands descensional reflection, a thinking that goes underground, beneath Leibnizian sufficiency and Cartesian clarity, below the surface upon which the horizon of the true and false once gathered. That fixed horizontal once gave us the latitude to collect and divide pure essences. We could scramble up divided lines and love-ladders and pull them up behind us, as Merleau-Ponty says, and that was a little bit like flying. Ours was the philosophy of overflight. Now Sartre, his grandmother and all his friends insist that in spite of our best will and piety we can no longer fly so high.

Whose fault is that? It is not Herr Nietzsche who plucks from the seabed the sponge that obliterates the horizon. All that is history by the time he writes, the history of nihilism, into which Nietzsche is plunged along with everyone else. The difference is that Nietzsche *thinks* about what has happened and is happening, about the unraveling of our destiny, and in that way Nietzsche upholds Adam's profession. For it is *Moira*, the fateful allotment, that requires the downgoing, nothing less. If my saying so seems overweening, clownish, it is because the clown prefers mortal foolishness to saintly *ressentiment*, because he elects to provide what criticism calls "comic relief" at the heart of tragedy.

But clowns do make room for Christian suicides: the gravediggers offer to Ophelia what was theirs and they come up. They ascend. Is Nietzsche's thinking purely descensional? Does he never come up? Nietzsche does ascend—at least he says he will do so—if only behind another mask. He calls that mask *die ewige Wiederkunft des Gleichen.* He describes the mask as an experimental thought and touchstone. At one point he labels it a consolation, as though there might be some comfort in it:

> A certain emperor always kept in mind the transiency of all things, in order not to take them too much to heart and to remain tranquil in their midst. To me, on the contrary, everything seems much too valuable to be allowed to be so fleeting: I seek an eternity for everything. Ought one to pour the most costly unguents and wines into the sea? My consolation is that everything that was is eternal: the sea spews it forth again. (*Der Wille zur Macht*, no. 1065.)

Indeed, Zarathustra's animals try to transform the thought of eternal recurrence into an image that traditionally serves as the surest comfort of metaphysicians: the circle, *ouroboros*, the friendly snake coiling itself about the neck of the eagle, itself circling through cycles of the same among the spheres of eternity. Is the thought of eternal recurrence an image fashioned to keep a drowsy emperor awake? Is it, as so astute a critic as Gaston Bachelard insists, redemptive and ascensional—which is to say, decadent?

The eternal recurrence of the same is Nietzsche's most difficult thought because it compels Zarathustra's pity for humankind, his nausea, to the surface. Yet, as the heaviest burden, it is the *Probierstein* of magnificent health because it requires that Zarathustra *swallow* what wants to come up.

How we might ascend to overman we really do not know. Gilles Deleuze is right when he says that we have no inkling of what human beings, stripped of rancor, would be like; we do not know how they can say yes without braying like an ass. To alter the image: we receive no instruction from the tradition on how to prune our old wings so that Eros' flood might nurture new growth. We have reason to fear that in any case our new wings would not support the burden, that they would serve us as the dodo's did it.

But Nietzsche says that we do not really have to fly in order to ascend. A few bars of curious birdsong in *The Dawn* (1886 Preface) provide the image that descensional reflection has been looking for:

> In this book you will find a "subterrestrial" creature at work, burrowing, digging, subverting. You will see him—presupposing that you have eyes for such work in the depths—see how slowly, reflectively, with what gentle implacability he moves forward. He scarcely betrays the destitution that prolonged lack of light and air imply; one could even say that he is satisfied in his obscure toil. Does it not seem as though some sort of belief guides him, some sort of consolation grants him recompense? As though he

perhaps wants to have his own long obscurity, his unintelligibility, his concealment and riddlesomeness, because he also knows what he *will* have: his own morning, his own redemption, his own *dawn*? . . . Oh, yes, he will turn back: do not ask him what he wants to do down there; he will tell you himself soon enough, this seeming Trophonios, this subterranean one, as soon as he has "become man" again. For one forgets silence altogether when one has been, like him, such a long time a mole, such a long time alone.

When Nietzsche's thinking ascends to the eternal recurrence of the same, it ascends *to the surface of the earth*. There it reaffirms its incarnation. Earth is as high as it will go. To mountains perhaps, some 6,000 feet beyond humanity and time, but no more, because moles cannot survive beyond 2,000 meters of altitude. To mountain caves, then, caves the thinker himself digs—piteously if we have not outgrown pity, alone if we cannot quit the sunlight and accompany him on the descent, relentlessly whatever we may or may not do.

These ups and downs, contours of earth, make out the search for the image, the water-soaked, incarnate *eidolon*: descensional reflection is metaphorics. With one eye on its own descent

descensional reflection is topography, its page a physical map, its pen the taupe-au-graph.

One final image. Nietzsche invokes "this seeming Trophonios." Apollo had granted the mortal Trophonios the finest gift that immortals can bestow once life has jerked into motion: the gift of death without pain. All mortals who desire an image of their fate come now to Trophonios' cave at Lebadeia. The cult practice is called

downgoing or descent. Two boys called *hermai* (after Hermes Psychopomos, the god of speech and interpretation, who leads souls to the underworld) bathe the body of the initiate as though he were still a

newborn babe or already a corpse. Then he is led to two springs, one
called Lethe, the other Mnemosyne. He drinks the waters of the first to
purge himself of all illusions, those of the second to enable him to
gather and preserve whatever is revealed during his descent. Pausanias
offers the following account:

> He looks at the statue they say Daedalus made . . . and then goes
> to the oracle. . . . The oracle is on the mountainside above the
> sacred wood. It is surrounded by a circular platform. . . . Inside
> the circle is a chasm in the earth. . . . There is no way down, but
> when a man is going to Trophonios they bring him a light, narrow
> ladder. . . . The man going down lies on the ground with hon-
> eycakes in his hands and pushes his feet into the opening. . . . The
> rest of his body is immediately dragged in . . . as though some very
> deep and swift river were catching him in its current and sucking
> him down. . . . People are not always taught the future in the
> same way: one man hears, another also sees. Those who go down
> return feet first through the same mouth. . . . When a man comes
> up from Trophonios the priests . . . sit him on the throne of
> Mnemosyne in order to learn from him what he saw and discov-
> ered. After they have heard it they turn him over to his friends,
> who pick him up and carry him to the house of the Good Daimon
> and Good Fortune. He is still struck with terror and hardly knows
> himself or those around him. Later his wits return unimpaired.
> To be specific, he can laugh again (*Guide to Greece*, IX, 39.)

Golden, superhuman laughter is the second divine gift, when life-
in-death, death-in-life, is the first. Such is the legacy of what Nietzsche
calls the death of God:

> the failure of dogmatic *logos*,
> collapse of the metaphysical project,
> and the emergence of mortal man.

Yet if overman—which says the same as mortal man—is to emerge at
all, it must be by virtue of a thinking sustained by anxiety, anxiety in the
face of death without resurrection. One of Nietzsche's students reflects
on the paradox of *over*man, whose task is to go *under*, and writes:

> Thinking does not overcome metaphysics by climbing still higher,
> surmounting it, transcending it somehow or other; thinking
> overcomes metaphysics by climbing back down into the nearness
> of the nearest. The descent, particularly where man has strayed
> into subjectivity, is more arduous and more dangerous than the
> ascent. The descent leads to the poverty of the ek-sistence of *homo
> humanus*.

A Personal Note:

Dear Ed,
  Not long after we first met, you grasped me by the lapels of my coat and threw me over your back onto the floor. No philosopher had ever done that to me before. They had moved me, it is true, but most often by remote control. They never threw me by gripping my body along with my mind.
  Merleau-Ponty speaks of the painter "carrying his body with him" whenever he paints. The judoka carries nothing. He is a gliding vector of force, a momentary fulcrum, a particular poise, "eye of the moon, soul of the lake," as my Korean instructor used to say. He is rest and motion, receptivity and perception, passivity and action, delay and decision. And his is a maieutic art.
  What I recall best from our judo sessions is the concealed strength beneath your gentleness. "The gentle art" demands such strength and you have it, I remember well, in your chest. Horse-lovers appreciate "depth through the heart." I hope you will not mind if I apply the epithet to you.
  Some readers of this Festschrift *may find it odd that I celebrate your chest and not–at least not yet–your mind. But those who know you best will recognize depth through the heart in your thought of "archaic experience." In the Introduction to* Philosophy at the Crossroads *(pp. 10–11) you speak of* thymos, *seat of both thought and feeling, located within a man's "lights" —as we used to call the lungs —breath, and blood. "Even as late as Aristotle," you say, "it was believed that conscious thinking was a function of the heart." Perhaps that conviction survives. Perhaps it may restore some lifeblood to our anemic Occidental* psyche, *which needs strength for the fateful, ever accompanying crossroads.*
  Thymos: *active thought, exercising all the ingenuity it can muster.*
  Psyche: *receptivity to whatever inspires, whatever is on the wind.*
  Fatum: *crossing boundaries that are flexible yet somehow ultimately fixed.*
  My own meager essay, which I began to write a decade ago, wants to invoke all of these. It senses the boundary-crossing as something significant, inevitable, irreversible, already accomplished in Western history yet hardly known and not at all accounted for. The language of my essay is all psyche, *in the undignified form of enthusiasm, struggling to find its way back down to* thymos, *to the lake, the way of the water. Forgive its excesses, imprecisions, vertigo, its inability to focus, and the air of self-assurance that tries to conceal all that. But now is a fitting occasion for me to ask myself what it is I have been doing these ten years since you last laid a hand on me and gave me to think on the descent.*
  I salute you and send warm greetings on your seventieth birthday!

Bibliographic References

Ballard, E. G., "On Ritual and Persuasion in Plato," in *Southern Journal of Philosophy*, Summer 1964, pp. 49 ff.
———, *Philosophy at the Crossroads* (Baton Rouge: Louisiana State University Press, 1971).
Cixous, Hélène, *Neutre* (Paris: Grasset, 1972).
Deleuze, Gilles, *Nietzsche et la philosophie* (Paris: PUF, 1967).
Granier, Jean, *Le problème de la Vérité dans la philosophie de Nietzsche* (Paris: Seuil, 1966).
Heidegger, Martin, *Nietzsche*, 2 vols. (Pfullingen: Neske, 1961).

———, *Basic Writings* (New York: Harper & Row, 1977).

Jung, C.G., *Von den Wurzeln des Bewusstseins* (Zurich: Rascher, 1954).

Merleau-Ponty, M., *Le visible et l'invisible* (Paris: Gallimard, 1964).

Nietzsche, F., *Werke in drei Bänden* (Munich: Hanser, 1954).

Sallis, John, "Tunnelings" (in manuscript, 1979).

Sartre, Jean-Paul, *Les mots* (Paris: Gallimard, 1964).

Shakespeare, W., *Hamlet*, V, 1.

Sophocles, *Oedipus at Colonus*.

Yeats, W.B., *Collected Poems* (New York: Macmillan, 1956).

John Sallis

2/Metaphysical Security and the Play of Imagination: An Archaic Reflection

Philosophy, then, is the interpretation of archaic experience

Edward G. Ballard,
Philosophy at the Crossroads

Gesture

Let me open with a gesture: Imagination transgresses nature, sunders its simplicity, installs difference.

This gesture is traditional. We can recover it through, for instance, the words of Rousseau. In *Emile* he writes: "It is imagination which extends for us the bounds of the possible . . ."—extends them boundlessly, one may add, since, by Rousseau's testimony, "the imaginary world is infinite."[1] The difference thus installed between the real and the imaginary is, however, no simple infinity but rather a radical indetermination, for the imaginary is no mere reproduction of securely bounded reality in a series of variations held safely beyond the boundary of the real; on the contrary, the imaginary flows back into the real, dividing it indefinitely from within.

Let me read further: "It is imagination which extends for us the bounds of the possible, whether for good or ill. . . ."

How for ill? Let me read still further, to the end of the sentence: "It is imagination which extends for us the bounds of the possible, whether for good or ill, and therefore stimulates and feeds desires by the hope of satisfying them." We are promptly warned that such hope is ill-founded and thus destined to produce only misery. Imagination kindles the passions, displaces man from innocence, casting him, in-

---

An earlier version of this paper was presented to the American Catholic Philosophical Association meeting in 1978. Some portions also appear in the author's book The Gathering of Reason *(Athens: Ohio University Press, 1980).*

1. *Oeuvres Complètes* (Paris: Bibl. de la Pléiade), IV, pp. 304 ff.; English translation by Barbara Foxley (London, 1974), pp. 44 ff.

stead, into that difference from which arise, in Rousseau's words, "all the sufferings which make us truly wretched."[2]

How for good? By the way in which imagination lends charm to nature so as, in turn, to warm our hearts.

Rousseau's words:

> It is fancy that adorns real objects; and if imagination does not lend its charm to that which strikes us, our barren pleasure is confined to the merely organic, while the heart remains cold.

Rousseau's example:

> In spring the country is almost bare; the trees give no shade, the grass has hardly begun to grow, yet the heart is touched by the sight. In beholding thus the rebirth of nature, one feels himself restored to life; the image of pleasure surrounds us. Those companions of pleasure, those sweet tears ever ready to accompany a delightful sentiment, tremble on our eyelids. . . . And why is this? Because imagination adds to the sight of spring the image of the seasons which are yet to come; to the tender shoot perceived by the eye, it adds flowers, the fruit, the shade, and sometimes the mysteries they may conceal. It blends successive stages into one moment, and views objects, not so much as they will be, but as it desires them to be.[3]

Rousseau could hardly be more explicit: This is the moment of the beautiful. Imagination extends our gaze beyond the immediately visible (the sparse traces of spring)—beyond through the stages to come (flower, fruit, shade), and, gathering these into one moment, it lets the ideal shine forth in and through the visible. In that moment unity is announced and ecstasy is born.

On both sides imagination is ecstatic: It transports us beyond ourselves, displaces us from the simple feeling of self in and through sensations, from what Rousseau could have termed the sensible *cogito*.[4] Installing difference, imagination disrupts simple presence to self, exposes us to the bonds of desire, delivers us over to the ecstasy of passion. And on the side of the beautiful, imagination, opening us to perfection, carries us beyond the merely visible, beyond what is sensi-

---

2. Pléiade, 305 (Engl. trans., 45). Rousseau is explicit regarding the link between imagination and the passions: "it is only at the flame of imagination that the passions are kindled" (Pléiade, 384; Engl. trans., 100).

3. Pléiade, 418 (Engl. trans., 122).

4. As outlined in the text (Pléiade, 570; Engl. trans., 232), in which the following sentences are to be found: "I exist and I have senses through which I am affected. . . . My sensations take place in myself, for they make me feel [*sentir*] my existence. . . ."

bly present—carries us beyond in that ecstasy to which the tradition has given the name love.[5]

This is, then, my opening gesture: the ecstasy of imagination, announcing unity as it installs difference, binding us to passion and love. Or again: one moment in which difference is inscribed, another in which the differentiated sides are connected as visible fragment and gathering one, as image and original. Both moments of the gesture trace out in different ways the same circle—the circle between image and original. The first traces it out in the manner of a differentiation; the second in the manner of a gathering. Imagination gives birth to the ecstasy of collection and division.

Though I have borrowed this gesture from Rousseau, the schema that it traces out is one that has been repeated again and again in the tradition; I could have recovered it, perhaps almost as readily, in certain texts of Plato, of Kant, or of Schelling. And my intention is in a sense just to repeat it again—not, however, in the way it has again and again been repeated in the tradition, but rather in a different space, a space whose axes have been radically displaced—so radically displaced that they remain, at best, only barely legible. Within this space the projection of the gesture onto the axes of morality, psychology, and aesthetics, projections with which Rousseau and even Kant could finally let matters rest securely—these projections now get indefinitely postponed, for the origin-point itself from which the axes would radiate has been displaced indefinitely. This is the space of what some have called the end of metaphysics, the space of nihilism. I want, then, to repeat the traditional gesture, to trace out its schema, within the space of a questioning that seeks to bring into question the deepest stratum of our metaphysical heritage, that seeks to dislodge our firmest securities. Among those securities there is one on which I especially want to focus: the distinction between the intelligible (to noeton) and the sensible (to aistheton). For this distinction may well be regarded the firmest of metaphysical securities, founding, as it does, the entire edifice of metaphysics as such—if I may for the moment make use of a classical metaphor which it is precisely my intention to disrupt at its source. Especially remarkable is the ease with which the opening gesture can be repeated within the framework of this distinction, as though it had belonged to it from the beginning. In a sense it has. We

5. In Book 5 of *Emile*, Rousseau presents the entire classical schema:

"There is no true love without ecstasy [*enthousiasme*] and no ecstasy without an object of perfection, real or chimerical, but always existent in imagination. . . . In love everything is only illusion, I grant; but what is real are the feelings which it awakens in us for true beauty which it makes us love. That beauty is not in the object one loves; it is the work of our delusion" (Pléiade, 743; Engl. trans., 354).

have only to recall the great myth of the *Phaedrus*: difference opened up in the fall from the grand procession of the gods around the heavens; mortals delivered over to desire, passion, the body, that is, sensibility as such in distinction from the intelligibility of those beings on which the gods feast their eyes when at the top of the heavens they celebrate their banquet; mortals, nevertheless, extended the hope of unity, granted the ecstasy of love. Yielding for the moment to this great founding myth, letting the opening gesture fall within its framework, almost everything becomes as clear as one could wish. The difference installed is that between intelligible and sensible; for ill, because of the bonds of desire and passion that bind us to the sensible; for good, because the ecstasy of love holds us still in sight of the intelligible. At most, we wonder whether imagination ought to be entrusted with this opening, whether it could in any sense be so entrusted—even though that myth within which we have just repeated the opening gesture would, admittedly, be difficult to separate from the play of imagination. One is tempted to suppose that we need only to divest the distinction of that garb with which it is clothed by myth and imagination, that we need only to repeat the gesture within a space removed from the play of imagination, to secure it within the space of the *pure* distinction between intelligible and sensible. But is such security possible?

Occlusion

The distinction between intelligible and sensible is constitutively linked neither to reflection nor to history. For this distinction is already in force in the very event of speech, which both reflection and history presuppose; it is opened once and for all in that moment when speech first transgressed the limits of sense, a moment in principle irretrievable, an absolute past. Such is the radicalness with which we are bound to the distinction. We are not given the choice of relinquishing it—not even in silence, which, always coming too late, is nourished precisely by the possibility of speech.

One might, correspondingly, attempt to isolate from history a *reflection on* this prehistorical distinction—or rather, one might be tempted, did not the attempt so quickly betray itself. For reflection is inextricably bound to expression and thereby to history: From the moment that one *expresses* the distinction, one has already broached a relation to the history in which are entangled the language and conceptuality that such expression cannot help but invoke. To express the distinction precisely *as* a distinction between intelligible and sensible is already to place the reflection within the history of metaphysics. It is to resume that history—necessarily, since we have no other choice except that silence of nonreflection which would deliver us over to a more inexorable necessity. We *must* resume that history. But can we?

Any simple resumption of the metaphysical tradition is today out of the question—even granting a quite genuine sense of resumption, granting, for instance, that resumption always requires an element of renewal, adaptation, reanimation. Why out of the question? Because one cannot today simply resume the expressed distinction that inaugurates that tradition, the distinction between intelligible and sensible, the distinction which, as expressed, compels our reflection to grant its rootedness in the metaphysical tradition. Or rather, one could simply resume the distinction, and thus the metaphysical tradition it inaugurates, only at the cost of putting out of question what is today most questionable, only at the cost of blinding oneself to the crisis of metaphysics.

Permit me here to allude to a historical phenomenon without attempting anything like a demonstration of it; I ask this because to determine in this case whether and in what sense a demonstration is even possible, to determine what sense demonstration could have here, would not only lead into an interminable analysis but would rather quickly get entangled in the very phenomenon that is here in question. What phenomenon? Nietzsche called it the advent of nihilism. I would prefer to allude to it with the word "occlusion"—to speak of the occlusion of the distinction between intelligible and sensible and, correspondingly, of the occlusion of metaphysics. Central to this phenomenon is the recurrent emptying of every refuge in which a pure intelligibility would be secure—that is, the recurrent appropriation of every alleged intelligible to the sphere of the sensible. Recall some moments of this attack: the reduction of the intelligible, in its theological aspect, to the human, all-too-human at the hands of Feuerbach, Nietzsche, Freud; the reduction of the noumenal, first in German Idealism and then radically in Nietzsche and in phenomenology; the reduction of the ideality of meaning, its empirical reduction in psychologism, its transcendental reduction in Husserl, its reduction to a system of differences in structural linguistics.

In referring to the occlusion of the distinction I want to retain all three senses of the word. There is, first, the sense of *absorption* as when in chemistry one says that a certain gas is occluded, for example, by charcoal; the distinction between intelligible and sensible is in this sense occluded in the absorption, the appropriation, of the intelligible to the sensible. There is, secondly and consequently, a *closing* of the distinction. And, thirdly, this closing *obstructs*, blocks, our passage; specifically, it obstructs that movement in which, resuming our metaphysical heritage, we would carry it onward. We, by contrast, are both too much within and too much without metaphysics—that is, suspicious of its every means, yet lacking any others. The occlusion of the metaphysical distinction recurs in each dimension in which the distinction gets reopened, and the examples cited allude to some of these dimensions. Occlusion recurs so insistently that one might well want simply to yield to it, were that choice open short of relinquishing reflection once and for all. But as soon as we reflect, as soon as we invoke the only conceptual and linguistic means really at our disposal, we have already reopened the metaphysical distinction and, if we require that the reflection be radical, have set for ourselves the task of reconstituting the distinction.

Here perhaps we can begin to discern a parting of ways: in one direction ever recurrent occlusion, indefinitely reiterated oscillation between means and end of reflection, from within metaphysics to without, exhaustion both manifest yet prohibited. But let us not retreat too quickly, too dogmatically. It seems to me that we ought instead to exercise a certain reticence about this direction—at least as long as we have not passed beyond its mere schema and made the effort to follow it up in a concrete and systematic way. Especially, I should want to postpone, perhaps indefinitely, the conclusion that this direction is *simply* one of hopelessness and anarchy; for nihilism is precisely *not anything simple* but a phenomenon of such complexity as to escape perhaps all previous measures. I should perhaps even want to grant that for some time yet it might be imperative to follow this direction— to linger on its way until one sees everywhere only the countenance of "this uncanniest of all guests."[6] Granted a certain sense of economy and strategy, one can in a limited context defer occlusion in such fashion as to turn metaphysics against itself. Who can yet say whether, beyond such deconstruction, an abrupt, eruptive leap outside the metaphysical tradition might be possible? Has such "active forgetfulness" as Nietzsche invoked yet been put to the test? Can we yet even envisage how Zarathustra might prove himself?

Nevertheless, the leap beyond the tradition, from man to overman, even if an alternative, is not the only one. There is another way—a way that *turns back* into the tradition, without, however, becoming either a mere resumption of that tradition or, at the other extreme, a deferent turning of the tradition against itself. To adumbrate this other way, let me use the title *archaic reflection*.

The structure of archaic reflection involves two principal moments. On the one side, such reflection is a regress to an *arche*, a return to a beginning, to an originary phase of the tradition, to a phase in which something decisive originated. It is distinctive of such phases that within them matters are never so secure as they become subsequently.

6. Nietzsche, *Der Wille zur Macht*, §1.

Within an originary phase there is an unsettling openness, and, in a reflective return to the texts in which such a phase is traced, in a de-sedimenting reading of those texts, we can bring again into play the manifoldness suppressed by subsequent tradition; we can stage again that play of different levels, different directions, different dimensions, which, irreducible to a closed structure, constitutes precisely the openness in which something decisive can originate. Yet we stage the play only in order that it might reflect something to us—that is, archaic reflection turns back into such an originary phase in order to let something at issue today be reflected in that beginning, in order to trace out in that beginning an image of the issue enriched by the openness of the beginning. This tracing constitutes, then, the first of the two moments of archaic reflection. The other moment, which is never guaranteed in advance, consists in the recovery and elaboration of the undeveloped possibilities freed through the tracing; reflection thus brings the means gained from the beginning to bear upon the issue from which and for the sake of which the reflection commenced. This moment may be termed the progressive moment of reflection in distinction from the first, regressive moment.

Regression

I propose to sketch an archaic reflection with respect to the issue of occlusion. The originary phase in which this issue will be reflected is that traced in Kant's critiques. The regressive moment of the reflection, the reflecting of this issue in the Kantian beginning, requires that I stage three scenes and trace in each the shape assumed by the issue of occlusion, by the distinction between intelligible and sensible. Let me date the three scenes. The first occurs at the end of Kant's so-called precritical period, the time of the *Inaugural Dissertation*; in this scene one can delineate the form in which Kant took over the distinction at issue. The second scene occurs during the time of transition to the critical philosophy; here one can observe a Kantian occlusion of the distinction. The third scene presents the unfolding of the critical system in its character as a reconstituting of the distinction.

Scene 1. Eleven years of public silence separate Kant's final precritical work, the *Inaugural Dissertation* of 1770, from the *Critique of Pure Reason*. Measured by the standards of the critical writings, the *Dissertation* is, in a decisive sense, a traditional work, even though one can quite easily isolate in this text certain major conceptions that mark an open break with the tradition and are carried over unchanged into the *Critique of Pure Reason*. Most notable in this regard is the conception of sensibility put forth in the *Dissertation*; according to this conception, objects as they affect the senses are invested with form by the mind, a kind of form for which Kant already uses the term "pure intuition" and which he identifies with space and time. With this conception Kant has clearly initiated the break that he will announce again in the Transcendental Aesthetic; and yet, at the same time, he suppresses what is radical and unsettling in this conception of sensibility by inscribing it within a general framework that remains thoroughly traditional—the framework of the traditional distinction between intelligible and sensible. In fact, this distinction gives the work its name; the *Dissertation* is entitled "On the Form and Principles of the Sensible and Intelligible World."[7] Yet, if the traditional distinction serves to suppress the unsettling conception of sensibility, that distinction is itself, by the same stroke, threatened from within.

But, however threatened, the traditional distinction remains intact in the *Dissertation*, and it is in this text that one can discern most clearly how Kant took over the distinction from the tradition. What tradition? Most immediately, the metaphysical tradition as reshaped by Leibniz and systematized during the eighteenth century by Wolff and Baumgarten. Thus, the distinction as Kant takes it over corresponds in general to the Leibnizian distinction between the realm of grace and the realm of nature—the intelligible world comprising things as they are, in distinction from the sensible world of things as they affect our senses. With this distinction on the side of things there is correlated a distinction on the side of the subject: just as the sensible is presented to sensibility, so the intelligible is presented to the intellect. And although intuitive knowledge of the intelligible—that is, intellectual intuition—is denied to man, there is nonetheless reserved a "real use" of the intellect by which are given, in total independence of sensibility, concepts of things as they are; through the real use of the intellect man is thus granted knowledge of the intelligible.

Here a very old schema is retained, a schema that one can easily trace in Book 5 of the *Republic*: That which truly is, is known through the pure intellect; that which appears, is known through sensible experience.

Scene 2 takes place during that long period of public silence leading up to the *Critique of Pure Reason*. Its main script is the well-known letter which Kant wrote to Marcus Herz on February 21, 1772—the letter in which Kant reproaches himself for having maintained a certain silence in the *Dissertation*, for having, as he says, "silently passed over the

7. "De mundi sensibilis atque intelligibilis forma et principiis," in *Werke: Akademie Textausgabe*, II. See esp. §3–6, 10, 12–15. English translation by G.B. Kerfeld and D.E. Walford in *Kant: Selected Pre-Critical Writings* (Manchester, 1968).

further question."[8] What question? The question of the concepts given in the real use of the intellect, the concepts through which one would know the intelligible, the concepts that now, in the letter to Herz, Kant terms "pure concepts of the understanding." How are these concepts questionable? What is the question regarding them? What is the question that Kant now reproaches himself for having "silently passed over"? It reads: "What is the ground of the relation of that in us which we call 'representation' to the object?" The structure within which this question is posed is perfectly symmetrical: If a representation in the subject is caused by the object, this causality is then sufficient ground for the relation; if, on the other hand, the object is caused by the subject in which the representation inheres, if the subject brings the object into being in the very act of representing it, this causality likewise sufficiently grounds the relation. The aporia is that neither type of grounding suffices for the pure concepts of understanding: They are neither caused by the object (since any such causality would involve sensibility, of which the real use of the intellect is totally independent) nor are they generated in the very creation of the object (since they are representations "in us"—i.e., in a finite subject). Kant's letter to Herz testifies that this aporia remained untouched in the *Dissertation*, passed over in silence—that is, the relation of pure concepts to objects remained simply ungrounded, merely posited. In the long interval, the years of public silence, the emptying of this relation is played out. By the time of the *Critique of Pure Reason*, Kant is prepared to deny man any knowledge of the intelligible; and those pure concepts, previously taken as supplying such knowledge, now serve only for knowledge of objects of experience. Intellect, understanding, is placed in service to sensibility; it becomes a moment within the full structure that belongs to sensible experience, to knowledge of appearances. Thereby the metaphysical schema that was still intact in the *Dissertation* is disrupted in decisive fashion. By the correlation it establishes, that schema had effectively cast the distinction between intelligible and sensible as a distinction between objects knowable by intellect and objects knowable through sensibility. The transition to the *Critique of Pure Reason* thus effectively abolishes one member of the distinction—or, more precisely, appropriates it to the other member: The purely intellectual is *absorbed* into sensible knowledge. Consequently, the distinction, *as* a distinction between two regions of knowable objects, is collapsed, *closed*.

The connections begin to take shape: In the transition from the *Dissertation* to the *Critique of Pure Reason* there takes place an *absorption* of the intelligible into the sensible and a consequent *closing* of the

8. Kant, *Philosophical Correspondence*, ed. and trans. by Arnulf Zweig (University of Chicago Press, 1967), pp. 70 ff.

distinction itself. Scene 2 thus traces the contours of a Kantian occlusion of the distinction.

Scene 3 begins amid ruins. The metaphysical distinction and all that it
supports—metaphysics itself—have collapsed. The ruined distinction
remains only in the form of an empty, limiting concept: From the thing
as it appears to sensible experience, that is, the phenomenon, is distinguished the thing in itself, the noumenon, which, utterly inaccessible to
human knowing, is posited by the critique of pure reason in order to
mark the limits of knowing. By rendering the limits legible, the concept
of noumenon serves to enforce the assimilation of pure thought to
sensible experience.

The retention of the traditional distinction, even though only as an
empty, limiting concept, would already suffice to suggest that the
Kantian occlusion is not total, that the obstruction piled up by the
collapse is not totally impassable. But even if it could be total, there
could be no question of merely granting utter occlusion—at least not as
long as one remained unwilling to relinquish questioning as such once
and for all. The aporia—as an aporia that attends the occlusion of
metaphysics—is expressed by Kant at the very outset of the *Critique of
Pure Reason*. The words with which he begins the Preface to the first
edition are familiar:

> Human reason has this peculiar fate that in one species of its
> knowledge it is burdened by questions which, as prescribed by the
> very nature of reason itself, it is not able to ignore, but which, as
> transcending all its powers, it is also not able to answer.[9]

There is no choice but to reopen the metaphysical distinction on a new,
more solid ground, to take up positively the question "How is
metaphysics as science possible?" A new edifice must be constructed
alongside the ruins. This work of construction constitutes the positive
task of Kant's three critiques.

In proposing now to retrace this construction, it goes almost without
saying that I can attempt here neither the rigorous demonstration one
could rightly demand nor the attentive and cautious reading of Kant's
texts that any such demonstration would presuppose. With due reservations, let me instead merely trace in three vignettes the contours of
the edifice constructed through Kant's critical labors.

The *Critique of Pure Reason* establishes a new conception of the
sensible—or, more precisely, it consolidates and extends that breach
with the traditional conception of sensibility that was already marked in
the *Dissertation*. Kant's celebrated comparison of the critical with the

Copernican revolution is composed on this new conception and thus serves to announce it: One can henceforth suppose that, like the movement of a planet, objects must be regarded as resultants to be calculated by taking a subjective factor into account, one can henceforth suppose that objects must conform to our knowledge, precisely because they are invested with their form by the knowing subject. The breach is obtrusive: The form by which objects are informed is grounded, not in a pure intelligible beyond sensible experience, but rather in the subject of such experience. In the consolidation and extension of this breach, form no longer designates merely form of intuition but is extended to categorial form, the form grounded in pure understanding; as a result, form takes on the sense of objectivity as such. Kant's "Copernican revolution" turns away from the intelligible ground, traditionally understood, to the subject as the ground of the objectivity of the object. In the new conception of the sensible, the constitutive opposition is not with the intelligible, traditionally understood, but rather with the grounding subject.

Nevertheless, this turning away from the traditional distinction between intelligible and sensible has the character of an *Aufhebung*, for the distinction is insuppressible, already reinvoked with the very speech that would banish it. It is a matter of reopening that distinction within the new conception of the sensible—or rather, a matter of establishing it, for in the assimilation of pure thought to sensible experience, the distinction has already been brought back into play within this new dimension. It is within this dimension that Kant finally situates the question that he silently passed over in the *Dissertation*: It is recast as the problem of the transcendental deduction of the categories, as the problem of vindicating the *a priori* applicability of pure concepts to objects of experience. The outline of the Kantian solution is well known: Pure concepts can have objective validity precisely insofar as they belong to the conditions of the possibility of objects of experience; in order to show that and how such concepts function as such conditions, Kant focuses upon their character as concepts of synthetic unity and thus is able to show that they are connected, in a constitutive way, to intuition and thereby to objects as they appear in intuition. More specifically, the categories are vindicated by exhibiting their connection to a synthesis: They are concepts in which are thought those forms of unity that are instituted through synthesis in the manifold of intuition. Yet the synthesis itself is accomplished neither by thought nor by intuition. Kant is explicit: "Synthesis . . . is the mere result of the power of imagination."[10]

The first vignette is completed: The *Critique of Pure Reason* estab-

10. A 78.

lishes a new conception of the sensible, its reference as object back to a grounding subject; within the sensible, thus conceived, the distinction between intelligible and sensible is reopened and established. What holds open the distinction? What allows its terms to be distinct yet connected? What repairs, within the new dimension, the occluded distinction? Kant's answer: imagination.

The *Critique of Practical Reason* establishes a new conception of the intelligible. This conception surpasses the relative form that was established within sensibility; and, using precisely the schema provided by that vestigial form of the intelligible formulated in the concept of noumenon, the practical conception surpasses that form in such a way as to restore to it a content. The orientation to the new conception is already prefigured in the first Critique—namely, in that turning to the grounding subject that comes finally to focus on transcendental apperception, the empty positing of self as subject of all representations. The second Critique, in effect, completes the turn by presenting the subject as self-determining, as free, intelligible. The course of this presentation is well known: a fact of reason, a unique consciousness of the moral law, a pure feeling rigorously dismantled in Kant's analysis of respect—this fact presented as irrefutable testimony to practical reason, to reason's capacity to determine the will, to the subject's capacity for self-determination—that is, as testimony to freedom. Kant expresses with utter directness the new conception of the intelligible that is established through the primacy of practical reason: "If freedom is attributed to us, it transfers us into an intelligible order of things."[11]

So, the second vignette: in the *Critique of Practical Reason* a new conception of the intelligible as self-determining, primarily practical subject, as freedom.

The *Critique of Judgment* completes the critical edifice by establishing the connection between the new conception of the sensible (established by the first Critique) and the new conception of the intelligible (established by the second Critique). It is a matter of mediation between nature and freedom, a mediation possible only through the concept of purposiveness. In the "Critique of Aesthetic Judgment" in particular one may distinguish three principal stages in which this mediation unfolds—the stages corresponding to Kant's theories of the beautiful, of the sublime, and of beautiful art.

The beautiful, determined as formal purposiveness, corresponds to a certain harmony between imagination, in its apprehension of intui-

---

11. *Werke*, V, 42. English translation by Lewis White Beck (Indianapolis: Bobbs-Merrill, 1956), p. 43.

tive form, *and* understanding, by which such form could be brought under concepts. What kind of harmony? One that is not aimed at, that is unintentional—a free harmony. Such harmony between imagination and understanding should be contrasted with the connection that obtains at the level of theoretical knowledge: In aesthetic judgment the concepts of understanding do not function as rules governing imagination and rigorously determining the course of its synthesis; this is why one may, as does Kant, speak here of play. The state of mediation corresponding to the beautiful thus takes place through a freeing of imagination, a releasing of it into its free play.

The second stage of the mediation between nature and freedom is broached by the violence done to imagination by the sublime in nature. Imagination is surpassed but precisely in such a way as to find itself directed beyond understanding and its realm—nature— to reason and its realm—freedom.

The unfolding of the mediation is completed in beautiful art, in the art of genius, in those productions of genius that Kant terms "aesthetic ideas." At this level there is no conformity whatsoever of imagination to understanding: Aesthetic ideas are representations of imagination that provoke thought but to which no concept of understanding is adequate. Now imagination is so freed from the rule of understanding that, conversely, it can govern understanding—though in its own playful way, by provoking thought.

The third vignette, bringing the entire Kantian play to conclusion, traces the freeing of imagination. Imagination is released to its free play, imagination becomes creative, at that moment when the mediation is genuinely accomplished. The keystone that crowns the arch binding into unity the critically reconstructed difference between intelligible and sensible is the *play of imagination*.

Progression

I propose to repeat the play—that is, to repeat within the space of nihilism the Kantian labor of reconstructing the metaphysical distinction. Thereby I shall also fulfill another intention, that of repeating within this different space that opening gesture which I borrowed from Rousseau; for it will undoubtedly have become clear by now that that gesture is, to say the least, a prefiguration of the structure that gets reestablished by Kant. This second, progressive moment of the archaic reflection ventures a hazardous recovery, ventures it within a space in which all ground is inhibited by that occlusion to which archaic reflection would be a positive response.

I propose to repeat the play—not only the play of Kantian reconstruction that I have just staged, but also the outcome of that play, what becomes preeminently manifest in it: the play of imagination. This is the undeveloped possibility that I want to gather from the Kantian beginning and bring to bear upon the issue of utter occlusion. Of course the Kantian theory of imagination has not gone totally undeveloped heretofore; on the contrary, during the period immediately following Kant's completion of the critical system, the theory of imagination was developed in decisive and original ways by Schiller, Fichte, and Schelling; one could rightly demand that attention be given to these developments, even if only to establish that they are not radical enough for our time. Be that as it may, I venture to suggest that the Kantian theory of imagination has, with only one exception, lain fallow ever since the end of German Idealism.

In order to install the Kantian play within the space of utter occlusion, let me outline a certain development pertaining to the relation between imagination and subjectivity as such. The development has as its point of departure a peculiar tension between these terms, a tension operative at several different levels within Kant's work. Most globally, it is the tension between the turning toward subjectivity that determines the entire critical system—in particular its reconstruction of the metaphysical distinction—and that ecstatic character by which imagination, though functioning as the keystone of the reconstruction, is, on the other hand, a turning of the subject away from itself, exposing it to captivation by the unruly play of images, threatening it with loss of self. One can trace the same tension at a simpler level and more explicitly in Fichte's reformulation. Within the section of his *Grundlage der gesammten Wissenschaftslehre* devoted to theoretical knowledge, Fichte takes up the Kantian problem of synthesis in a radical form, which, though discernible in Kant's texts, is mostly suppressed within a more traditional framework. Fichte shows, more unequivocally even than Kant, that the fundamental synthesis is the work of imagination—that it is imagination that composes in their opposition those opposites whose synthesis is required: thought and intuition, phenomenon and noumenon, subject and object. What makes Fichte's formulation more radical, however, is that he foregoes simply installing imagination and its synthesis within an already constituted subject; on the contrary, the synthesis becomes the very condition of the possibility of finite subjectivity. On the other hand, returning to Kant's text, imagination is "one of the fundamental faculties of the human soul."[12] The tension is obtrusive: On the one hand, imagination is that by which subjectivity is first constituted as such; on the other hand, imagination continues to be reduced to a mere power possessed by the subject. Imagination is freed with one hand only to be suppressed, bound, with the other. But

12. *Critique of Pure Reason*, A 124.

let me cut the knot! Let me free it once and for all!

By freeing imagination from subjectivity, by so radicalizing it that it ceases to be anything subjective at all, it is possible to transpose the issue of imagination into one of the primary dimensions opened up in that assault on the purely intelligible that has led to the utter occlusion of metaphysics. What dimension? That of the dissolution of the subject, the dismantling of subjectivity. This dimension must be distinguished from that in which Kant took up the antinomy of freedom and natural causality: It is not a matter of an alien causality that would invade an already constituted subject but rather of a force, a structure, an openness, that would constitute the subject "from within"—a "force" such as will to power, such structure as has been unearthed by structural anthropology, the openness of ek-sistent *Dasein*. However, the moment one takes up the dismantling of subjectivity, one thereby abandons the Kantian edifice and initiates its collapse by launching an assault against its conception of intelligibility as self-determining subject. One cannot transpose the issue of imagination into the new dimension without eventually undertaking a radical redetermination of imagination as such.

In order to prepare such a redetermination—and here it can be a matter only of preparation, with all the discontinuities and reservations thereby entailed—let me transpose the issue still more radically beyond subjectivity. Or rather, let me simply shift discontinuously from imagination to that play of images to which imagination, however it be determined, is always to some degree given over. Let me repeat the Kantian play within the space of nihilism by replacing Kant's turn toward subjectivity with a turn toward the play of images.

Yet images in their play are also turned toward something which they image, and it would appear that in turning toward images one inevitably passes through them in such fashion as in the end to be turned away from them. The turn toward images would thus appear to revoke itself. But what is the character of that to which one would be turned by images? What is imaged in the play of images? Kant's answer is assured, at least at the level where imagination is genuinely freed to its play: In the play of images there is imaged the intelligible—that is, practical freedom. This assurance is expressed in the title of the last major section of the "Critique of Aesthetic Judgment": "Of Beauty as Symbol of Morality." If, however, one lacks that assurance, that security, if one openly confronts the utter and recurrent occlusion of metaphysics, then there can be no question of simply establishing a new intelligible. On the other hand, an image is by definition attached to a dyadic structure—that is, it is an image *of* something, *even if* that of which it is an image cannot be declared an ultimate intelligible, an original beyond all imaging, a final security aloof from the play. It is not a matter of a domain of originals which, set apart from the play of images, would themselves be incapable of entering that play, of playing the role of image. Nothing escapes the play; one finds everywhere only the play of imaging, the play of indeterminate dyads. In turning toward images one is, in the end, turned to the play of imaging.

This turning, initiated by turning back into the metaphysical tradition, is not, however, a return to metaphysics, for it issues in no new determination of the intelligible. On the contrary, the metaphysical distinction between intelligible and sensible is radically displaced, decisively unsettled, by the turn to the play of imaging, for in that play there is incessant opening and closing of the distance between what the tradition, since its beginning in the Platonic dialogues, has thematized as intelligible and sensible. The play of imaging is nothing but the play of occlusion itself, of absolute occlusion.

A redetermination of imagination is now prepared: Imagination is original ecstasy; it is a standing out into the play of imaging, a being set out beyond oneself into that play, a being outside oneself in such radical fashion that the self is first constituted in a recoil from this ecstasy of imagination.

Within the space of nihilism I have resumed that opening gesture in which was enacted an imaging of imagination: Imagination as original ecstasy implants one in the play of imaging, in the play in which, incessantly, difference is installed and unity announced.

Let me close with a gesture taken from Plato's *Laws*. The words are those of the Athenian: Man, at least his best part, is a plaything of the god; And so we should live out our lives playing at the most beautiful play—sacrificing, singing, and dancing—so as to be able to win the favor of the gods and to repel our foes and vanquish them in battle.[13]

13. 803 c-e.

Andrew J. Reck

3/Hodgson's Metaphysic of Experience

The appeal to experience in philosophy is a hallmark of traditional empiricism. In the seventeenth and eighteenth centuries it was employed to deflate the cognitive claim of reason to reach ultimate reality or Being transcending human beings and human society. By the beginning of the twentieth century, however, the appeal to experience had been transformed into an instrument of metaphysical theory-construction.

Experience itself had, of course, been reinterpreted. Whereas the traditional empiricist had viewed experience as a private affair of the individual mind, consisting of atomic sense data connected by mechanical laws of mental association, late nineteenth and early twentieth-century philosophers regarded experience as a social stream of contents and relations from which concepts could be wrenched by active and purposeful thought. Bergson, James, Dewey, Whitehead all resorted to the appeal to experience in metaphysics, and embracing a radical or broadened empiricism, the appeal to experience dominated metaphysics in Europe and America during the first quarter of the twentieth century.

Writing nearly a half-century later, Ballard returns to the appeal to experience. In his penetrating and profound survey of Western philosophy and its contemporary predicament, *Philosophy at the Crossroads*, Ballard defines philosophy as "the interpretation of archaic experience."[1] An archaic experience, Ballard relates, "is not only an experi-

Research for this essay was made possible by a grant from the Penrose Fund of the American Philosophical Society, to which the author expressed his gratitude.

1. Edward G. Ballard, *Philosophy at the Crossroads* (Baton Rouge: Louisiana State University Press, 1971), p. 4. Hereafter this work will be designated PC and cited in parentheses in the text.

ence having the character of a first temporal moment; but it is also first in the sense of evidently embodying a principle" (PC, 281). Thus on Ballard's analysis an archaic experience both terminates a temporal epoch and, grasping or recollecting an insight or principle, ushers in a new temporal epoch. Returning, it begins.

Permit me to observe that what Ballard's magisterial interpretation of our philosophic tradition suggests, particularly with its sober understanding and sympathetic assessment of the achievements of Husserl and Heidegger, is that the appeal to experience in metaphysics has been transformed, in a return to its beginning in Greek philosophy, into an appeal to Being itself.

It is fitting on this occasion when we do homage to our teacher and colleague to remember another thinker—Shadworth H. Hodgson (1832-1912). Although assigned a permanent resting place in "the vast cemetery of the history of philosophy,"[2] Hodgson deserves to be revived on this occasion, not merely because it coincides with the centenary of the Aristotelian Society, which he founded, but also because his philosophy initiated the century-long epoch in which the appeal to experience dominated metaphysics and which Ballard's interpretation terminates by turning back to a new beginning toward Being.

When, during the mid-nineteenth century, Hodgson was grappling with the ideas that were to fructify in his system, idealism and positivism were the dominant philosophical movements in Europe, Great Britain and America. Hegel was the towering giant of idealism, and Auguste Comte of positivism. Then came the shock of Darwin's theory of evolution; its impact on philosophy was profound and extensive. The leading British philosophers worked in the shadows of these giants. To name the three most famous British philosophers whose lives were contemporaneous with Hodgson's is to name exponents or allies of the three main movements: John Stuart Mill, Herbert Spencer and F.H. Bradley. Yet Hodgson's philosophical career is unique; he was unaffiliated and even antagonistic to those movements.

Today Hodgson is best known as the founder of the Aristotelian Society and also for his influence on William James. Certainly he counts as one of a large company of philosophers and psychologists whose investigations separated psychology from philosophy for the sake of endeavoring to establish the former as a natural science. Hodgson also anticipated (and possibly influenced) doctrines of other philsophers—for example, Henri Bergson's theory of time, Husserl's phenomenology, Santayana's ontology of essence/existence and epiphenomenalism, and Russell's theory of logical constructions.

2. Rudolf Metz, *A Hundred Years of British Philosophy*, transl. by J.W. Harvey, T.E. Jessop and Henry Sturt (London: George Allen & Unwin, 1938), pp. 481-83.

Metaphysical Method

It is Hodgson's metaphysical method that has excited most recent attention, because it suggests, in germinal form, Husserl's psychological-phenomenological reduction.[3] Hodgson first unveiled it in 1865 in his book *Time and Space*. This work is a pioneering effort, among other things, to separate psychology from philosophy, which he then called "metaphysic." Whereas psychology, a branch of "empiric," studies "mind, or consciousness in relation to the bodily organs which are its seat," [4] metaphysic asks: "What are the facts? What is their analysis?—and Is there any phenomenon answering to a given definition?" (TS, 4).

To answer its questions, metaphysic focusses on consciousness and its states; Hodgson called it "the applied logic of the universe" (TS, 8). Because metaphysic, moreover, is excluded from explaining the causes of the existence of consciousness and its states, it is "an entirely statical and not a dynamical theory. . . . It is the *causa essendi*, or nature, of the world of existence which metaphysic undertakes to examine; to analyse the structure of objects, as objects of consciousness, and to resolve them into their elements" (TS, 30–31). The consciousness under study by metaphysic, furthermore, is "consciousness as existing in an individual conscious being" (TS, 5), and not some absolute mind. Further, metaphysic studies "consciousness in relation to its objects" (TS, 30).

Intentionality is for Hodgson a mark of consciousness. Utilizing the medieval distinction between first and second intentions in a singular fashion, Hodgson declared that "any object, however complex, may be made a first intention by keeping it alone before the mind and separating it from other objects" (TS, 41), whereas to take an object in relation to other objects is to have it before the mind as a second intention. Inasmuch as metaphysic considers its object as a first intention, it makes no assumptions concerning the conditions for its existence whether inside or outside consciousness. As he prescribed, "Take now any empirical phenomenon, from the simplest to the most complex, isolate it from others, treat it as an object of the first intention, and analyse it as such, without asking how it came to be what it is, or whence it derived its characteristics, or what other things it is like" (TS, 45).

To study an object or phenomenon in the first intention is to have it before consciousness just as it is and nothing else. The object of

3. See Stuart F. Spicker, "Shadworth Hodgson's Reduction as an Anticipation of Husserl's Phenomenological Psychology," in *Journal of the British Society for Penomenology* 2 (1971) 57–73; and Karl Schumann, "Husserl and Hodgson: Some Historical Remarks," 3 (1972) 63–65. See also Stuart F. Spicker, "The Fundamental Constituents of Consciousness: Process Contents and the *Erlebnisstrom*," in *Man and World* 6 (1973) 26–43.

4. Shadworth H. Hodgson, *Time and Space; a Metaphysical Essay* (London: Longmans, Green, 1865), p. 30. Hereafter this work will be designated TS and cited in parentheses in the text.

metaphysic is just such an object; it is an object on first acquaintance, given in a sort of pure experience, before the intervention of any conceptual interpretations linking it existentially with other objects. The metaphysical analysis of this object, moreover, is in terms of form and matter, a distinction Hodgson borrowed from Kant (TS, 33).

On the side of matter, an object is qualitative, having the characteristics of color, sound, taste, odor, and so forth. Hodgson's term for such qualitative material is "feeling." On the side of form are time and space, ". . . [the] particular forms in which these feelings appear. Every feeling must exist for a certain length of time, and some feelings must exist also in a certain position in space, and some also in a certain extent of space" (TS, 45–46).

Although metaphysic grasps its object in its first intention by means of deliberate intellectual effort, or reflection, Hodgson justified the analysis by an appeal to experience in observing that, "every phenomenon as such contains these two elements, time, or time and space, on the one side, and feeling on the other. This is empirically and experimentally certain; on this as a verifiable fact I take my stand, and shall appeal to the experience of everyone whether it is not so" (TS, 46–47). The appeal to experience is paramount in Hodgson's 1884 article, "The Metaphysical Method in Philosophy." As the first rule of metaphysical method, he emphasized, "Throw yourself frankly on experience." The business of philosophy, he continued, "is with the stream [of consciousness], and the features which belong to it as a stream of consciousness. . . . Now subjective analysis of the stream of consciousness, *without assumptions*, is the whole business and function of philosophy."[5] At the same time Hodgson's empirical method in metaphysic, involving a reformed empiricism that he dubbed "experientialism," is intellectual, or reflective, and also far-reaching in its grasp.[6]

The Metaphysic of Experience (1898), in the first of four huge volumes, articulates Hodgson's conception of metaphysical method in its most mature form. Metaphysic is "the method of analysing experience as a subjective phenomenon, discarding assumptions."[7] It starts from "the common-sense form of experience, which is shared by all men prior to their commencing to philosophise" (ME, I, 109). Common sense is a form of experience with assumptions and unanswered questions, and

5. Shadworth H. Hodgson, "The Metaphysical Method in Philosophy," *Mind* 9 (1884) 55.

6. For the term "experientialism" and its relation to British empiricism, see Shadworth H. Hodgson, *Philosophy and Experience* (London: William & Norgate, 1885), pp. 9 ff.

7. Shadworth H. Hodgson, *The Metaphysic of Experience* (London and New York: Longmans, Green, 1898), I, p. 18. Hereafter this work will be designated ME and cited in parentheses in the text.

science is a form of experience continuous with common sense and consequently replete with assumptions, but, in addition, intent upon the grouping of phenomena in order to discover laws and uniformities in nature. By contrast, philosophy is no such assumption-bound, fragmentary enterprise. Rather philosophy is "the form of experience which must be taken by the most exact, organised and comprehensive system of knowledge of which the human mind is capable, after all possible doubts and questions have been raised and pondered, and in which, therefore, it must perforce acquiesce as its nearest possible approach to the whole truth" (ME, I, 17). Analyzing experience to uncover its ultimate elements and aspects metaphysic eschews such common-sense assumptions as "(1) the idea that what I am experiencing is a part of the world of persons, things, actions, and events, and . . . (2) the idea that *I* as a real person am experiencing it or them" (ME, I, 39). These assumptions involve objects or characters that are not immediate experiences, but when analyzed may prove to be constructions of the fundamental components of experience or inferences from experience. "Experience, alone, without assumptions, is the ultimate source of all our knowledge under this head" (ME, I, 43).

Twenty years before the publication of *The Metaphysic of Experience*, Hodgson had sought to formulate his entire system of philosophy in his two-volume work, *The Philosophy of Reflection* (1878). Here he spelled out the critical and intellectual features of the experiential basis of his metaphysical method, which, despite subsequent revision, he never abandoned, so that for Hodgson the appeal to experience was never—as later for James and Bergson—anti-intellectual.

Reflection is "the cardinal point" of his system; it "is the foundation of metaphysic because, being the moment of distinguishing the objective and subjective aspects of phenomena, it gives us our notion of *existence* as well as cognition, so that we cannot speak or even frame a notion of anything beyond it. Whatever notion we frame lies within it, is subjective as well as objective or imaginary."[8] Reflection is consciousness of consciousness; it is, to use another word, self-consciousness. And it is distinguished from other moments of consciousness: on the one side, from prereflective consciousness or, in his terms, "primary consciousness"; on the other side, from postreflective consciousness or "direct consciousness."

In his first book, *Time and Space*, when striving to articulate a theory of consciousness, Hodgson distinguished three orders: the order *essendi*, the order *existendi*, and the order *cognoscendi* (TS, 333–41). This

8. Shadworth H. Hodgson, *The Philosophy of Reflection* (London and New York: Longmans, Green, 1878), I, p. 6. Hereafter this work will be designated PR and cited in parentheses in the text.

distinction was to survive in his later works, and to remain a useful instrument of analysis. The order *essendi* is the philosophical order; it has to do with what a thing is. The order *existendi* is the historical order investigated by science; it has to do with existence and the causes of existence. The order *cognoscendi* is the order of knowledge.

Confined to science in the first book, the order of knowledge is subsumed under philosophy not only as the complete system of knowledge in later works, but also as the starting point of philosophy when it entertains the order *essendi*. Here reflection is the key. As Hodgson said:

> Reflection is with me, as it was with Kant, the basis of the whole of philosophy, but—and here is the important difference—*not* as the *causa existendi* of consciousness, *not* (which soon developed itself out of Kant) as the *causa existendi* of existence, but as a particular kind of *causa cognoscendi*, namely, as the perception of the *ti esti*, the analysis of the *essentia*, of consciousness and its states. Reflection is reexamination of the states of consciousness from which it is derived, of that series of states of which it is a prolongation [PR, I, 229].

Stemming from reflection, philosophy encompasses the analyses of things that reveal their natures; it is critical, presuppositionless and systematic. By contrast, science springs up when we inquire into the causes or conditions of things and investigate genesis or history instead of nature or essence; it assumes existence and existents, and it is partial.

Grounding science in a philosophical distinction drawn by reflection, Hodgson undertook, by means of philosophical principles, to explain and justify verification, upon which he insisted positive science depends. In his 1865 book he had foreshadowed later pragmatism and positivism when he defined truth as "the agreement of our perceptions with others which are or shall be the result of more accurate investigation" (TS, 503), and denied that any investigation is ever completed in science by the discovery of an absolute truth, inasmuch as its test always "depends upon the future" (TS, 503). As he then explained: "It is the thought of yesterday which we address as truth; the thought of to-day, which warrants that of yesterday, needs itself the warranty of to-morrow" (TS, 504–5).

Is there no stop to any line of scientific research, its truth forever escaping over the horizon toward which it is directed? Hodgson's answer in 1865 was pragmatic:

> Here the rule of practice is to adopt a principle or a system as a limit of enquiry, a terminus *a quo* and *ad quem*, and to work from it and live by it as if it were true. . . . The will says Here we take our

> stand. The result of metaphysical enquiry, just as that of practical experience, shows us that there is no absolute or ultimate empirical truth, but every where relative and approximate truth. It is an inflexible law of consciousness—*Nihil absoluti* [TS, 504].

Within positive science, there is no final epistemological foundation, because the scientific test for truth is verification. Only philosophy provides the ultimate foundation of knowledge. Among the first to emphasize the centrality of verification to scientific knowledge, Hodgson was nonetheless early to recognize that, although verification terminates in perceptions of direct consciousness, it requires a conceptual order and processes of reasoning that involve reflection.

In 1878 he stated his formula for the philosophical foundation of all knowledge, including scientific knowledge, both objectively and subjectively. The objective statement, one that James was to reiterate often in his pragmatism and radical empiricism, is: "A thing *is* what it is *known as*." The subjective statement is: "the objective and subjective aspects are inseparable." Both statements, according to Hodgson, expressed "the way in which the same truth appears in reflection itself" (PR, I, 149).

In his two-volume work *The Theory of Practice* (1870), Hodgson had designated the discovery of the distinction between the subjective and objective aspects of phenomena "the cardinal point of philosophy."[9] He ascribed these aspects, distinguished at the moment of reflection, to all phenomena, and insisted that, although neither is derived from the other, they are inseparable.

In acknowledging distinct but inseparable elements or aspects of phenomena, Hodgson departed from traditional empiricism that followed Hume in regarding every distinction a separate existence. To illuminate the inseparability of the subjective and objective, Hodgson invoked his distinction between nature and history. The nature of phenomena, as a feeling or complex of feeling in space and time, is its subjective aspect. The existence of phenomena, moreover, has its subjective aspect in its counterpart in consciousness as "the reflection, or imagination, or perception, or belief of it" (TP, I, 101–2). At the same time phenomena display an objective aspect. For the individual, the objective aspect consists "in the fact of his presenting, representing, imagining, or believing in, the objects which he is said to have in his mind, the objects of his states of consciousness" (TP, I, 105).

Thus, on the one hand, the bare existence of a phenomenon for

9. Shadworth H. Hodgson, *The Theory of Practice, an Ethical Inquiry* (London: Longmans, Green, 1870), I, p. 97. Hereafter this work will be designated TP and cited in parentheses in the text.

consciousness is subjective; and, on the other hand, the existence of acts, moments or processes within consciousness is objective; and these two senses of existence for phenomena are inseparable. Yet neither sense, according to Hodgson in 1870, is germane to historical existence. "The world, then, which exists with its objects and its forces independently of our puny existence and our feeble thoughts, though its nature, its *ti esti*, its bare existence, is to be actually or possibly present to consciousness, is yet in its certainty, its permanence, its causative agency, and its inherent power, no counterpart of the consciousness of any of its individual members" [TP, I, 104].

In *The Metaphysic of Experience* Hodgson retained his formula of the inseparability of the subjective and objective aspects, but in radically altered form. He no longer held the distinction between subject and object to be the primary distinction of method. Rather he deemed "the distinction between consciousness apprehended simply as a process-content in the relation either of real condition or real conditionate" to be primary (ME, I, 31-32). The content of any moment of experience is its *whatness*, and the process—the fact that the content is experienced or perceived—is its *thatness* or existence as at present known. Distinguishable, inseparable and commensurate, the *whatness* and the *thatness* are characterized as

> opposite *aspects* of each other, and of the experience, yet without taking the experience as a third thing, or anything but their inseparable union. It is the most general truth about experience. . . . The meaning of *esse* is *percipi*. Simply being or existence in its lowest terms is known as the *thatness* of a *whatness* [ME, I, 61].

Yet neither that whatness nor the thatness is the object of the other. The content perceived, the whatness, is not a perceiving. Nor is the perceiving a part of the content perceived. Nevertheless, these distinct aspects of every phenomenon hold together in every moment of experience and perdure through to the next moment, when indeed the perceiving in a past moment is part of the content perceived. The unity and the continuity of the double aspects of experience fall to reflection. It is reflection that grasps what is now a past moment of experience, and distinguishes its whatness and its thatness. It is reflection, too, that apprehends this moment of experience as a total whatness for the process present now as thatness.

Hodgson's discussion of metaphysical method adumbrates several meanings of the terms "existence" and "reality." Although on many occasions he paused to analyze these terms, his definitive clarification is to be found in *The Metaphysic of Experience*, where he discriminated four senses of the term "reality." In the first sense, "reality" means "something simply in consciousness" (ME, I, 457). This sense is represented by the formula: *esse* is *percipi*. In the second sense, "reality" means "something which has a definite place in perception, or objective thought" (ME, I, 457). This sense further amplifies the formula *esse* is *percipi*; it holds that to be is to occupy "a definite place in a context of perceptions in the time-stream of experience" (ME, I, 362).

Whereas these two senses of "reality" pertain to objective thought, the next sense applies to objects thought about. In this third sense, "reality" signifies "a place and a function in an external world"; it means "independence of the circumstance of being perceived or not perceived by any consciousness" (ME, I, 362). "Reality," in the third sense, means "something which has existence independently of whether it is perceived or unperceived, thought or not thought of, at any given time" (ME, I, 457). Whereas all three senses of "reality" postulate the synonymy of "reality" and "existence" or "thatness," the first two senses, applying to what is in consciousness, provide for the doctrine of nature, essence, content or *whatness*.

The central problem of knowledge is how the essences or natures in consciousness relate to the objects existing outside consciousness. This leads to the fourth sense of "reality" — "reality in the sense of *efficiency*" (ME, I, 457). It means "something which has efficiency as a real condition" (ME, I, 457). Once the quest for reality in the sense of real efficiency or conditions is begun, science is born.

Acknowledging that these four senses of "reality" express different meanings, Hodgson nonetheless held that "all alike refer to feeling and form taken together, that is to say, to complete or empirical objects. . . . *Reality*, taken as common to all four classes, means simply the *fact that* experience takes place — a fact which is incapable of degree, that is to say, of being either less or more real than it is" [ME, I, 458].

Theory of Consciousness

In *Time and Space*, Hodgson defined the subject matter of metaphysic to be consciousness and the facts of consciousness. In fundamentals he never departed from this definition, however differently he may have elaborated its details in his later writings. Basic to his theory of consciousness was his espousal of what in contemporary philosophical discussion is called "the intentionality of consciousness." Metaphysic, he declared, studies "consciousness in relation to its objects" (TS, 30). And he underscored the coextension of consciousness and existence: "suppose consciousness, and it is consciousness of an object, that is, of existence; suppose existence, and it is existence in consciousness, that is, an object" (TS, 346).

To exist is to be an object, and to be an object is to be present in some mode of consciousness. The primary mark of existence, in this sense, is "that of being present in consciousness, taking consciousness in its widest sense and including therefore both possible and actual presence in consciousness. . . . Whatever therefore can be perceived, conceived, or imagined, exists; exists either potentially or actually, in the past or present or future" (TS, 60).

Long before James and Bergson, Hodgson had revised the associationist psychology of traditional empiricism, and had presented a philosophy that pictures consciousness as a stream or a field. In his mature work he had analyzed the ultimate moments of experience from which metaphysic starts as "process-contents." Process characterizes both the sequence of the moments of experience making up consciousness and each moment as well (ME, III, 278).

Viewed as a succession of perceived moments, consciousness consists of percepts separated into different groupings. In *The Philosophy of Reflection* the separative consciousness, which groups percepts into various bundles, of which the body is one, the soul another, the external world still another, is called "primary consciousness." A second method of consciousness, termed "direct consciousness," accepts the groupings of primary consciousness and strives to establish causal connections between them. Inveterately dualistic, direct consciousness is "the point of view from which the sciences start as their basis, and which they do not attempt to transcend" (PR, I, 115). More fundamental than either of these modes of consciousness, and the starting point of philosophy, is reflective consciousness.

Reflection takes consciousness itself as its object; it discovers that consciousness is a stream. As Hodgson reported: "What I find, when I look at consciousness at all, is, that what I cannot divest myself of, or not have in consciousness, if I have consciousness at all, is a sequence of different feelings" (PR, I, 248). Within the sequence or stream, the minimum of consciousness requires two different feelings: a single feeling alone "would not be felt," so that a second feeling is needed to bring the "first into consciousness together with itself" (PR, I, 249–50).

Reflection analyzes consciousness in terms of elements and aspects. The elements are formal and material; the aspects, subjective and objective. So far inquiry remains philosophical. When, however, it reverts to the method of direct consciousness and seeks to find the causes by correlating the physical and mental groupings of percepts, psychology springs up as a science separate from philosophy.

The material element will be discussed briefly here. In *Time and Space* Hodgson designated "feeling" or "quality" to be the material of all phenomena (TS, 92). He subdivided feeling into sensations and emotions.

In his theory of sensations Hodgson followed the standard psychological authors of his time (Lewes and Bain); sensations are defined scientifically as organic feelings by reference to the different organs or parts of the body or nervous system on which they depend. Because sensations are the matter of presentations, he further emphasized that the meaning of the latter is to be found in sense.

In *The Theory of Practice* (1870), Hodgson proposed a thoroughly novel theory of emotions. Distinct from sensations, emotions are the matter of representations; and no less than sensations, which have their objective aspect as the sense qualities of things, emotions also have an objective aspect. For "every representation with its pervading emotion has an objective aspect, the thing represented with its qualities of sensation and its qualities of emotion" (TP, I, 99). Furthermore, instead of construing emotions to be effects of sensations, presentations or representations, he viewed emotions as a new kind or mode of feeling, similar to sensations in that both are produced by the constitution and operation of nervous matter, but different in that sensations result from the motion or impact of matter on the nervous matter, whereas emotions arise from the motions of the nervous matter itself, the same motions that support the representational framework.

For Hodgson emotions, better than sensations, constitute the material of the objective world. Emotions and their frameworks are "the deeper, latest evolved, character of the tangible, visible, and otherwise sensible world" (TP, I, 268). Materially, "the meaning of this world which we inhabit consists of the feelings, and chiefly among them in the emotions" (TP, I, 333).

The formal elements are space and time. In *Time and Space* Hodgson declared that "every feeling must exist for a certain length of time, and some feelings must exist also in a certain position in space, and some also in a certain extent of space" (TS, 46). Of the two forms, Hodgson's treatment of time is the more significant. Following Kant, Hodgson understood space to be the form of all phenomena composing the physical world, and time to apply to the very nature of the subject as well.

As early as 1865, Hodgson espoused a temporalist metaphysics. He admitted time to be "the so-called substance of the soul" (TS, 1878), and described the subject itself as nothing but "the incomplete moment of time" (TS, 184). The primacy of time is recognized by reflection, whose object—consciousness—has time as "the only constant element" (TS, 178).

Consciousness is inherently retrospective. Indeed, it is because of the temporal nature of consciousness that reflection distinguishes subject and object. Moreover, "the fact that consciousness is fleeting in point of time, that it escapes observation in the moment of consciousness, so that we are never conscious that we are feeling but only that we have felt,—the fact that we are never able to seize consciousness itself but only its product, warrants us in distinguishing a Subject from an Object" (TS, 177–78).

Hodgson's temporal distinctions were later adopted by James in *The Principles of Psychology*. The empirical present Hodgson apprehended in 1878 to be unreal, or in the term James used, *specious*; it is sharply distinguished from the strict present, thus "crudely and popularly we divide the course of time into Past, Present, and Future; but, strictly speaking, there is no Present; it is composed of Past and Future divided by an indivisible point or instant. That instant, or time-point, is the strict *present*" (PR, I, 253). Consciousness needs both presents. The empirical present makes both perception and memory possible; the overlap of past feelings in the present pointing toward the future is "what is meant by saying that all consciousness is in the form of *time*, or that time is the form of feeling, the form of sensibility" (PR, I, 252). The strict present is "the instant of change" (PR, I, 253). It is due to "the stimulus or shock given to the nerve, or the change between the two intensities of stimulus, which is the psychological condition of the feeling" (PR, I, 253). The minimum of feeling that is the empirical present, therefore, contains "two portions, a sub-feeling that goes and a sub-feeling that comes. One is remembered, the other imagined" (PR, I, 253).

Although Hodgson's conceptions of the empirical present and the strict present later played a central role in the development of temporalism and process philosophy, it is doubtful that he himself would have embraced a system of process metaphysics. He distinguished two points of view: one forward-looking, the other transverse-looking. According to the forward-looking view, "taking the flux of percepts by itself, everything is *new*, a new creation. No moment of the flux is repeated; it is a train of *differents*. From the transverse-looking point of view, on the other hand, everything is *old*, already existing, the future as much so as the past" (PR, II, 159).

A comparison of consciousness and existence with a fly on a mosaic illustrates this conception of time. When the fly moves across the mosaic, what is in front of it represents the future, what is behind it the past. As long as the fly moves, things are in flux. It is the position of the moving fly that determines the distinction between the part of the mosaic that has already appeared to the fly—the *past*—and the un-known and apparently nonexistent part of the mosaic that lies in front of the fly—the *future*. Regard the fly as part of the mosaic, and suppose "that the mosaic *grows*, beginning from one side of the floor and spreading like a ripple so as gradually to cover it, carrying the fly with it on the crest of the wave" (PR, II, 160). For Hodgson this last picture conforms to the ordinary notion of existence where we are ourselves "part and parcel of the onward movement" (PR, II, 160). Hence "the flux and its arrest [are] equally essential. The *content* of the mosaic belongs to the flux; the picturing it *as a content*, the picturing any part of it as a part, or of the whole as a whole, belongs to its arrest" (PR, II, 160).

Perceiving and percept are the subjective and objective aspects of the same phenomenon—perception. In *Time and Space* Hodgson defined perception as the "minimum of cognition, the subjective name for an object" (TS, 296). By taking perception to be the minimum of cognition, Hodgson in effect denied that sensation is the ground of consciousness and awareness, inasmuch as there could be no sensation unless it were perceived. Consequently, he undercut the sense-datum theories that were to flourish in the early twentieth century. The objective aspect of perception, percepts are "the ultimate empirical objects of metaphysic." As the quantifiable and measurable effects of shocks, stimuli or changes in nerve forces, they are also "the ultimates in psychology" (PR, I, 269–70).

The stream of consciousness depends upon the association of feelings (percepts and concepts)—in other words, upon a flow of feelings uninterrupted by feelings that come from the outside. Following Sir William Hamilton, Hodgson called the association of percepts or ideas "redintegration." He accepted as a general law of redintegration the principle "that every object, which has occurred in a variety of combinations, has a tendency to redintegrate, or call back into consciousness, all of them" (TS, 267). Redintegration, in the first place, is spontaneous, although interest plays a crucial role. In a passage later quoted by William James, Hodgson described the redintegrative processes of consciousness in these terms:

> Two processes are constantly going on in redintegration, the one a process of corrosion, melting, decay, and the other a process of renewing, arising, becoming. Unless by an effort of volition, which is here out of the question, no object of representation remains long before consciousness in the same state, but fades, decays, and becomes indistinct. Those parts of the object, however, which possess an interest, that is, those which are attended by a representation of pleasure or pain, resist this tendency to gradual decay of the whole object [TS, 266].

When the stream of percepts is broken up into parts by means of attention, the redintegration in the second place is voluntary; its products are concepts. To Hodgson's theory of concepts the debt of William James, who quotes the British philosopher often and at length in *The Principles of Psychology*, is immeasurable.[10] In 1865, the same year

10. For references to some of the major derivations of William James from Hodgson in psychology, see Andrew J. Reck, "Epistemology in William James's *Principles of Psychol-*

Hutchison Stirling's *Secret of Hegel* appeared to usher in the era of neo-Hegelian idealism in British philosophy, Hodgson criticized Hegel in just those respects that a half-century later pragmatists, naturalists and realists exploited in their assaults.

Hodgson's thought professedly took "the opposite route" from Hegel's (TS, 353). Whereas Hegel's logic employs the concept form that both includes and excludes the same content, and consequently erupts in a flux of concepts, each concept entailing its opposite, Hodgson restricted the flux to percepts and defined concepts as fixed meanings embodying content selected voluntarily. Logical conceiving, he said, is "a voluntary process. No one forms concepts without effort, nor without a purpose in view" (TS, 356).

Voluntary redintegration, attention, will transforms the stream of consciousness, the chain of percepts, into a conceptual order. As Hodgson explained in *The Philosophy of Reflection*, "A flash of light, a loud sound, and so on, intervening in the redintegration, arrest the attention, as it is called; we pause to say, what is that? We dwell upon it and keep it in representation, long after it has died out of presentation, that is, has ceased to be actually seen or heard" [PR, I, 292].

Concepts therefore are products of attention; they are answers to the question, What is that?

As a stream, consciousness displays two characteristics: it is actual, and it is expectant. A moment of consciousness when actual is "a Percept; in its expectant character it is a Concept" (PR, I, 294). The concept as expectant is, in Hodgson's words, "a provisional image" (PR, I, 301). It involves objectivity and relatedness.

In this regard, Hodgson restated his theory of first and second intentions. Percepts are first intentions, and concepts are second intentions, inasmuch as "objects considered in their relation to consciousness alone are percepts, while objects considered in a certain kind of relation to other objects of consciousness are concepts" (PR, I, 295).

The transformation of the stream of consciousness into a conceptual

---

ogy," in *Tulane Studies in Philosophy* 22 (1973) 79–115. Pertinent to Hodgson's critique of Hegelianism, particularly in psychology, is his exchange in *Mind*, 1886 and 1887, with John Dewey, then a Hegelian. See Shadworth Hodgson, "Illusory Psychology," in *Mind* 11 (1886) 478–94, a critical reply to John Dewey's "The Psychological Standpoint," 11 (1886) 1–19, and "Psychology as Philosophic Method," 11 (1886) 153–73. Dewey responded in " 'Illusory Psychology,' " 12 (1887) 83–88; and Hodgson replied in " 'Illusory Psychology,' a Rejoinder," 12 (1887) 314–18. All but the last mentioned article by Hodgson in the *Mind* series has been reprinted in John Dewey, *The Early Works, 1882–1898*, Vol. I (Carbondale: Southern Illinois University Press, 1969). Hodgson convinced William James of the cogency of his case against Dewey; see Lewis E. Hahn, in John Dewey, *The Early Works*, Vol. I, Introduction, pp. xxvii–xxx.

order is not arbitrary, because "we do not and cannot change its content at our will, in the sense that we can choose what content it shall offer us, yet . . . we can and do reject what it offers until it offers what suits our purpose" (PR, I, 300). Thus the stream of consciousness is remolded voluntarily or, in Hodgson's own metaphor, "the chain of differents" is broken up, groupings are introduced and the links are changed. The pieces in the chain "are now connected together, not as they are given us in perception, but in an order of thought, the connection of which consists in similarity and graduated differentiation" (PR, I, 301).

In contrast with the perceptual order, the order of thought exhibits a new nexus produced by voluntary redintegration. Despite the differences between the perceptual nexus and the conceptual nexus, "the content of the two orders is the same, there is no content in the order of thought which is not a derivative of something or other in the order of perception" (PR, I, 301).

The perceptual order is transformed into the conceptual order for the sake of knowledge. This transformation, however, does not eliminate the perceptual order. On the contrary, the perceptual order remains as the bedrock of scientific knowledge. As Hodgson declared: "The conceptual process is instrumental and intermediate. It begins with perception simply, and it ends with perception again" (ME, II, 150–51).

Ahead of his time, Hodgson had apprehended that his theory of consciousness as a stream eliminates the doctrine of a substantial mind or soul with separate psychological faculties. He observed that, "there is no longer a mind, an immaterial substance, with its several distinct and ultimate faculties. . . . But there is a single broad and ever broadening stream of consciousness, the phenomena of which, sensations, emotions, reasonings, volitions, and so on, are given by observation, analysed by experience, and classified under the ultimate distinction of consciousness simple and reflective" (PR, I, 101).

As early as 1865, he had defined the ego in the order *essendi* as the correlate of all existence, and as an ever elusive subject that reflects but never catches itself as an object; in the order *existendi* as the empirical ego and also the subjective aspect of world; and in the order *cognoscendi* as "the conscious life of the individual being, that is, the feelings or cognitions of the empirical ego together with those feelings or qualities which are called the body, and with which they are constantly connected in experience" (TS, 340).

At the time, he restricted the ego as the topic of metaphysic to its sense in the order *essendi* and, working in the shadow of Kant's doctrine of the transcendental ego, he viewed it as existing solely in the order of logic as "the limit, point, a line of demarcation between the empirical ego and the universe of qualities" (TS, 341). In the order *existendi*, however, science works where metaphysic does not enter, and it seeks to find the genesis of consciousness and its states.

Hodgon's theory in his first book was interactional. Conscious states and physical events are connected causally, so that phenomena of either type may be the cause or effect of phenomena of the other type as well as of the same type.

Among the theories alternative to dualistic interaction that Hodgson then advocated was the theory called epiphenomenalism or automatism, which—ironically, because he rejected it at the time—he described superbly. According to epiphenomenalism, consciousness is like "a mere foam, aura, or melody, arising from the brain, but without reaction upon it" (TS, 280). Although he located the origin of consciousness in the nerve substance of the brain, he still insisted that there is interaction between states of consciousness and events in the brain and nervous system.

Five years later, in *The Theory of Practice*, Hodgson yielded to the scientific materialism of his time and withheld causal efficacy from consciousness and its states, confining them to being solely *causae cognoscendi* of physical objects and events:

> The sequences and combinations of feelings form, as it were, a kind of mosaic picture, the separate stones of which both support the picture and keep each other in their places; the stones are the states of the nervous organism, the colours on the stones the states of consciousness which are supported by the nerve states. The states of consciousness, the feelings, are the effects of the nature, sequence, and combination, of the nerve states, without being themselves causes either of one another or of changes in the nerve states which support them [TP, I, 335–36].

Later still, in *The Philosophy of Reflection*, Hodgson professed to be a materialist in psychology, as "indeed in all the sciences" (PR, I, 226). In this work he defined the soul nominally as "*a series of conscious states among which is the state of self-consciousness.* And the agent or substance which becomes conscious, or in which resides the force of becoming so, or which *has* the states of consciousness, is not the series of any one or more of the states which compose it, but (in man) the brain or nerve substance" [PR, I, 226].

In *The Metaphysic of Experience* Hodgson distinguished two processes: on the one hand, the process of consciousness itself, a process that resides in the continuity of moments of experience; and on the other hand, "the process of its proximate and real conditions, consisting of some neural or other action in the Subject, which is not consciousness, and of which it is a dependent concomitant" (ME, I, 58).

Amending the language of causation, Hodgson deemed consciousness and its states to be the conditionate of physical objects and events, which are the conditions. By "condition" he meant *"the real de facto order of existence"* (ME, II, 287). This order is the one great object of all science, which seeks to discover its laws, not causes, because the old conception of causes implies necessary linkages between particular events, whereas the conception of laws represents uniformities between classes of events of given types. Moreover, a conditionate itself does not necessarily react on the real condition. Consequently, to designate consciousness a conditionate is to maintain "that neither the nature of consciousness as awareness, nor the qualities of the ultimate modes of consciousness or awareness, as distinguished from their occurrence, are, or can be, or are held to be, accounted for by assigning their real conditions" (ME, II, 287–88).

Hence the notion of a special immaterial agent of consciousness is discarded, and "the way is at once opened for an experimental and observational psychology, devoted to discover the real laws which govern the genesis and history of consciousness in all its modes and ramifications, by referring that genesis and history to the action of that special physical tissue with which we find it connected in actual experience, when observation is tested by experience" (ME, II, 287–88).

Hodgson illustrated his theory by comparing the relation of consciousness and its physical conditions to a measuring tape wound upon a reel enclosed in a case (ME, I, 59–60). The reel with the tape on it, not yet drawn through the slit, stands for the real conditions of consciousness. The slit is the threshold, consciousness in the present moment. The part of the tape drawn through the slit represents the whole of consciousness, mostly memory and imagination.

Thus Hodgson sought to explain the unity and continuity of consciousness by reference to connections of the moments of experience within the stream. Instead of positing a mental subject with agency at the core of consciousness, he identified the subject with "connected consciousness *plus* this central, constant, material object" represented by a group of percepts always present in consciousness and commonly called the body (ME, I, 300), so that the body is perceived "as not only the seat but also the proximate real condition or subject of consciousness" (ME, I, 349). As he explained:

> When we say, *I think, I feel, I remember, I desire, I choose, I resolve, I purpose, I act*, and so on, there is involved in each case a nerve process, and this process, which is not expressly described, is included in the act which is described, as a whole, by any of the terms in question, these being terms of consciousness. And the real agency lies in this undescribed nerve action, which is not affected by the concomitant consciousness which is used to indicate it [ME, II, 344].

it [ME, II, 344].

Within the body, it is brain substance, the neurocerebral system, or simply the brain that is "the highest known kind of real conditions" (ME, III, 277).

Upon Hodgson's analysis the total human individual is a compound being consisting of two heterogeneous parts, matter and consciousness:

> The conscious being is double in this sense throughout his whole life, and in every state and process of it. What *he* is said to do, or feel, or think, is really done, felt, or thought, by his nerve organism. His nerve organism is the real agent of Subject. . . . His consciousness is some mode of feeling or thought, or both combined, concomitant with, and conditioned upon, some physical nerve process, or some physical nerve action, to which latter alone his deed belongs [ME, II, 283–84].
>
> The "conscious agent" which common sense does not analyse, and which we all feel that we *are*, is thus, in what is at once physiological and philosophical psychology, analysed into two component parts, the really conditioning and neural cerebral processes, and the process-contents of consciousness which accompany and depend upon them [ME, I, 448].

Concluding Remarks

What commands our appreciation of Hodgson's philosophical achievement, restricted in the present essay to consideration of his metaphysical method and his theory of consciousness, is the striking originality of his views, perhaps the seeds and clearly the anticipations of later thought. He invented a philosophical method similar to Husserl's phenomenological reduction. He introduced the description of consciousness as a stream, discovering corollary theories of redintegration and of concept-formation, all of which William James assimilated, with implications for functional psychology and for pragmatism. He uncovered the principles of temporalism in the immediate data of consciousness long before Bergson, and in important respects he scouted the terrain of categories to which process metaphysics made claim in the twentieth century.

Hodgson offered a theory of whatness (essence) and thatness (existence), which the critical realists—for example, George Santayana—developed in the epistemologies and ontologies that flourished in the period between the two world wars. He acknowledged the centrality of the principle of verification by reference to sense experience for science; but he stressed that perception, which involves reflection, is epistemically ultimate, so that he avoided the pitfalls of positivism and of the sense-datum epistemologies. He underscored the intentionality of consciousness, and discovered the role of interest or purposiveness in thought as the key to concept-formation. At the same time he proposed the epiphenomenalist theory of consciousness, and prepared the way for the establishment of psychology as an experimental, physiological science.

He nonetheless considered every science to be but a partial and fragmentary glimpse of the panorama of knowledge and existence whose province is philosophy. Hodgson was undoubtedly one of the most original British philosophers and perhaps the most seminal British metaphysician of the late nineteenth century.

PART TWO

Archaic Experience in Myth and Art:
Philosophical Supplements

Charles E. Scott

4/Freedom with Darkness and Light
A study of a Myth

The question about the essence of man is not a question about man
Martin Heidegger
Gelassenheit

I shall assume in this discussion that a significant part of our language and tradition is Greek in origin. That part—as well as the other equally significant parts that come from the Hebrews, from Africa, the Anglo-Saxons, and other sources—forms groups of meanings in our awareness that are imbedded and transmitted in our language and tradition. These meanings give determination and identity in our lives.

I shall also assume that the myths and mythological thinking in our Greek heritage deal with commonalities for the human condition, that we are determined partially by a conglomerate expression in this heritage of how we are together in the universe. This expression forms a cultural way of seeing that is, at least partially, unavoidable. When we think *with* the myths, as distinct from thinking *about* them with non-mythological purposes in mind, we are in touch with determinations that are depth meanings in our world.

Probably one of the most important aspects of thinking with myths is openness to the myth itself. That is like being open with dreams, not reducing them to nondream structures, but moving with them as much as possible on their terms and certainly on their ground. One becomes less bound and absorbed by the ordinary practices and assumptions of one's waking life. One becomes freer and more open, more aware of possibilities and other realities that lie outside routines, habits and customs. Above all one becomes accustomed to a region of happening quite distinct from the usual places of waking awareness—a region that is one's own happening, but one that is not governed by the way "things ordinarily happen." By dwelling openly and nonreductively with dreams and fantasies we become freer in relation to the arbitrariness of the usual in our waking lives.

The same can be said for thinking with myths. They come from a

51

region of our heritage that is distant, but they form part of our present heritage, and so are, like the unexpected dream, close. As we think with them, trading criticism for appreciation and "objectivity" for involvement, we find that we draw closer to regions of our awareness that we in no sense originated, but which are ours and in which we are together. That discovery of commonality in myths will tend to be veiled or hidden if we think about them in nonmythological ways, as we do when we analyze them to find out what the Greeks thought about nature or the gods or whatever. In such cases of scholarship and learning we generate helpful information that allows us to report on differences and similarities. But that information must be rethought —reimagined—and freed from the very apparatus that unearthed it before we can experience the depth of our awareness in it.

As we gain more feel for meanings in the myths common in our language and tradition, we become more alert not only to meanings that relate us and constitute us in the depth of our inherited awareness, we also gain touch with how the myths express our human commonality, our being in common. An extraordinary double edge: shared, given, unchosen meanings that have to do with how we are shared, given and unchosen.

Greek myths often express profound experiences of determinations given in the way the world is and pervasive of our kind. And like an artist of this century, the myths, in their iteration, engender a freedom of consciousness, a capacity to be free by telling the determinations and by naming and personalizing the movements of inevitability.

I share with my age the pursuasion that determinations and inevitabilities are historical. The inevitabilities that led to the tragedy of Romeo and Juliet depend on the existence of brutal family rivalries, a semimedieval Catholicism, and so forth. The destinies of our inherited awareness, though not appreciably alterable in any one lifetime, may well not exist for a people in quite a different culture. Destinies come as histories, and inevitabilities come in how things have presence with a people.

In our history, two inevitabilities—much brooded over—are light and darkness, with their attendant spatial imagery of height and depth. We expect light and darkness—with their close associates of life and death, memory and forgetfulness, gaiety and terror, growth and decline, wakefulness and sleep—to carry meaning everywhere. I suspect that nothing carries more depth and power in our Western history than the relation of illumination and darkness, a relation closely in touch with haleness and madness.

Light and darkness have a cosmic dimension. They betoken a certain pervasiveness of all things, a slant on how things are given, the shades of presence. No light at all cannot mean for us a complete absence. It might mean an edge of total darkness, like a far horizon as night falls on a prairie, or the coming of no consciousness at all, or the total loss of something. But light, consciousness and possession are meant at once in these particular instances. Hence, my deepest attitudes regarding both light and darkness are lived in my relation with all things.

I propose to explore a dimension of light and darkness, writ large, in one small portion of Greek mythology. I shall make therapeutically related observations along the way, holding always in mind that these notions are fateful in our lives and that freedom means, in part, being imaginatively open for the determinations that have determination as their issue. The underlying thesis is that *freedom occurs as imaginative openness in determined states*. When these states of determination become the subject of profound fantasy, a remarkable freeness occurs, in which the determinants are slightly transcended in their telling. That occurrence reflects what I take the Greeks to have addressed when they spoke of one cosmos filled with irreconcilable differences.

The Elements of Hades and Zeus

Zeus and Hades are brothers. After they and their allies defeated Cronos and the Titans, Hades received the Underworld as a gift, and Zeus found his sway and aegis at Olympus. The element of Hades is darkness, not the moonlit kind or even a moonless, starry kind, but a pitch darkness, a lightless realm of divinity impenetrable by living mortals. His realm is not at all like the Isles of the Blessed, to appear later in Greek imagery, where heroes find timeless fellowship together. Hades' place, a residence of the dead, is more like a prison, and being taken there is like violent capture or rape. It is a heavy place—down, down, down—and is probably more akin to Saturn's element than it is even to Hades' mother, Gaea, whose children replaced empty chaos. Saturn freezes and rigidifies. But Hades captures too, in darkness and invisibility, if with greater warmth.

Hades, in fact, took Erebus' place. Erebus was not spawned from Gaea, but from Chaos alone. Chaos "was" total emptiness until Gaea founded and brought forth the world. Erebus was a void under the earth, a vast emptiness in which nothing came together or happened: no spawning, no growth, no harvesting, no speaking, no sound, no decay; not a soul there; nothing. With Hades came place, darkness over against light, death, condemnation, imprisonment. The goddess Night, also the child of Chaos and not of Gaea, is closely related to Hades' place. She gave forth both Aether and Daylight, as well as Fate, Destiny, Death, Sleep, Dreams, Memesis, Old Age, and Strife, among others. (She is also the grandmother of Strife's children, including Murder, Lying Words, Lawlessness, Famine and Ruin.)

Hades' place is not a womb. But it *happens*: it is manifest in its darkness, and therein is Gaea's heritage and victory over Erebus. She enjoys part of her victory in the occurrence of death — death too, like all else, was absent in Erebus. And the misery and fate and condemnations and violence and putrid hatreds and all that is dark and ugly and deathly have their place in Gaea's son's region, in which much that is awful and lifeless *happens*. This awful place means life.

Invisibility happens there too. Hades' gift from Gaea's monsters, the Cyclopes, was a helmet that made its wearer invisible. He received it at the same time that Zeus received the gift of lightning and thunderbolts from the Cyclopes, as they all prepared to defeat Cronus and send him and the Titans to the Underworld, to be guarded by the monsters of Gaea. Darkness for Hades means invisibility: not seeing, not coming out into the light, no cancellation of Lethe, no truth. One might wonder if Erebus is not to be preferred — if one might choose — given the totally evasive and ungraspable region of Hades in all its terror. But Hades is there, quite utter and divine, forever cancelling absence in his dark and elusive way.

Zeus' element is Aether. This is not to be forgotten. Aether, daughter of Night, granddaughter of Chaos, not the child of Gaea or of Uranus or of Cronos. As far as I know Erebus and Night were the only children of Chaos. For being Nothing at all, Chaos did a lot, giving as it did the element of Hades and, through Night, the element of Zeus. But Zeus' element is once removed from Chaos, and the distance between Aether and utter darkness must itself be considered divine.

Aether is not mortal light, and though related to Day, is not the same as the light of Day. That light vanishes and comes back, it is suffused with Night, circumscribed by it, and reflects the mortality of human beings. Aether, to the contrary, is as pure as Hades' darkness is utter. Clear luminosity, ever light, total absence of darkness, clean separation from Mother Night. But grandchild of Chaos nonetheless. As awful for humans in its purity as Darkness in its density, but in a totally different way. Zeus could see as far as he wanted in it. Vision was not obstructed. It neither held things up nor weighted them down. All that is in Aether appears. Its touch is manifestness. No closure, no hiddenness, no necessity, no requirements, not even one principle of order. Old and condemned Chaos, once removed, smiles absently in the no-order, no-destiny, no-history, no-person, no-good, no-evil, the luminous and absolute indifference of Aether, Zeus' element.

But Zeus is also Gaea's son, who defeated Cronos, the victor over Chaos' victor. He gathers and produces wonderfully. Eos, Helius, Silene and Caephalus, the dawn's cold wind, are evoked and ordered divinely to keep humans in light. And Eos and Caephalus together gave persons the morning star of hope, in the direction of light, as the cooling breeze announces the rising, cloud-reddening illumination. But Zeus also brought together, in Aether, gods and goddesses, not for the sake of humans, but for divine fellowship. In Aether, where there is no dawn or darkness, there was no natural order at Zeus' arrival at Olympus. Only absolutely uncompromised light. Chaos gave no order.

Zeus' situation is not enviable, given its history. Uranus angered and overworked Gaea. Cronos was a tyrant, selfish and alone, and Gaea would not tolerate his self-protective, ingesting refusal of a chancey kingdom and of growth and expansion. She did not like for her begotten to be closed off and held captive, and she was already giving Zeus, who had the Titans imprisoned, trouble when he emerged as king of heaven. Aether gave the conditions for divine sight, but nothing else. No guidelines, no protection. In this unimpeded luminosity, the gods, now great and wonderful in their victory, gathered. And Zeus had to figure out how to rule with no precedent and with considerable danger.

What did the gods do in their element? Among many other things, they partied, counseled, were angered, were envious, sang, danced, had entertainment by the Graces, made love, gave birth, ate, listened to the Muses sing, thought, held games, were worried, were eloquent, recalled things, built, were jealous, cultivated, tended, were violent, were deceitful, were creative, were fearful. Olympus was not an abstract place, but a place where much that we think of as finite and fallible went on. Limited orders were forever forming, new alliances were made. There were reconciliations and agreements, friendships and complicated forms of opposites.

And through all this ran old Chaos' indestructible heritage through the parentage of Night: immutable, mysterious, marblelike, unbending Fate that Zeus had to live with and respect. Grandfather of Fate, Chaos was omnipresent, imprisoned or not. Zeus might have control over mortals' lives, but he was in a universe he did not make, with an element that was foreign to his own lineage, with a company of deathless, headstrong gods who would pay him only so much attention. The element Aether and the company of gods were absolutely present with anything Zeus might do in the direction of order, and we must not forget that Fate and Aether combine at Olympus to mean that orders of divinity, and consequently of mortals, occur in directions and in luminosity that are absolutely indifferent to even the god of sky, contracts, oaths and the protection of guests. What Cronos set in motion, Fate and the Light spawned of Night, are immutable in the place where Zeus rules.

The elements of the brothers, Hades and Zeus, have the same parentage and are not related at all to Hades and Zeus. I suppose one could think of mortal light—Day—as between Darkness and Aether.

But however they relate, they are in the same cosmos, and we have to think of this cosmos as one with their radical difference.

Their sameness needs also to be noted. It is named as absence of order, as impenetrableness, as mystery, as most utterly other vis-à-vis the human. And they are both where the gods are, even though they are not related to those gods who indwell Darkness and Aether. They are each elements of the presence of life. They each cancel their grandfather Chaos by defining places. They occur as the depth and vault of Gaea. In Aether Zeus could see to Hades, who dwelt in a kingdom that eliminated all Aether. Aether always made visible—the opposite of forgetfulness. They are the same in the sense that neither is mortal, neither is a kind of energy, and that the immortality of both together is reflected in the mortality of a Day's passage.

When we interpret this situation of the gods and the difference and sameness of Darkness and Aether as expressing aspects of the realm of awareness, we are put in touch with a world of a remarkably wide and variant range. Particularly when we do not collapse the situation into an order dominated by any one part or group of the parts. Chaos is remembered in both concealment and illumination. Being alive is remembered in being deathly. Totally incomprehensible movement (Fate) is remembered in the highest and most divine orders, of which we are not the authors. The nonpartiality of growth, nurture, fecundity and life itself is remembered in the process of continual emergence and overthrow of the greatest of powers. Even sleep, forgetfulness and deterioration recall death, loss of brightness, passage of all lumination.

The nonorder of simple, unpolluted clarity for sight means also the strength of ordering, the community of divines, the escapades, fights and lives of the greatest powers, the present distance of utter darkness. The very presence of Hades (as well as Persephone, Charon and particularly Dionysus) means that Darkness is endurable and dwellable. We are in a cosmos, a region in which the whole is implicated in the parts and in which the parts immediately reflect each other in their relations and discontinuities. Above all, in the situation of the gods, we are able to see that awareness is a region of relations, organically related, and not subject finally to explanation, but subject to description.

I am paying particular attention to the presence of Aether and Darkness in this account of cosmological extremities. I am assuming that these mythological elements reflect fundamental and given states of the realm of awareness, and that by reflecting these reflections we draw closer to our own immediacies and see them more clearly. Our therapeutic sensibility will also be affected as we find out what is at stake in an individual life as one lives out denials and acceptances of these outer regions of the human cosmos.

(a) *Aether and Darkness are the progeny of Chaos, once removed. They are not engendered by Uranus, Cronos or Gaea.*

This most remarkable insight in the myths shows that hiddenness and luminosity, in their utterness, are not produced by any ordering direction. They do not reflect personality or intentionality or a cosmic plan. Although Uranus, with his power of generation, overcame Chaos, nevertheless Night and her children remained, unrelated to all powers of decay and growth that were to emerge.

Manifestness and hiddenness do not mean anything, although they constitute the boundaries of the world and are the elements associated with the highest and deepest dimensions of reality. They are both timeless in the sense that they have no structure or movement. That does not mean that they occur without reference to time or movement or structure. It means that with all time and differentiation occurs an element or aspect, pervasive and ever and utter, that is not the same as what goes on or as the going on itself—a freedom, if you will, that is no choice, no identity and no history.

These regions are violated as I make anything of any sort finally definitive of my being or the being of the world, such as: identity, substance, what-I-want, definiteness itself, a virtue or all virtues, or volition. Aether and Darkness are present as not-identity, not-substance, not-what-I-want, not-definiteness, not-a-virtue, not-all-virtues, not-volition. They are what I fear most if I define my life by identities.

Aether is where I can seem to fly endlessly and worldlessly. Darkness is where I can cease to see, grow, remember, and the like. Each, in other words, can be remembered or forgotten in how I live. And each can mean absorption and loss of world. But together they are the regions that give place for all that is divine and free of human constriction. They are present as the awful regions that mean awe, wonder, self-transcendence, depth, profundity, inspiration for us in our particular ways of being aware. As the grandchildren of Chaos they are free of everything that happens in their realm. They are never seen as objects or subjects or things or images. They are utter. And they mean for human identities an incomprehensible endlessness that has not begun and that is present, but on no terms, exactly.

(b) *Aether is the element related to Fate in which Zeus takes counsel.*

Zeus is the father of the Fates of human being. As the grandchildren of Cronos they draw thread from a distaff, wind it and cut it off. They have control over the time of birth, life and death. But Fate is someone else. It was born of Night, too. It decrees, and Zeus has nothing to do with that.

Fate does not mean anything that mortal minds can grasp. Fate is the it-is-done or it-is-to-be-done quality of experience in which one knows that one has no say, and not because someone else is more powerful, but because others are in the same decree. Surely a descendant of Chaos, with no perceptible overarching intuition or wish, but ever-present in human experience. It both pervades structures of life and passes out of human comprehension, and it is not informed by the interests of human personality and character.

Zeus has interests and can be influenced by particular, human concerns and gifts, as well as by human beauty. He protects — and I suppose that he needs to protect — divine prerogatives. He is terrible in his power as far as individual mortals are concerned, but he is always having to do something. Aether has nothing to do. Fate does things, but without interest as far as I can tell. But Zeus is a ruler — a passionate, working, protecting, seeking god. He establishes. He is capricious and irrational. But he wants order among the gods. He wants order among humans (he *will* have hospitality, for example). Even when he is doing just what he feels like doing, for no good reason, a person can see what he is up to and what is going on. His order is fallible, and he is always punishing, shoring up, taking sides and repairing damages. His divinity is found in his ordering power.

That power occurs in Aether, which is not a power, and is compromised by Fate, which has no known relation to ordering and generating powers and has plenty of relation to Chaos. The very element of Zeus' sight (and hearing too, I assume) offers no nurture for what he sees, wants or plans. And Fate's iron decrees do not reflect his capacity for planning, much less his interestedness and passion. Fate and Aether do reflect each other in the absence of purpose, concern, personal meaning, and character. I suppose that means that in the acceptance of inevitability one draws closer to the pure light of divinity in its absence from all personal intent.

In this absence Zeus also finds an unestablished region that means that the very condition of his divine perceptivity and sensibility make inevitable the contingency of all specific (divine) relations and situations. His unending activity reflects this nonfamilial element that does nothing and thereby relativizes all his doings. Pure luminosity, in its absence of meaning, means to us the light of everything as it is and the nonnecessity of all orders. Just as Fate does with its ungrounded decrees.

(c) *Day, the light of mortals, alternates with Night, her mother.*

Night reclaims her regency regularly vis-à-vis her daughter. Day, aligned with Helios, Eos and many other deities, has a daughter's power. But she is never free of her mother. Aether seems to have total freedom in its unaltering, pervasive luminosity. It is constant and reflects Night in its absence of content and its incomprehensibility. That is a reflection of total independence. But Day dawns and dies. Her light, which gives us our perceptivity, comes and goes. She and Night together are the elements of mortality. Day means that our sight fails, even as she means that all things are visible for us—for a time. She gives no order except in being born and dying. She always means Night, who has an encompassing power: Night is not born; she is found there in the depth of day—always there, a primordial absence. Night is in an order, but she escapes it in the sense that she will be present when this order ceases or when Order is gone. Even Gaea has no power over Night.

Being in Day and Night, mortals are limited moments in the progeny of Chaos. Best not look for meaning in that. Meaning happens in Day and Night with their support, to the extent that one is not ensnared in Fate. Mortals reflect, limitedly, the directions of the gods, in the weaker sister of Aether. Being free is being in light and darkness and doing what one finds worth doing in living reference to the company and history of those who are to die.

If I expect Aether in Day, I shall be terribly confused by dawn and twilight. No joy, no serenity. If I live as though day leads to Aether and not to Night, I shall be repeatedly confounded by Night (and by Day as well): I shall be depressed in Night, instead of living with her daughters Sleep and Dream before Day is reborn in the gift of Caephelus and in the bright distance of the morning star. The hopes and rests and directions and meanings of mortals happen only in the realm of no-hope, no-rest, no-direction and no-meaning.

The elements are not to be denied in our being. They are our place, our region, even when they are not our specific place and have no meaning in particular.

(d) *The elements of Hades and Zeus do not weep or laugh.*

Through the myths I have been hearing aspects of awareness, which go far beyond personality, character and individual identity. The elements of Utter Darkness and Aether are not objects of speculation or names for something outside the range of awareness. They name kinds of occurrences that are outside the range of our creating, ordering abilities. They name dimensions of all events that cannot be had, objectified or comprehended.

With all orders—ontological, social, psychological—Utter Darkness and Aether are density and clarity that cannot be achieved or lost or incorporated by an order. They name those most awesome dimensions, usually forgotten and avoided, that are with, but totally free of, the most intense and important passions and powers of reality. They name the nonpowers of awareness that are ever and utter, and appear to us as boundless in themselves, but bounded by each other. They refuse resolution or reduction. They are the elements of pure sight and pure hiddenness with which we share intimacy in being utterly different from them. They are reflected in the light of day and the darkness of night, in circumscribed insights and nightmares, in thinking and confusion, in elucidation and oblivion.

On our owning their presence depends our alertness with divinity and with the mortal freedom of our being. I shall not be free to live and die until I countenance the utter differences of Hades' and Zeus' elements.

We have already noted some of the things that go in these elements or regions of occurrence. We have noted too that the Cosmos involves them both in their radical difference. If I fail to live out of this difference, I shall most probably "humanize" everything, even Night (into relative darkness, missing the quality of darkness itself), Chaos (into uncooperativeness, ignorance, bad upbringing, and so forth), Cronos (tick-tock, tape measures, and dots on a line) and Lethe (repression, bad memory, or psychological blockage). If I give one dominance over the other, losing again part of old Chaos' progeny, I will not see the manifestness or the hiddenness of Aether. Either the underworld or the highest regions will dominate my way of being with things, such that Gaea tends to mean to me total obscurity or mystic luminosity. She is both at once and will not be without sky horizon or inner darkness.

This at-onceness is the center of our final emphasis. The difference of the elements of Zeus and Hades is not the last word. Hades and Zeus are great gods in elements not of their own making. How they are together is part of how (the meaning of) being human is in Day and Night, and these elements of the soul are not affective or intuitional or passionate at all. They are Utter Darkness and Pure Light, without tears and without a smile.

(e) *Hades and Zeus are brothers; Darkness and Aether have the same parentage.*

The oneness of the Greek Cosmos, with its overpowering diversity of divinities, each of whom is far greater than human character, will not be denied. The pervasive Darkness that is Hades' realm and the pervasive Light that is Zeus' realm are as related as are Zeus and Hades. Coming from two different parentages, the four relate like royal, intermarried families. They are related deeply in their histories —their being, as we know it, involves a tellable story of power, reign, murder, conspiracy, defeat, creation of kingdoms, and peaceable conjunction.

That Chaos, through Erebus, becomes a place through Hades, and that Chaos, through Night, becomes a region of sight through Zeus, is terribly remarkable. As remarkable as seeing that is never resolved into what is seen, as light that is so deeply related to darkness that in being light darkness is revealed, and in being darkness light is revealed.

The cosmic nature of the whole story means each of the divinities, and the place of each, manifests all the others in their relatedness. And the reflection of these divinities and realms in all our lives means at once a cosmos of infinitely related differences.

Nietzsche, teacher of classic literature, forever in service of Dionysus and Apollo, speaks out of this world of the soul:

> You higher men, what do you think? Am I a soothsayer? A dreamer? A drunkard? An interpreter of dreams? A midnight bell? A drop of dew? A haze and fragrance of eternity? Do you hear it? Do you not smell it? Just now my world became perfect; midnight too is noon; pain too is a joy; curses too are a blessing; night too is a sun—go away or you will learn: a sage too is a fool.
>
> Have you ever said Yes to a single joy? O my friends, then you said Yes too to *all* woe. All things are entangled, ensnared, enamored; if ever you wanted one thing twice, if ever you said, "You please me, happiness! Abide, moment!" Then you wanted *all* back. All anew, all eternity, all entangled, ensnared, enamored—ah, then you *loved* the world. Eternal ones, love it eternally and evermore; and to woe too, you say: go, but return! *For all joy wants—eternity* [*Thus Spoke Zarathustra*, trans. Kaufman, Viking, p. 323].

Chaos with definiteness. Night with light. Aether with Utter Darkness. And always at once.

The at-onceness of the Cosmos of related eternal differences means that we are with each other always in the reflection of the whole. When the whole is not reflected in a dominance by one or more of the parts, a usurpation occurs that will not long be tolerated by the Cosmos itself.

Freedom and Fantasy

I have read these mythical relations as an account of how being human happens in a related universe far beyond its compass or meaning. Their power is in their indirectness: to be literal with them is always to miss them as myths. Their power to describe how things are, as well as their evocative and suggestive power, is in their nonliteral manner. I believe that is because "what" these myths describe is not "objective." They give account of the happening of things in an "at once" that pervades even the most fundamental elements of all real things. Myths consequently have their meaning for human understanding in how they are appropriated, never in literal application.

One must live with them as one might live with a dream, until the gods begin to interact, as in a waking dream, alive and present without our guidance. Only then, I believe, will the full power of the myths of our tradition become consciously efficacious for the philosopher or therapist: not as a pattern for pathology or health, but as a region of powers with which we dwell, sane or not, as we interpret ourselves and our world.

Freedom with such powerful determinants? Hades found his freedom and his space of life in his element, Utter Darkness. And Zeus, in Aether. These nonorders, nonmatters were the regions, the place-qualities, in which these gods could make their mistakes, establish their domains, suffer and perhaps even die. I do not mean to suggest that we are like Hades or Zeus or both together. They are not like persons. They are powers considerably in excess of all human character. I do mean to suggest that Utter Darkness and Aether, in the lineage of Chaos who countenanced no order, named the freedom of these two gods, and that like them we humans have our freedon, our "element." Is it found in, shall I say, "mything"? Or in free imagining? Or in countenancing fantasy? Or in naming things as they have to be? I mean to say all those things.

Our "element" is the orderless region of dreaming, fantasizing, concocting, seeing, imagining, intuiting. I say "orderless" because the range of orders and worlds that can take place in this most awesome region appears unlimited. Who has counted the number of dream orders that occur in dreaming? Does the region of fantasy tell us how to put things together? Do myths, as such, teach as right and wrong? They thrive on contradiction, battles of orders, differences among gods.

What is my life like if there is little imaginative psychic movement? Intelligent perhaps, distracting, involved with things, but banal. Attentive to detail or visionary, responsible or irresponsible, but flat behind the surface. The absence of psychic movement is like an absence of vital meaning or lively images in addition to whatever else is going on. At an extreme, it is that dead sense that gives backdrop to whatever a suicidal person does. In a more ordinary way, the absence of psychic movement is lived as an absence of imagination, as a vague boredom with everything, as a feeling that nothing is deeply arresting, as not being very moved by anything.

In that absence, I do not get inside different ways of seeing or different ways of being, and find how to confront those differences. I live a straight-out identity of my own, no matter how devious or how upright, without being able to experience that identity from different postures and in different ways of being. I tend to be literal about everything. I like the finality of certainty. I want nonambiguity. Fantasy seems the opposite of truth. Dream seems the opposite of reality.

And I seem vaguely distant behind whatever closeness I may achieve. When there is little imaginative, psychic movement in my life, I live as though I were not free.

Our freedom is found as we open to the region of fantasy without guarantees of stability, of life with multiple *teloi*, this region of fecundity that does not support for long anything that we hold dear, but engenders yet dearer, as well as more dreaded, things. We may also come to our element as we dwell with the myths, finding ourselves strangely free as we imagine the inevitable and discover that we are ourselves of an element that casts doubt on even the most stringent of all inevitabilities.

Carol A. Kates

5/Myth and Art:
The Authentic Image

The theater, poetry: these techniques can communicate new experience; they can open up new possibilities and elicit new kinds of feeling, new self-interpretations . . . Poetry and drama . . . often awaken in us . . . a new and lively self-feeling and awareness of our possibilities and destroy old roles and routine responses

Edward G. Ballard

Edward Ballard's claim that art works constitute a means of self-interpretation provides a clue to the vexed question of identifying authenticity in art. Some works, one feels, do not reveal an essential or ontological truth about human existence. Indeed, there are artworks that distort the truth; in some subtle way, they diminish rather than enhance our sense of self. And yet how is one able to make this judgment? If one already knows the truth, one has no need of art. But without prior knowledge, how does one detect an inauthentic vision? More fundamentally, what sort of human truth does art reveal?

I shall argue that Ballard's ontological description of the self as a free subjectivity identified within a "nonobjective dialectic" provides a basis for distinguishing authentic and inauthentic art. Specifically, I shall claim that authentic art reveals the self in its ontological dimension within a changing experiential context.

The context for self-interpretation is provided by the social order, which offers to each subject a set of social values implicit in the behavioral conventions or roles of society and in the social myths and "world-symbols" that express and legitimize that social order. Thus, artworks have a social or, as I shall call it, a mythic aspect. As I hope to show, it is characteristic of inauthentic work that it distorts the truth of human existence through an unself-conscious treatment of social myth.

Nonobjective Dialectic of the Self

In *Man and Technology*, Ballard developed the concept of the "nonobjective dialectic" through which a self enters into dialogue with itself to establish an accurate self-image. As Ballard sees the matter, such a dialogue does not produce a final, definitive answer or general truth about the nature of some individual self, except perhaps within the limits of an ironic recognition that the identity of a self both is and is not manifested through the roles it carries out. In the end, an individual self eludes definition because it is a subject. Thus, the self attempts to take itself as an object of knowledge that might be given, say, in the way that physical objects may be apprehended in their presence or under-stood through reflection on their properties. (Ballard distinguishes between a spontaneous—or one might also say sensuous—form of intuition and a reflective interpretation of a presentation.) However, what is uncovered through the intuitive awareness of one's existence and through reflective self-interpretation is the self as an activity: specifically, an awareness-of-existence or a reflection-on-self. The intending self, the individual act of awareness or reflective interpreta-tion, is not an object.

At this point one might simply conclude that the self is a subject—that is, has a subjective nature—and point to this as its essence. Thus Husserl's conception of the intentional structure of consciousness provides a kind of definition on the self as subject. Furthermore, if consciousness is always embodied, one might understand the structure or essence of an *individual* consciousness in terms of its unique space-time location. An individual consciousness or "self," then, might be grasped in its existence as something like "this embodied awareness now" and understood reflectively as the locus of a unique set of experiences resulting from its placement in the world and resulting in a specific personal identity.

Such an analysis of the self may serve as a description of subjectivity in general, but it also points to the essential difficulty in defining an individual self. What I as an individual want to know about my self is not merely what are my ontological properties as a being-in-the-world but what am I as an individual: a unique embodied awareness with my own limits and possibilities, a unique perspective on the world. Evi-dently, the only way to discover what I am is to "catch" the self, as it were, "in action." As Ballard puts it:

> The presented self is interpreted in terms of an elaborated world view, a familiar profession, or a kinship system. . . . In a social group, a person aware of himself as a part of this whole and perhaps obligated to it, tends to interpret himself by understand-ing himself in an accepted manner and by assuming a role, a function, or profession which is defined clearly enough within the social context and possesses definite object-like properties. By thus acceding to the demands of role and of the social forms

which define it, the elusive self seems to be caught and fixed like an object in the net of a familiar structure.[1]

In short, to discover my own nature I must objectify myself through action. I cannot know my own thoughts until I think them. I cannot know my character until I have been tested. Without work to do, I have no sense of my powers; without failure, no grasp of my limits.

As Ballard points out, society offers the individual a number of preconceived identities from which one may select during the process of self-interpretation. In general, there is a social demand that everyone assume certain roles (e.g., "citizen," "family member"), while other roles are options that may be selected by (appropriate) individuals. In one sense, if an individual is successful in carryong out some role, one may say that the role, or the individual's way of playing the role, objectifies or manifests the identity of that person. At the same time, however, the self that takes on some role retains the power to reject that form of activity and find a new direction. The subject that interprets is free to reinterpret and choose again from the set of available roles.

Thus Ballard understands "subjectivity" to be "a man's power of standing outside of himself, as it were, or of separating his powers from their directedness and modifying or redirecting them."[2] In sum, an individual self is always more than what is manifested. The freedom of the self lies in this horizon of possibilities. However, it is a limitation resulting from that very freedom that in choosing a role in order to discover what one is, one is simultaneously shutting out other directions of self-discovery.

The fundamental limitation on self-definition is compounded by the fact that an individual is changed by experience as well as by changes in the body, in the natural and social environment, and in the culture. For this reason Ballard characterizes the dialogue of self-discovery as "dialectical." In a given situation the self responds at first to a mute perception of its possibilities through feelings, which may in turn provoke a reflective interpretation through action, imagination or critical thought. But these manifestations of the self will lead in turn to a new response in feeling, leading again to new interpretations. This dialectic of the self in flux ensures that there can be no definitive self-image. The nature or identity of an individual self both is and is not objectified through roles: the self that reveals its powers and limits through activity is always only partially seen, in limited ways and in

---

1. Edward G. Ballard, *Man and Technology* (Pittsburgh: Duquesne University Press, 1978), pp. 34–35.
2. *Man and Technology*, p. 88.

specific situations, and the self thus manifested is always the self at that point in time and before it is modified through the event.

Although there is no final truth about oneself, Ballard argues that one is obligated to pursue the truth. Philosophical analysis has uncovered the ontological structure of the self as "an intrinsically limited set of possibilities."[3] The self is dependent on external factors determining its existence and, in part, its identity, and the self is essentially finite and, ultimately, "non-identical with any of the type-identities offered by a culture."[4]

Thus individuals who deny their subjectivity and attempt to live a life of unself-consciousness are denying (one might say, repressing) an awareness of the self, and in that sense are denying the essence of human existence. For that reason Ballard speaks of a "primary obligation" deriving from our human nature as subjects to acknowledge that nature, in particular the distance of the self from its roles, and to take responsibility for one's freedom as a means of discovering the truth about oneself. Failure to engage in nonobjective dialectic is failure to live a human life, and such a failure of the self entails what one might call ontological guilt. In Ballard's words:

> The ways of guilt are many. One need only avoid reflection upon oneself and accept without question some conventional mode of life, or one may identify oneself so completely with some function or role that one fails to become aware of oneself as something other than the role-player, or one may disguise one's future and imagine oneself to continue somehow infinitely in a non-terminating role, and the like. In effect all of these ways of avoiding oneself are ways of imagining the self to be fate, or even superior to fate; they are hybritic, and invite the revenge of fate.[5]

The references to "fate" and "hybris" recall Greek tragedy, which Ballard takes as a paradigm of the dialectic of the self. Tragedy reveals the archaic human experience of role trial and change of role. To be successful in this trial is to make an ironic or self-conscious choice of a role that is in harmony with one's actual powers and limits. If one is fortunate, the world will allow one to "be" that person; if one is not fortunate, one will follow Socrates along the path of martyrdom. Tragedy occurs when one misidentifies oneself, either by ignoring one's ontological limits as a subject or through blindness concerning individual limitations. The "revenge of fate" is a revelation of human dependence, finitude and "Socratic" ignorance.

3. *Man and Technology*, p. 146.
4. *Man and Technology*, p. 146.
5. *Man and Technology*, p. 147.

The circumstance that Greek tragedy provides an archetypal image of nonobjective dialectic suggests that art may serve an ontological function. Art that pointed to general (ontological) conditions of human life, thus revealing essential human limits, would clearly have a universal significance and a distinctive type of authenticity or truth. Similarly, artworks that distorted the nature of human life might be accused of a fundamental falseness or inauthenticity. Art critics and aestheticians have applied such categories to artworks but they have not, thus far, achieved any notable success in clarifying the distinction in the art context.

I shall show that Ballard's concept of nonobjective dialectic provides a convincing model of the nature of authentic and inauthentic art. Before turning to art, however, I must first consider the nature of myth as a social product that contributes essential cultural content to works of art.

Myth and Social Reality

As Ballard notes, human beings interpret their experience through certain "world-symbols." One thinks, for example, of the Anglo-Saxon "hall" representing the light and warmth of the world in contrast with the cold darkness of the unknown. It is in this darkness that Grendel lies in pain, waiting to destroy those sheltered within the hall. Christianity provides another world-symbol: the tree of life that becomes the crucifix and an image of redemption as a promise of eternal life in compensation for wordly suffering. In general, a world-symbol is an image pointing to the basic values or the worldview inherent in a culture. Thus it constitutes a means of self-interpretation.

World-symbols might be said to have a religious significance in the sense that they express a cultural judgment about the meaning of life: the events that are taken to be of ultimate concern, and then provide a context for the interpretation and evaluation of one's own life. Religious myths are stories that incorporate such world-symbols and, in Eliade's terms, provide paradigmatic or exemplary models to be imitated by the men and women of a given society. In societies that recognize no significant secular activities, all social roles or ritualized social behaviors are legitimized as imitations of the paradigmatic gestures of gods, culture heroes or mythical ancestors.[6] However, even societies that differentiate between secular and narrowly religious behavior—the latter concerned with formal worship of a god—utilize ritual and myth to structure social life and to legitimize a social order.

What one might call "social myths" are deeply rooted beliefs or

6. Mircea Eliade, *The Sacred and the Profane* (New York: Harper & Row, 1961).

value-judgments that bear two relations to social structure.[7] First, such myths "express" or imitate social reality in the sense that they reflect a given social order or ritualized system of behavior. The connection between social ritual and myth may be direct or indirect — for example, some beliefs may reflect analogies from the social order. But in any case, to discover the myths of a given society one must examine the underlying social order. Second, myths serve an instrumental function by directing persons toward certain forms of behavior and away from others. Social myths are conventional expressions of conventional ideas. As such, they reinforce a given social order.

It is always difficult to become aware of the myths within one's own society. To become aware of myths in a critical way means to see them as myths — that is, as models presenting values or beliefs that serve a particular social function. Typically, judgments that some behavior is "proper" or "improper," "natural" or "unnatural," reflect unexamined social myths. The "socialized" but unself-conscious person may be expected to adopt conventional attitudes and behaviors unreflectively, simply because certain things have always been done a certain way and therefore should always be done that way.

This notion calls to mind Eliade's category of rituals that imitate the paradigmatic gestures of mythical ancestors. If one is pressed to defend some such conventional idea, one might try to find a rational (i.e., empirical or logical) basis for one's belief, but this is always potentially threatening to an established social order. If one should discover that one is defending a particular set of social values rather than "objective" truths, there is always the possibility that one will reconsider and try to change society. Of course one might also make an entirely deliberate choice to defend a set of social values understood as such. In a broad sense, then, it is the process of critical examination that distinguishes a "rational" from a "mythic" affirmation of values.

In addition to providing paradigms of socially desirable behavior, social myths also channel behavior through cultural stereotypes that create a "bad image" for those who are socially marginal (without a proper "niche"), or who in some way threaten the social order. For example, in societies having witchcraft beliefs, including European societies in the Middle Ages, it seems to be generally true that the primary targets of witchcraft accusations are individuals who are in some way socially anomalous.

Among the Nupe of Nigeria the women, rather than the men, have become traders.[8] For this reason they generally have much more

7. See Mary Douglas, *Purity and Danger* (Penguin, 1966) for a recent elaboration of Durkheim's insight into the social basis of myth.

8. S. F. Nadel, "Witchcraft in Four African Societies: An Essay in Comparison," in *American Anthropologist* 54 (1952) 18–29.

money than the men and in that respect are of greater social importance. These women frequently leave their children in order to go on
trading expeditions. In fact they often refuse to bear children, or they
perform abortions without male consent. Needless to say, the males of
the tribe, who are legitimately dominant as tribal and family lawgivers,
are very resentful of the situation. Their response to this threat to the
"ideal" social order is to accuse the more aggressive and independent
women of witchcraft. In fact it is taken for granted that the leader of
the female traders is also the leader of the witches. Thus, if there are
any social disasters, such as crop failure or epidemic that might be a
result of witchcraft, one of the women will be blamed and secretly
beaten or murdered by the men. The social effect of such a threat is to
maximize social conformity among the women, or to inhibit them from
asserting their social power. An attack upon witches is, in this instance,
a moderately successful means of punishing those who threaten established social values.

Within our own Western context one might recall the story of Joan of
Arc, that archetypal social intruder. She was, as Mary Douglas observes, "a peasant at court, a woman in armour, an outsider in the
councils of war," surely something like the social equivalent of the
"beetles and spiders who live in the cracks of the walls and wainscot-
ing," an intruder who must attract fear and dislike owing to her
"ambiguous" status.[9]

Though it may perhaps be less obvious, there is also a social message
(a kind of warning) in such common stereotypes as "interfering
mothers-in-law," "domineering wives," "hen-pecked husbands" and
"aggressive women as (dangerous) lesbians." One would expect such
warnings to intensify during periods of social change, when traditional
roles may be threatened. Thus, as wives are forced to join the work
force, there is an almost hysterical concern to ensure the survival of
traditional family life and preserve the "femininity" of the "total
woman" (in Britain, the "superwoman" who pursues a career while
remaining a housewife, mother and devoted spouse).

Social myths are expressed in a "positive" form through the glorifica-
tion of certain roles and the creation of culture heroes who embody
social values. Such images provide, in Eliade's terms, paradigms or
exemplars of socially desirable types. It is, for example, somewhat
interesting to ponder the cultural significance of the images of James
Bond and Superman as archetypal "defenders of Western values."
Despite their differences these two figures share a common trait.
Neither is able to succeed on the basis of natural human power and
intelligence. Bond relies on sophisticated technology, and Superman's

9. Mary Douglas, *Purity and Danger*, p. 124.

body is itself a kind of inhumanly powerful machine. Thus, both reflect what Ballard has suggested is a "world-symbol" of modern technological society: the image of a cyborg or heroic machine-person.

If the cyborg image does truly symbolize our "world" or make explicit the basic values underlying our social myths, the implication is that we are moving toward what Ballard calls a religion of technology or "technism" inconsistent with humanistic culture. A humanistic view of technology would see it as a means to the humanly desirable end of a maximally free and aesthetic mode of life. As Lewis Mumford puts it, "Every manifestation of human culture is directed ultimately to . . . the expression of the human personality." Thus technology provides a means of "purposeful self-identification, self-transformation, and . . . self-understanding."[10] Technism, in contrast, represents a denial of subjectivity and freedom. As myth, technism points away from the nonobjective dialectic of the self toward a view of the human person as a tool or a more or less efficient cog in a powerful machine that serves no purpose beyond that of "conquering" nature. In the world of technism there is no freedom, no self, only a set of more or less useful roles to be carried out by efficient machine-persons who have identified with an inhuman power as a way of denying and overcoming individual weakness.

I think the real point of Mumford's statement is not that the humanist alternative to technism is one of many ways of responding to technology, but that it is the only way we can respond as human beings. If it is indeed an ontological truth that we are subjects—in Sartre's words—"condemned" to the freedom of self-definition, then the denial of subjectivity is paradoxical and self-refuting. One can no more deny one's point of view, one's consciousness, than one can deny that one exists. Thus one may say that the worldview of technism is false, in the sense that it denies an essential truth of human existence, from which it follows that no authentic work of art can represent the project of living as a "person of technism" without also revealing it as a form of self-deception.

Authenticity and Inauthenticity in Art

It is characteristic of inauthentic artworks that they distort the nature of human existence and for that reason do not "ring true." I believe that this distortion occurs on an ontological level. Thus the judgment of authenticity does not concern such contingent matters as the accuracy of some portrayal of a social type or setting, or the credibility of a

10. Lewis Mumford, *The Myth of the Machine: Techniques and Human Development* (New York: Harcourt, 1970), p. 10.

plot. Works that are flawed on this level are merely inept or "bad," and
such flaws may well infect authentic as well as inauthentic productions.
The distortion introduced by inauthentic works is fundamental: a
failure to exhibit the self in its freedom as it emerges ¿hrough a
nonobjective dialectic. Such works cannot ring true no matter how
accurately they portray specific conditions of social experience, because they conceal the freedom that is the essential condition for that
experience.[11]

In our society one frequently encounters inauthentic works that
serve as a kind of social propaganda or ideology by promoting social
myths that support a particular social order. Such works serve as
persuasive elements in the social machinery of manipulation through
the social myths they express. Social values are reproduced unconsciously as "objective" facts and the self is reduced to a set of "given"
social roles. Artworks that in this way deny the essential structure of
human possibility or freedom may be experienced as oppressive or
deadening, though they might also strike some as profound revelations
of human "nature" and thus as liberating in a Spinozistic sense.

One thinks of D.H. Lawrence, for example, who for many strikes a
deep emotional note through his "revelation" of the dominant male
and subordinate female "nature." When Kate Millett attacked Lawrence's work as sexist propaganda,[12] she was in turn roundly criticized
by the academic literary establishment for attacking an acknowledged
master. This conflict suggests the difference between traditional art
criticism, which concerns itself with the factual level of plausibility
("realism"), expressiveness and technique, and a more radical form of
criticism concerned with the essential dimension of human freedon.

John Berger's recent discussion of the category of the nude in
modern painting provides another instance of a critical concern for
essential truth in art.[13] Berger distinguishes between nakedness and
nudity as follows: to be *naked* is to be oneself, without disguise, whereas
to be *nude* is to be seen naked by others and yet not to be recognized for
oneself. As he puts it, "A naked body has to be seen as an object in order
to become a nude."[14] In the European tradition (beginning with the
first medieval representations of the shame of Adam and particularly
of Eve in Eden), the naked body is almost always female and is
conventionally represented as a nude: with an awareness of being seen
by a (male) spectator. Thus, through such conventional themes as

11. In his book *Loss of the Self in Modern Literature and Art* (New York: Vintage, 1962),
Wylie Sypher describes what may be the loss of a romantic image of the self as an
autonomous and powerful center of the world. However, the self remains as a center of
receptive attention or as a point of view.
12. Kate Millett, *Sexual Politics* (Garden City: Doubleday, 1970).
13. John Berger, *Ways of Seeing* (Penguin, 1977).
14. *Ways of Seeing*, p. 54.

"Susannah taking her bath" or "the judgment of Paris," as in modern pornography, the naked female body is displayed with a consciousness of being anonymously given to the male who looks at it. (In an instructive scene in Charlotte Bronte's *Villette*, Lucy Snowe is severely reproved by a shocked male companion for "surveying" a nude painting as coolly as any man.)

Throughout the European tradition there have been exceptional canvases which have violated the conventions of the nude by painting nakedness. One thinks of Rubens, who gives us the nuances of skin tones and "fat softness" in such detail that each body takes on an extraordinary particularity. Not all of these bodies are objects to be possessed by the voyeur. For example, Helen Fourment, his second wife, is painted as a naked individual who is very much loved.

There are other examples of this type: the woman Rembrandt painted in *Danäe* is naked for him alone; and, as Berger suggests, Manet's *Olympia* is "somewhat defiantly" questioning her role as a nude. Once the ideal was broken in painting, this way of seeing women passed into advertising, television, popular films and pornography. However, an inauthentic view of women to be found in Titian, Rubens, Tintoretto, Cranach and others is clearly not to be blamed on "popular culture."

Nor should one assume that artworks critical of a given society must be authentic. It is quite possible to criticize a given set of roles and values in an entirely unself-conscious way and to present such criticism in works that conceal the self. There is, for example, good reason to dismiss Gorki's "revolutionary" novel *Mother* as simpleminded propaganda. Gorki's novel reverses the values of social roles in a capitalistic society by presenting all the factory owners and bourgeois landlords as evil and corrupt, in contrast to the uniformly virtuous and idealistic revolutionary workers. Such revolutionary mythology is not a revelation of freedom. Oddly enough, it is not even an effective condemnation of capitalism, inasmuch as it seems to depict moral virtue as a function of sincerity and intelligence rather than of economic conditions, despite the gratuitous assumption that it is correlated with class.

The Gorki novel raises a central issue concerning the authenticity of any artwork that expresses some ideological worldview. Marxist critics of Western bourgeois art contend that it expresses the values of a social order in decline. Thus Ernst Fischer contends that modern art is "decadent," because it obscures the meaning of social reality.[15] Only art informed by Marxist principles can, he says, understand and express the real significance of modern life.

Karsten Harries replies that the modern artist is searching for the

15. Ernst Fischer, *The Necessity of Art* (Penguin, 1963).

meaning of human life with an awareness that it may have no definite meaning.[16] From this Nietzschean perspective, the Marxist faith in "scientific socialism" appears excessively optimistic, even absurd and ideological. A number of critics seem to agree with Harries that the authentic style is sceptical and searching rather than confident and dogmatic, and that an artist who begins with a definite theory about the meaning of human life is to that extent hampered by an ideology that interferes with authentic vision.[17] Sartre expressed the same idea in another context when he remarked that Mauriac could not be considered a genuine novelist, because he was a Catholic.[18]

One way of approaching the debate about ideology in art would be to try to determine which social or political theory was true and which false. One might then argue that artworks that incorporated a true analysis of social experience were authentic, whereas those that promoted false theories were ideological or inauthentic. This is the position taken by those Marxist critics who condemn Western art and who praise, for example, Gorki's "masterpiece of social realism" (*Mother*) on the ground that the Marxist analysis of class warfare is the only true ("objective") account of social reality. On the other hand, the artist who assumes that a Marxist or some (other) religious account of the meaning of social experience is false, and operates on the theory that human life has no definite meaning, might also be said to be projecting a theoretical viewpoint into art. If then one holds such a viewpoint one might consider such sceptical or nihilistic art "realistic" or authentic.

My own view is that artworks that promote social myths without revealing the process of self-definition are ideological regardless of whether they favor a socialist or capitalist system, or a religious or atheistic worldview, and so on. In contrast, works that present social values and analyses of social experience within the context of ontological truth about subjectivity and freedom may be called authentic regardless of the truth or falsity of the social, political or religious theories favored by an artist. Artists who have different social and religious values and who disagree about the causal factors influencing human decisions will create very different representations of ideal social behavior and of the conditions that limit individual self-interpretation and action. The essential point is that authentic art must reveal the subjectivity and freedom of those who, wittingly or unwittingly, must define themselves within some context and who in doing so are committed to certain actions.

16. Karsten Harries, *The Meaning of Modern Art* (Evanston: Northwestern University Press, 1968).

17. Roy McMullen, *Art, Affluence, and Alienation* (New York: Mentor, 1968).

18. Jean-Paul Sartre, "François Mauriac and Freedom," in *Literary and Philosophical Essays* (New York: Collier, 1962).

A Marxist work could meet this condition of authenticity *and* show that human beings are inevitably alienated or oppressed under a capitalistic system. One might, for example, create factory owners of great "goodwill" (of whom there are some) and workers of an evil, exploitative disposition (of whom there are many), and try to show how the good intentions of the former are frustrated by the nature of the economic system, while the selfish impulses of the latter create tensions pointing toward a final dissolution of that system. Such a work would not, of course, prove the Marxist thesis, but it would provide an imaginative "test" of a theoretical claim. However, the authenticity of the work would not depend on the truth or falsity of the Marxist theory of economic determinism but rather on its illumination of the universal process of self-definition within a specific set of social conditions.

Although an artwork that depicts the self authentically may suggest a criticism of current social values or of the conventional roles available within a given society (for example, through the character of Becky Sharp in *Vanity Fair*), such social criticism is not a necessary condition of authenticity. Artworks overcome the ideological function of social myths and in fact contribute to a rational examination of such myths if they represent social values as possibilities chosen or rejected by those who play specific social roles.

For example, the author of the Icelandic epic *Njal's Saga* was a Christian who was also sympathetic to the heroic values of pre-Christian Germanic society. In the saga he depicts Gunnar as a mar-tyred hero who deliberately chooses his fate and is finally destroyed as he carries out his obligations in a vendetta. Despite the destructiveness and ultimate injustice of the Germanic code regarding blood feuds, Gunnar chooses not to "turn aside" from his fate, much as Homer's Achilles chooses to fight and die young rather than live unheroically. In contrast, Njal chooses the Christian role of peacemaker and tries unsuccessfully to end the vendetta before he is drawn into it. In the end, Njal's fate is tragic; the social code ultimately requires him to participate in the violent struggle. In one sense the saga might be said to criticize heroic values by showing their destructive consequences. At the same time one is led to understand and perhaps to admire Gun-nar's character as he deliberately chooses his role with full awareness of those consequences.

Authentic works illuminate the roles, images, symbols or, in general, the myths of a society by showing how they may be understood as manifestations of freedom, or possibilities of self-interpretation and action available in a given social context. For this reason it is generally assumed that art can overcome clichés, prejudices, stereotypes and meaningless or "dead" images by rethinking them and uncovering their living truth in self-experience. Consider as an instance the Gothic church as a world-symbol of late medieval Christianity. The Gothic structure was originally intended as a specific image of the redemption of matter, an overcoming of the darkness and weightiness of matter by the "light" of spiritual reality. As such, it was a visible manifestation of God's transforming presence on earth. (At an earlier stage, the Romanesque church provided a visible "fortress" keeping out the invading "powers of darkness.") Today it is difficult if not impossible to respond to such a supremely confident expression of faith. The modern world is predominantly secular, despite the fact that churches in the Gothic style are still erected by those of a "conservative" bent.

To the extent that such a style of church architecture has become merely conventional rather than expressive of a contemporary religious experience or of a conviction about the meaning of life, one would expect a contemporary artist to reject it and create a more authentic form. I think that LeCorbusier has done precisely this at Ronchamp, where he built a church that, in effect, throws itself away from the earth in a direction without revealing the (otherworldly) "space" to which it points. Such an image says that God is not present but that to be religious means to look for God. It is not a confident image, and the religious myth it expresses may very well be pointless (if God does not exist). However, it may be called authentic insofar as it provides a plausible, contemporary means of self-interpretation for those in pursuit of a religious dimension within a secular environment.

It is, I think, a significant comment on the worldview implicit in modern industrial society that modern art has become increasingly philosophical in its focus on the ontological dimension of the self. The social ideal represented by technism is to fit into the system smoothly, as an efficient machine. The more efficient the machine, the more highly it is valued. To an alarming degree, one's social value, one's very identity, is tied to some organization, and there is a relentless pressure within organizations to increase efficiency through a system of constant evaluation ("feedback") and rewards.

However, though one may define the goals of such organizations in mechanical or economic terms (e.g., to produce goods or provide services in a cost-efficient manner), it remains for human beings to specify the value of the system, or the human purpose it is designed to serve. The "religion" of technism might express the social values implicit in the system, but it tells us only that we should become machines working to produce better machines. Traditional religion provides an otherworldly purpose without justifying some manner of "worldly" existence.

Although many philosophers have emphasized the intrinsic value of human freedom and happiness, the worldview of secular humanism has not been widely understood or acted upon in our society. Thus it is left to individuals to identify themselves within a society that does not tend to value the process of self-discovery or purposeful self-identification, and that rewards those who function well as unself-conscious, uncritical, unemotional machines. Perhaps it is this lack of a generally accepted humanistic vision of the self that explains the abstract, intensely self-conscious, philosophical character of modern art.

In 1913 Marcel Duchamp began exhibiting machine-made objects purchased in stores as "ready-made" art works: a bottle-carrier and bicycle wheel, a typewriter cover, a steel comb, a urinal. In 1966 David Bainbridge presented his *Crane*, a mechanical object declared to be both crane and art object at certain times, and simply crane at other times. In 1918 Kasimir Malevich exhibited his "empty" canvas *White on White*; other artists followed suit with a series of blank, "hidden," black or extraordinarily minimal canvases. In 1968 Mel Ramsden attached the following note to his *Secret Painting* (a black canvas): "The content of this painting is invisible: the character and dimension of the content are to be kept permanently secret, known only to the artist." In 1967 Ian Burn produced *Mirror Piece*, consisting of an ordinary mirror hanging on the wall of a gallery, displayed with notes describing three possibilities: (a) an ordinary mirror hanging in a room, identified as a mirror, (b) the same mirror hanging in a gallery, without notes, where it *might* be taken to be art, and (c) the same mirror in a gallery with notes explaining the art intention behind the piece. In 1969 Terry Atkinson published an essay entitled "Introduction" (*Art-Language* I:1) describing a theoretical essay about art as itself an artwork (whether or not placed in an "art context" such as a museum).

Obviously these conceptual pieces are concerned with the nature of art. They are not simply developing new art forms or techniques, but are suggesting that art is a matter of context. Thus anything may function as art by virtue of its presentation within an "art context."[19]

The avant-garde focus on a kind of meta-level of art significance (i.e., on the artwork as a statement that it is to be seen as art) is one aspect of a characteristic preoccupation with epistemological issues. Modern art seems obsessively concerned with the truth of its presentations. Thus Robbe-Grillet rejects character, plot and what he calls

19. The conceptual artist Joseph Kosuth has appointed himself a philosophical spokesman for the conceptual art movement. Thus he offers the following definition of art: "Works of art are analytic propositions. That is, if viewed within their context—as art—they provide no information whatsoever about any matter of fact. A work of art is a tautology in that it is a presentation of the artist's intention, that is, he is saying that that particular work of art *is* art, which means, is a *definition* of art. Thus, that it is art is true *a priori*. . . . " ("Art After Philosophy," in *Conceptual Art*, Ursula Meyer, ed. [New York: Dutton, 1972], p. 164). Unfortunately, Kosuth does not tell us how to identify the "artist" or characterize the "art context."

commitment: a convincing presentation of what purports to be "the" truth about something.[20] Style is never "innocent," and therefore the writer must do whatever is necessary to interfere with "belief" and avoid pursuasive "rhetoric" by presenting the novel *as* a novel, which can never do more than construct a game of possibility on the surface of the arational presence of the world. There are also novels about language, and about the novel as a certain use of language: specifically about the dissolution, fragility and arbitrariness of language and the silence that threatens it or that it promises (Joyce, Beckett). Whereas the traditional novel attempted to "tell a story well," the "art" novel makes itself visible as a certain arbitrary form.

The deliberate "artiness" of modern work emphasizes the relative—one might say phenomenal—status of an art presentation. In one sense, then, modern art might be called sceptical. It lacks confidence in its power to express an absolute truth, to reveal the essence, the "reality," of some event.[21] By the same token, however, it seems convinced about the ontological status of its images: they are "possibilities," "points of view," "(new) ways of experiencing," which are framed by the art sign. There is an underlying philosophical assumption that reality itself is phenomenal and thus conditioned by the viewpoint of a subject. From this phenomenological perspective, then, the artist is free to create the conditions for a new experience or point of view.

Thus Bruce Nauman produced these "art instructions" in 1969:

> Drill a hole into the heart of a large tree and insert a microphone. Mount the amplifier and speaker in an empty room and adjust the volume to make audible any sound that might come from the tree.
> Drill a hole about a mile into the earth and drop a microphone to within a few feet of the bottom. Mount the amplifier and speaker in a very large empty room and adjust the volume to make audible any sounds that might come from the cavity.

Some artists have provided new experiences of standard logical paradoxes. For example, Frederick Barthelme filled out a form that stated "Instead of making art I filled out this form" and presented it as art (February 22, 1970). Gregory Battcock produced the "art-statement": "Art I Am Not Nor Have I Ever Been Gregory Battcock Art I Am Not Nor Have I Ever Been Gregory Battcock" (1972).

20. Alain Robbe-Grillet, "On Several Obsolete Notions," in *For A New Novel* (New York: Grove, 1965).
21. Even the recent, somewhat more conservative, photorealist style in painting might suggest an epistemological interest in the "objectivity" that is commonly attributed to photographs.

Other artists use techniques that cause ordinary objects to be seen in unexpected ways. Rosemary Castoro (one of the more interesting conceptual artists) used tape to divide a gallery room in *Roomcracking* (1969), interrupting the ordinary function of the room and presenting it as a cracked surface. In her *Eclipse* (1970) she uses language in the form of an elaborate but arbitrary record of certain "bits" or "points" of activities gone through in one day, producing a strange and oddly significant experience of passage through time. Lawrence Weiner threw water on the wall of an empty gallery room, and exhibited the (dry) wall as *A Wall Stained with Water* (1969).

John Cage has perhaps gone further than anyone else in the direction of interrupting expectations and undermining conventional modes of experience. He uses chance techniques to produce combinations of words, sentences, images, sounds or gestures, and his art may consist of odd sounds of an amplified cartridge scraping over various objects (*Cartridge Music*), or random sentences such as "A bird flies. Slavery is abolished. The woods. A sound has no legs to stand on. The world is teeming; anything can happen" (*2 Pages, 122 Words on Music and Dance*, 1957). Walter De Maria shows more humor than most conceptual artists in his *Beach Crawl* (1960), which involves a systematic placement of three stones, ending with the direction: "Then shout as loud as you can. 'Well that's new isn't it?' Then throw the three stones into the ocean."

With its emphasis on the nature of the art frame, both in its limitation as a point of view and in its power to modify experience by creating new contexts or viewpoints, the modern work is calling attention to the self. Ordinarily, in such art, the human person is absent in any obvious, comforting way. There are few great roles in avant-garde theater or memorable characters in art novels. If the human person has become something of a cypher in literature, it has virtually vanished in painting.[22] But the human subject is powerfully present in such works as the observing intelligence that questions, entertains possibilities and moves freely from convention to the unconventional, from the familiar to the novel, as it engages in the nonobjective dialectic of self-interpretation.

Modern art is often faulted for its remoteness and obscurity, as though it were deliberately avoiding the task of clarifying social experience or revealing our world. Sometimes the "failure" of modern art is blamed on the lack of myth in contemporary life. Traditional artists

22. As Wylie Sypher observes, there has been a loss of confidence in a romantic image of the self. Postromantic works may stress the finite, dependent nature of the self. Thus Dubuffet shows us a human form barely distinguishable from stone or earth. We are viewed from outside as a rather limited part of nature. Or again, Nathalie Sarraute shows how our freedom is limited by "tropistic" habits of thought and behavior that mark us as surely as a fingerprint. She is a kind of ethologist of individual behavior.

could communicate a shared worldview already articulated through religious myths, whereas the modern artist is required to invent myths or do without them. But in fact no one can invent a myth. Myths express a specific social reality, and no society lacks myths.

Ballard has suggested that our own myths reflect a society in which, generally, the self is unrecognized and unvalued. If this is true, then until there is some change in society, or in the values incorporated in social myths—perhaps a fundamental change in worldview—authentic art can interpret the self only as it has been doing: by insisting on its freedom and irreducible subjectivity.

Michael Zimmerman

6/Archetypes, Heroism and the Work of Art

In this essay I propose to examine certain related themes of Carl G. Jung, Erich Neumann and Edward G. Ballard concerning the nature and purpose of artistic creation and the art object. Jung and Neumann claim that the artist is the cultural hero who plunges into the depths of the unconscious to win the "treasure" of the archetype to which he or she gives expression in the artwork. The work of art is a symbol, the contemplation of which enables beholders to reintegrate their conscious experience with the primordial archetypal patterns the symbol represents.

Ballard, who agrees with much of what Jung says, offers further insight into the artistic experience, particularly in his interpretation of Aristotle's view of the cathartic function of tragic drama. According to Ballard, in the drama spectators witness a representation of the tragic character of their own existence. Each person begins with a self-definition, which eventually proves to be inadequate. The calamity that often arises from attempting to act according to inadequate self-understanding opens the way for the insight necessary for a more appropriate self-understanding. The *telos* of art in general and of drama in particular is to provide symbols that mediate between the conscious ego and the hidden depths of the self. If the tragic hero is the one who is seized by overconfidence in his powers, then contemporary Western man can be understood as such a tragic figure who fails to see the limits of the self-understanding that spawned the technological project.

Jung, Neumann and Ballard all agree that a new world-symbol is

The author would like to thank Professors Theresa Toulouse and Martha Sullivan for having read and contructively criticized the first version of this essay.

needed to disclose to modern man the inherent limitations of the rationalistic, egoistic viewpoint. They also agree that the self becomes whole, healed and holy only when the ego acknowledges its roots in and dependence on its cultural traditions, which are symbolic expressions of the unconscious archetypes. Ballard maintains that only by assuming the primary Western obligation of full self-knowledge (Socrates) will we be able to perceive the limitations of the technological project. The question is, however, whether there will be a hero capable of providing a world-symbol equal to this enormous task.

C.G. Jung

Jung's major presupposition, unsettling to those who identify the psyche with the self-reflective ego, is that ego-consciousness is but a thin skin floating atop the dark and powerful ocean of the unconscious.[1] The unconscious is that vast expanse of psychic life of which the ego, with its narrow focus, is simply unaware but on which it is quite dependent. Jung claims that "the really fundamental subject, the self, is far more comprehensive than the ego, since the former includes the unconscious whereas the latter is essentially the focal point of consciousness."[2] In having elevated the rational ego to the level of God, modern man has forgotten that much of life is controlled by the autonomous forces of the unconscious.[3] Failure to give adequate expression to these forces can lead to an invasion by them that destroys the ego-consciousness that is so highly prized and took so much effort to win in the first place.

According to Jung, ego-consciousness is a late development of the human species. Even educated persons in the twentieth century spend much of their life in a condition where the ego disappears, as in dreaming. A fully unified or integrated person is one who opens up adequate channels between ego-consciousness and the unconscious.

Jung divides the unconscious into the personal and the collective. The former refers to the particular memories and images that belong to each particular person; the latter refers to the universal memories and images that belong to every member of the human species. Jung opposes the empiricists' claim that the mind is a *tabula rasa* at birth and the Cartesian claim that the true self is the independent, timeless,

---

1. C.G. Jung, *Analytical Psychology: Its Theory and Practice* (New York: Vintage, 1968), p. 21.
2. *The Portable Jung*, Joseph Campbell, ed., translated by R.F.C. Hull (New York: Viking, 1971), p. 32; see also pp. 126, 142–43, 232, 295, 350–51, 365–66, 452–53.
3. See C.G. Jung, *Symbols of Transformation*, translated by R.F.C. Hull (Princeton University Press, 1976), pp. 430–43; C.G. Jung, *Man and his Symbols* (New York: Doubleday, 1964), p. 101.

rational ego-subject. He insists instead that the mind "carries with it the traces of [its] history, exactly like the body, and if you grope down into the basic structure of the mind you naturally find traces of the archaic mind."[4] Jung was led to the conception of the collective unconscious when he became dissatisfied with Freud's refusal to interpret dream images symbolically. Freud used dreams as the starting point for free associations through which patients might come to see for themselves the psychic disturbances of which they were unaware in waking life.[5] Jung had long been intrigued by the startling cross-cultural similarity of myths and by the archaic, mythical nature of his own dreams. Moreover, the dreams and experiences of many of his disturbed patients resembled in uncanny ways mythological motifs, which many of them (including uneducated persons) could never have come across in everyday life. Jung came to regard schizophrenia in particular as an instance of regression to an archaic-mythological and hence to a preego-conscious psychic condition.[6]

He used the word "archetype" to refer to these patterns found in all human minds and represented in symbols (dreams, works of art, myths, etc.). "An archetype means a typos [imprint], a definite grouping of archaic character containing, in form as well as in meaning, mythological motifs. Mythological motifs appear in pure form in fairytales, myths, legends, and folklore."[7] One of the major motifs, to which we shall turn our attention later, is the myth of the hero.

Archetypes are not images or symbols but the propensity to produce certain kinds of symbols. Archetypes are "the unconscious images of the instincts themselves, in other words . . . they are the patterns of instinctual behavior."[8] Jung's psychological practice convinced him that certain situations elicit universal and necessary reactions from persons. These reactions are conditioned by the unconscious mind's projection of an archetypal image upon the situations.

In a lecture first read in 1919, Jung remarked that the history of Western philosophy involves the progressive rationalization (and hence attenuation) of the archetypes, beginning with Plato's interpretation of them as "forms" and going all the way through Kant. "Just as certain biological views attribute only a few instincts to man, so the theory of cognition reduces the archetypes to a few, logically limited

4. *Analytical Psychology*, p. 45; see *Symbols of Transformation*, p. 29.

5. See Jung's essays "Sigmund Freud in his Historical Setting" and "In Memory of Sigmund Freud," in *The Spirit in Man, Art, and Literature*, translated by R.F.C. Hull (Princeton University Press, 1972), pp. 33–49.

6. See *Symbols of Transformation*, pp. 139, 408.

7. *Analytical Psychology*, p. 41; see *The Portable Jung*, pp. 34, 38–39, 44–45, 159, 261; *Man and his Symbols*, pp. 67, 75, 79; *Symbols of Transformation*, pp. 102, 158, 178, 228, 293–94, 308–9.

8. *The Portable Jung*, p. 61.

categories of the understanding."[9] In 1935 he described the archetypes of the collective unconscious as "*a priori* categories of imagination."[10]

As a psychologist, Jung was interested less in philosophical theories about the meaning of "reality" and more in discovering the conditions necessary for the possibility of a *meaningful* life. One of these conditions is for persons to understand their life as a reenactment of a heroic saga that is part of the history of all humankind. Such understanding is available through a culture's myths, religions, sagas, literature, art and other symbolic forms, which are particular historical projections of the universal archetypes of the unconscious. Symbolic forms provide mediation between individuals and their unconscious. For so-called primitive peoples the archetypes were projected in the form of myths, the recounting of which during rites of passage helped the young to make sense of the painful separation from their parents and of their entrance into adult life.

For the most part, the behavior of individual members of the primitive collectivity was governed by the collective unconscious, which left little room for what we call individual consciousness. Even today, however, when conscious individuals can interpret their suffering in terms of a heroic myth, they are lifted from their isolation so that their suffering is transformed.[11] The myth of the hero—for example, the biblical account of Christ dying in order to be reborn—is so enduring because it sets off an archetype that infuses an individual's life with deeper significance.[12] For Jung, the archetypes are inborn psychic patterns that arose in the course of human development; they function to integrate the psyche during the unfolding of a person's life.

Erich Neumann

In his monumental work *The Origins and History of Consciousness*, Erich Neumann elaborates the theme first touched on in Jung's *Symbols of Transformation*—namely, that "in the course of its ontogenetic development, the individual ego consciousness has to pass through the same archetypal stages which determined the evolution of consciousness in the life of humanity."[13] The similarity of Neumann's program to that of Hegel's *Phenomenology of Spirit* is not accidental; Hegel's book uses the mythological motif of the hero to describe the journey of spirit to absolute consciousness. The Hegelian aspect of Neumann's in-

---

9. *The Portable Jung*, p. 55; cf. Erich Neumann, *The Origins and History of Consciousness*, translated by R.F.C. Hull (Princeton University Press, 1971), p. 335.

10. *Analytical Psychology*, p. 42; see *The Spirit in Man*, pp. 80–81.

11. See *Analytical Psychology*, p. 116.

12. See *Symbols of Transformation*, pp. 247, 262, 290, 345, 392, and passim.

13. *The Origins and History*, p. xvi.

terpretation of the history of the psyche becomes more evident when he says that "the development of consciousness in archetypal stages is a transpersonal fact, a dynamic self-revelation of the psychic structure, which dominates the history of mankind and the individual."[14]

According to Neumann, the history of Western culture to the present can be regarded as the endeavor by the species to produce individual ego-consciousness not totally dominated by the autonomous power of the archetypes. Just as the human species had to struggle for thousands of years to develop individual consciousness, so too each individual must recapitulate that struggle in order to become a separate person. Just as the first conscious individuals experienced enormous guilt, suffering and isolation when they escaped from the domination of tribal mythological consciousness, so too each of us experiences guilt when we separate ourselves from our parents.[15]

In mythology, this painful separation necessary for the development of ego-consciousness is described in terms of the myth of the hero, which symbolizes the archetype of separation, death and rebirth. The hero is called away to adventure from the secure, comfortable life spent within the restrictions of his mother's world. If he stays in that world, he will never become a fully formed individual, so he must forsake all that he has loved for something higher. The event of separation is depicted as the struggle by the hero to slay the Terrible Mother, who represents the desire of the psyche to remain at the unconscious, collective level. The hero must also slay the Terrible Father, who represents the cultural limitations that hem in the development of the individual's own unique capacities.[16]

The guilt produced by the birth of the ego is reflected in the fact that negativity is essential to all conscious discrimination. I become self-conscious only when I can recognize that "I am *not* that"—that is, only when I have left behind the *participation mystique* that unites me totally with the objects I encounter, as is the case with children and primitive peoples.[17] Once he has slain his enemies, the representatives of the old order, the hero must then rescue the captive or find the treasure, which represents the reconciliation of the ego with the unconscious depths from which the ego originally emerged. The individual who only achieves the stage of autonomous, active egoconsciousness and who does not acknowledge his roots in the collective unconscious becomes maniacal, selfish and destructive:

14. *The Origins and History*, p. xxii.
15. See *The Origins and History*, pp. 114–24.
16. See *The Origins and History*, p. 173. On the myth of the hero, see Joseph Campbell, *The Hero with a Thousand Faces* (Princeton University Press, 1973), and Otto Rank, *The Myth of the Birth of the Hero*, Philip Freund, ed., translated by F. Robbins and Smith Ely Jelliffe (New York: Vintage, 1964).
17. See *The Origins and History*, pp. 120–23.

Too much stability can cramp the ego, a too independent ego
consciousness can become insulated from the unconscious, and
self-esteem and self-responsibility can degenerate into presump-
tion and megalomania. In other words, consciousness, standing
at the opposite pole to the unconscious, and originally having to
represent the personality's striving for wholeness, may lose its
link with the whole and deteriorate.[18]

The fully developed self has passed from the stage of domination by
the collective unconscious to the stage of ego-consciousness, and has
then gone on to establish links with the unconscious that bring about
the full unity of selfhood.

Spiritually fulfilled existence is described by religious sages as the
state of blessedness or detachment:

By the displacement of the center from the ego to the self, the
inmost experience of the individuation process, the transitory
character of the ego is relativized. The personality is no longer
identified with the ephemeral ego, but experiences its partial
identity with the self, whether this experience takes the form of
"godlikeness" or that "cleaving to the godhead" (adherence) of
which the mystics speak. The salient feature is that the personality's sense of no longer being identical with the ego prevails over
the mortality which clings to egohood. But that is the supreme
goal of the hero myth. In his victorious struggle the hero proves
his godlike ascent and experiences the fulfillment of the primary
condition on which he entered into battle, and which is expressed
in the mythological formula, "I and the Father are one."[19]

To put this development of the self in Hegelian terms: consciousness
first becomes individuated when the ego affirms its own identity and
negates the Other. But this negation alienates ego from Other and
leads to the desire or longing for reunion, which can be achieved only
at a higher, transformed (aufgehoben) level of consciousness. The price
of freedom (individuation) is the loss of innocence. Consciousness
becomes fully self-conscious with the negation of the original
negation—that is, with the recognition by the ego that fundamentally
ego and Other are elements of an all-embracing whole.

Jung says that we must become again as little children, in the sense of
acknowledging our dependence on the collective unconscious (symbolically expressed in cultural traditions), which transcends the limited

18. *The Origins and History*, p. 384; see also pp. 188, 388–89, 421–44.
19. *The Origins and History*, p. 359; see also pp. 256, 311–12, 319, 412; cf. Jung,
Analytical Psychology, p. 187.

ego.[20] Life itself calls us to independence and responsibility. If we lack the courage necessary to heed the summons, the price we pay is neurosis, the modern word for sin.[21]

Both Neumann and Jung say that mass phenomena such as National Socialism result from the fact that millions of persons have reached the bare level of ego-consciousness but are not genuine individuals, for they are not in touch with their unconscious roots. In attempting to live as pure egos, as wholly separate conscious centers whose sole purpose is to use reason to manipulate others and nature for gratification of desire, modern persons do not give adequate expression to the instinctive powers at work just beneath the veneer of ego-consciousness.

We have not come so far as we think from the level of primitive humankind, for whom the mere sight of certain symbols was sufficient to set off behavior wholly determined by the demands of the archetype represented by the symbols. Triggering the archetype had then and still has now a "knockout" effect on an ego-consciousness that is not sufficiently developed to resist the autonomous power of the archetype.[22] If the conscious mind does not provide for symbolic projection of these archetypal forces—for example, through creating or enjoying works of art—if the ego does not complete the hero's task of rescuing the treasure of the unconscious, the ego is in a precarious position, for the unconscious will ultimately demand compensation for having been repressed. Such repression is the source of mass psychosis in societies that repress whatever impulses or feelings seem to conflict with the demands of authoritative ego-consciousness. Jung says:

> what the unconscious really contains are the great collective events of the time. In the collective unconscious of the individual, history prepares itself; and when the archetypes are activated in a number of individuals and come to the surface, we are in the midst of history, as we are at present [1935]. . . . The archetypes are the great decisive forces, they bring about the real events, and not our personal reasons and practical intellect. . . . Sure enough, the archetypal images decide the fate of man.[23]

Neumann points out that mass movements are a destructive regression by millions of persons to the level of consciousness belonging to members of primitive groups. Because these modern individuals are

---

20. See *The Portable Jung*, p. 337; see also Jung's "Psychological Commentary" to *The Tibetan Book of the Great Liberation*, W.Y. Evans-Wentz, ed. (New York: Oxford University Press, 1975), p. xxxi.

21. See *Symbols of Transformation*, p. 304.

22. See *The Origins and History*, p. 329.

23. *Analytical Psychology*, p. 183.

fragmented and isolated egos, the "group" they form is only external and artificial. Once they surrender their self-responsibility and allow themselves to be taken over by the archetypes that have become autonomous once again, the masses become bestial and participate in untold evil and destructiveness.[24] Such destruction might be regarded as cosmic punishment for humankind's original sin of separation—that is, the winning of individual ego-consciousness.[25] The only way to avoid this retribution would be for the members of modern society to acknowledge that the ego is not absolute but dependent on something more enduring and significant, which Kant described as the "treasure lying within the field of dim representations, that deep abyss of human knowledge forever beyond our reach."[26] Like Nietzsche before them, both Jung and Neumann understand the full implications of the "death of God."

Given this account of the human psyche, it should not be too difficult to anticipate Jung's and Neumann's views on the nature and function of artistic creation. Because a healthy humankind must remain open to the insight offered by the archetypes of the collective unconscious, but because a total return to the unconscious would eliminate the ego-consciousness won at a terrible price, symbols are needed to mediate between ego-consciousness and the unconscious. These symbols are created by the culture hero who must often break through worn-out traditions in order to help his people regain touch with the archetypal patterns of which traditions are symbolic representations.

Too often the traditional norms become one-sided and hence do not promote the development of whole individuals. The culture hero risks and often even loses himself in his effort to compensate for what his culture has denied or forgotten. Neumann writes:

> The hero is not creative in the sense that he decorates and embellishes the existing canon, although his creativeness may also manifest itself in shaping and transforming the contents of his age. The true hero is one who brings the new and shatters the fabric of old values, namely the father-dragon which, backed by the whole weight of tradition and the power of the collective, ever strives to obstruct the birth of the new.
>
> The creators form the progressive element in a community, but at the same time they are the conservatives who link back to the origins. . . .
>
> By means of the symbol, the archetypes break through the creative person into the conscious world of culture. It is this

24. See *The Origins and History*, pp. 421–44.
25. See *The Origins and History*, p. 118.
26. *The Portable Jung*, p. 119. The quotation from Kant is from his *Vorlesungen über Psychologie*.

deeper lying reality that fertilizes, transforms, and broadens the life of the collective, giving it and the individual the background which alone endows life with a meaning.[27]

Jung rejects Freud's attempt to reduce the artwork to the personal product of neurotic individuals and insists that the artist is a vessel for forces that are transpersonal and collective.[28] The creator is seized by the power of the archetype that demands expression so that it can gain compensation for long neglect by a culture that has become dessicated, fragmented and unbalanced. In his essay "Psychology and Literature," Jung points out:

> The artist is not a personality endowed with free will who seeks his own ends, but one who allows art to realize its purposes through him. As a human being he may have moods and a will and personal aims, but as an artist he is "man" in a higher sense—he is "colective man," a vehicle and moulder of the unconscious psychic life of mankind. That is his office, and it is sometimes so heavy a burden that he is fated to sacrifice happiness and everything that makes life worth living for the ordinary human being.[29]

A little later in the same essay, he says that the artist's conscious ego is swept away by the power of the archetypes at work through him. Hence, "it is not Goethe that creates *Faust*, but *Faust* that creates Goethe."[30] In another essay written some years later, Jung remarks that there is no essential difference between the artist's creative seizure and an invasion by the unconscious that results in insanity.[31]

Neumann provides a helpful corrective to this view of the creative individual by noting that the creator is heroic precisely because he is not entirely destroyed when he descends into the depths to gain the treasure of the archetype:

> The Great Individual . . . who really is a great man in the sense of being a great personality, is characterized not only by the fact that the unconscious mind has him in its grip, but by the fact that his conscious mind also has an active grip on the content. It is immaterial whether his assimilation of the content takes the form of creation, or of interpretation, or of action; for common to all these is the responsible participation of the ego in coming to

---

27. *The Origins and History*, p. 377.
28. See Jung, *Modern Man in Search of a Soul*, translated by W.S. Dell and Cary F. Baynes (New York: Harcourt, Brace & World, 1933), p. 168; cf. Jung, *The Spirit in Man*, pp. 68–69, 93, 100.
29. *The Spirit in Man*, p. 101.
30. *The Spirit in Man*, p. 103; cf. Jung, *Modern Man in Search*, p. 115.
31. See *Analytical Psychology*, p. 37.

terms with the invading content and not only its participation, but its ability to take up an attitude.[32]

Were the creator totally swept away, he could not give formal expression to the nonformal vision he has had. The creator is heroic precisely because he holds himself open for the insight pouring through him. Here we are reminded of Martin Heidegger's remark that "It is precisely in great art . . . that the artist remains inconsequential as compared with the work, almost like a passageway that destroys itself in the creative process for the work to emerge."[33] When the passageway breaks down, as in the case of someone like Nietzsche or Van Gogh, the archetype no longer finds symbolic expression. The broken hero is finally seized by the archaic forces within him. His gift, however, outlasts him as an individual. His deed or creation remains as a powerful symbol, in the contemplation of which individuals can undergo a psychic reordering of the relation of ego to unconscious.

In this symbolically guided interplay between ego and unconscious, there can occur the experience of the unity of selfhood. What Heidegger has called the "moment of vision" (*Augenblick*) seems to be similar to what Neumann has in mind when he says:

> At particular moments of emotional exaltation, or when the archetypes break through—that is, in certain extraordinary situations—there comes an illumination, a momentary uprising of consciousness, like the tip of an island breaking the surface, a flash of revelation which interrupts the humdrum flow of unconscious existence.[34]

Edward G. Ballard

In his book *Art and Analysis*, Ballard offers a theory of aesthetic experience that draws on and elaborates many of the themes found in Jung's analytical psychology. In his attempt to describe the interplay between the viewer and the work of art, Ballard claims that the artwork symbolizes the "forms of feeling" (cf. Cassirer) that *are* the experience of that work.[35] That is to say, the work of art is a symbol of those forms of feeling that we intrinsically value and through which the artwork is appreciated. Ballard maintains that the artwork—particularly

---

32. *The Origins and History*, p. 426.
33. Martin Heidegger, "The Origin of the Work of Art," in *Poetry, Language, Thought*, translated by Albert Hofstadter (New York: Harper & Row, 1971), p. 40.
34. *The Origins and History*, p. 286. For a discussion of Heidegger's idea of authentic temporality, see my essay "Heidegger and Nietzsche on Authentic Time," in *Cultural Hermeneutics* 4 (1977), 239–64.
35. Edward G. Ballard, *Art and Analysis* (The Hague: Nijhoff, 1957), p. 94.

poetry—usually represents to us the journey of the self away from home and back again. In Jung's terms, poetry symbolizes the archetypal pattern of separation (dawn of ego-consciousness) and return (reunification of ego with unconscious). Ballard says:

> Poetry is an example of the sort of activity which the human being is always engaged in; poetry is, in greater or lesser degree, always a turning of the mind homeward, a nostalgia for the peace of one's final rest. Both the journey and the return are essential to poetry, but the return is usually most important. . . .
> The Bible . . . is an epic. In it there are many minor wanderings and revolutions, but through it runs another all inclusive theme; that of the journey of man begun at the Fall and continuing through time until his final return in a reborn and glorified state to the New Jerusalem, the City of Peace.[36]

A significant work of art is one that manages to engage the interest of appreciators and lead them to attempt to form themselves in the image of the work. For example, in contemplating the poetic account of the hero's journey home, readers let their own psychic structure—which includes the archetypal pattern of journey and return—be moved to align itself with what is taking place in the poem. Appreciators thus let themselves be placed under the sway of the work and do not regard the work as something useful for or manipulable by the ego. They let the work play on their feelings in a way that integrates them and makes them whole:

> The subject then conforms to the work for its own sake. By means of this conformation, the form of the work is recreated within his psyche. It is precisely this recreated form within the appreciator which the work is said to symbolize. The form, however, is the very identity of the work. Then in symbolizing the form reembodied within the appreciator, the objective work of art is symbolizing itself, it is referring to its very identity as shared by the appreciator. It is being self-significant. A work of art, we conclude, is a self-significant natural symbol which is intrinsically valued.[37]

The artwork is a symbolic projection by the artist of the archetypal feeling patterns that are usually hidden from the rest of us. Freed from the constraints of the rationalizing ego,

> the artist's imagination is much more primitive and childlike. His mental processes are dreamlike and are in closer touch with the

---

36. *Art and Analysis*, p. 85; cf. Jung, *Symbols of Transformation*, p. 324.
37. Ballard, *Art and Analysis*, p. 94.

irrational depths of his being, the dark forests of the mind where tigers burn and which shelter one from tigers.[38]

In enjoying the artwork, the perceiver recreates the constellation of feelings that led the artist to create the work.[39] The work of art makes such self-recreation and self-renewal possible because it is to a large extent a myth at least partially divested of its religious character.[40] According to Ballard, myths are verbal transformations of the feelings and movements of primitive ritual. The rites of passage performed by ancient societies arose as an automatic response of the human psyche to the painful guilt that accompanies the separation needed for consciousness to emerge. Ritual gave expression to the powerful experience of loss and rebirth that characterizes the various passages a human being makes from birth to death. Mythology brings to language these hitherto unexpressed but definitely experienced patterns of feeling.

Ballard suggests that with the appearance of drama in the Greek world, there occurred a major shift for Western culture from myth to art, a shift that corresponds to the growing self-consciousness of the human species. In the Greek world, humankind began consciously to produce symbolic representations (tragedy, for example) that elicited in the spectator a sense of the loss and renewal that hitherto had been available somewhat unconsciously in hearing the tribal myths. Ballard uses his own understanding of aesthetic experience to reinterpret Aristotle's unparalleled interpretation of Greek tragedy.

Following Nietzsche's lead, Ballard notes that for the Greeks the principal gods of art were Dionysus and Apollo, whose chief characteristics correspond to Aristotle's famous distinction between matter (potency, receptivity) and form (act). The Dionysian person is primarily passive, receptive and imitative of others. His erotic attraction to and empathetic identification with others leads him to lose himself. The Apollonian type, who seeks to be wholly self-sufficient and self-defining, maintains a distance between himself and the other. The Greek tragedy can be regarded as the "process in which the hero (the matter) acquired certain forms."[41] At the beginning, the hero identifies himself with an attitude that ultimately turns out to be inappropriate. In attempting to live in accordance with this misguided self-understanding, the hero encounters a catastrophe that brings him the insight needed to grasp the "formal harmonies" hidden in his previous

38. *Art and Analysis*, p. 55.
39. See *Art and Analysis*, p. 122.
40. See *Art and Analysis*, p. 147.
41. *Art and Analysis*, p. 158.

resolution and to seek a more adequate self-interpretation in the future:

> The rhythm of tragedy, then, is an articulation of the myth of progress. It moves through this cycle: one passes from a decision made under the aegis of Dionysus through the catharsis to insight, seen by grace of Apollo. The form (Apollo) becomes active only through matter; matter acquires identity through form.[42]

Just as the hero's journey from calamity to insight purges him of an inharmonious identification, so too the audience, in identifying itself with the travails of the hero, experiences a kind of purging (catharsis) of certain of its own inharmonious identifications. The structure of the drama resembles the structure of the myth of the hero, which in turn resembles what Ballard has called the "myth of progress."

In light of Jung's theory of the nature of the psyche, we might say that the tragic drama is a projection of the archetype of the heroic journey to individuation. In symbolizing for us the pity and terror involved in any period of growth, the tragedy is a medium for the expression of the archetype, an expression that gives us some insight into the nature of our own particular struggles. According to Jung, our lives take on meaning only when we can interpret them in terms of universal themes that are part of the psychic equipment developed through the ages to assist in the healthy development of the self.

A brief consideration of Ballard's idea of the myth of progress will help us see the essentially tragic character of the present age. The myth of progress "refers to a revivifying movement from the secular to the sacred, from the routine to the novel, from convention to insight. It is to be observed that during the history of art this movement has been understood in two ways: the classic and the romantic."[43] For the classicist, the movement of progress is a kind of circle or spiral in which the individual learns to accept his limitations (fate) and always ends up returning with new vision to everyday life. The classic hero is one who resolves to reappropriate his traditions in order to bring them (and thereby himself) new life. In terms of Jung and Neumann, we might say that the classic hero has passed beyond the stage of separateness and egoism (false self-identification) by plunging into the unconscious depths (catastrophe) in order to win the treasure of genuine selfhood (insight). The hero revitalizes his culture's traditions by recasting them in the light of his vision of the archetypal patterns that form the basis

---

42. *Art and Analysis*, p. 159.
43. *Art and Analysis*, p. 182.

for all tradition but are usually inaccessible to the average person except through symbols fashioned by culture heroes.

For the romantic, the myth of progress involves not a circle but a line. The romantic hero strives endlessly for the infinite, unbounded, novel, grandiose, for that which is entirely free from the fetters of tradition:

> The classic is like Homer's Ulysses, who after voyage and adventure returns home a renewed man, the better for his suffering; the Romanticist is more the Ulysses of Tennyson who sails without ceasing beneath all the Western stars and bears always before him the tantalizing vision of some infinite home beyond the things of earth.[44]

In the hands of the romantic, the myth of progress—that is, "the faith that the trammels of convention can be enlightened by understanding and that the irrational world or fate which rims us in is an order ultimately permiable by human vision"—ultimately becomes a source of despair.[45] For one can never gain a meaningful understanding of life as long as one is driven by the Faustian ego-mania that is essential to the romantic spirit. As Neumann points out, if the hero

> acts in the arrogance of egomania, which the Greeks called *hybris*, and does not reverence the *numinosum* against which he strives, then his deeds will infallibly come to nought. To fly too high and fall, to go too deep and get stuck, these are alike symptoms of an overvaluation of the ego that ends in disaster, death, or madness.[46]

If Ballard is right in his claim that the history of art is the faith of a culture becoming explicit and is thus the means for a culture's self-contemplation,[47] then on the basis of much of modern art we might conclude that our culture has lost its faith. The despair, fragmentation and isolation so characteristic of modern art might be explained by saying that modern Western man has modelled his culture on the *romantic* version of the myth of progress. Instead of accepting his limitations and recognizing that real progress is ultimately spiritual, Western man has defined himself primarily as a self-grounding, self-willed ego whose rational capacities enable him to transform the planet with technological means designed to gratify his limitless desires. The myth of progress has degenerated into an incredible scheme: to make man the master of the cosmos. Jung asserts that modern man, far from

44. *Art and Analysis*, p. 182.
45. *Art and Analysis*, p. 182.
46. *The Origins and History*, p. 188.
47. *Art and Analysis*, p. 181.

being the culmination of the historical development of the human species, is in fact "the disappointment of the hopes and expectations of the ages."[48]

In *Man and Technology*, Ballard explains the rise of the technological version of the myth of progress in the following way. The ancient Greek version of the heroic myth suggested that man was intrinsically capable of putting himself in harmony with fate. Progress was measured by the degree to which the individual understood and accepted his limitations. For the Christian, on the other hand, the heroic myth was essentially changed by the claim that man is intrinsically incapable of saving himself. Humankind's corruption is so thorough that only the intervention of God himself in the form of the heroic Christ could release it from the pain of sin.[49] Along with the notion that only an external agency could bring salvation, Christianity offered a linear interpretation of history that conflicted with the Greek cyclical view. Human history came to be seen as a dramatic journey toward a decisive historical moment when God would intervene against the forces of evil to establish a new covenant that would make possible the New Jerusalem.[50]

This view of history is operative in the optimistic humanism that arose in Europe around the sixteenth century. Man believed that he was headed for a new age in which evil and suffering would be eradicated by means of the scientific-technological conquest of nature, which was regarded as the external fate preventing man from achieving happiness. As Ballard notes in *Philosophy at the Crossroads*, once fate gets understood in terms of the constraints of the natural world, then man's efforts are directed toward a transformation of nature instead of the self. By knowing nature "men may, and should according to the knowledge-is-power ideal, subdue the whole of nature according to their inclinations."[51]

Just as the intervention of an external agent, God, was necessary in the Christian view to free humankind from its fallen condition, so too the intervention of another magical agency—technology—was necessary in the Enlightenment view to free humankind from the grip of natural forces. Such a view of man and history is essentially Romantic, in the sense that it regards man as constantly striving for a goal that may be in principle impossible to attain and dangerous even to seek. The "rationalistic" Enlightenment, then, is in fact Romantic and "irra-

48. *Modern Man*, p. 199.
49. See Ballard, *Man and Technology* (Pittsburgh: Duquesne University Press, 1978), pp. 38–40, 122.
50. See *Man and Technology*, pp. 118–53.
51. Ballard, *Philosophy at the Crossroads* (Baton Rouge: Louisiana State University Press, 1971), p. 277.

tional" insofar as it goes against the proper *logos* of man. Rationalistic humanism's hybristic understanding of man leads Jung to call it a "sham enlightenment."[52]

The so-called Romantic reaction against the excessive rationalism of the Enlightenment in no way countered the yearning for the infinite, but instead fostered it under the guise of the recovery of the forgotten powers of the self. Both rationalism and Romanticism were secularized versions of the Christian eschatological longing for the Golden Age. As Ballard observes in *Man and Technology*, the Romantic person in particular

> is intoxicated with a sense of creative inspiration, of the power to originate. This fascination with the possibilities opened up by birth induces the Romantic person to attempt to become free of all limitations and to ignore human dependence; it has led the sphere of art, some believe, to chaos, the political world to the brink of barbarism, and the economic and industrial worlds into an increasing commitment to a supposed omnipotent technology.[53]

The Romantic reaction was not without merit, however. It suggested that there were aspects of the self that were hidden from the gaze of scientific rationality and that much of human behavior is guided by forces that cannot be controlled by will. Whereas Christianity regarded such forces as the will of God, "a will from which man fell but to which he might return by way of personal rebirth," modern psychologists such as Jung demythologized such talk and reinterpreted these compulsive forces as "arising from the depths of the self."[54]

Jung, Neumann and Ballard hold out hope that these primal impulses can be harnessed appropriately by the mature individual who acknowledges the limits of ego-consciousness. But the question is whether humanity will recognize in time that the technological myth of progress is flawed by hybris and leads to a totally rationalized industrial society from which all links with tradition have been excluded. Neumann says:

> In these circumstances the disoriented, rationalistic consciousness of modern man, having become atomized and split off from the unconscious, gives up the fight because, understandably enough, his isolation in a mass which no longer offers him any psychic support becomes unendurable. For him the hero's task is

52. *Symbols of Transformation*, p. 77.
53. *Man and Technology*, p. 137. On the "Myth of the Golden Age," see Jung, *Man and his Symbols*, p. 85; on Romantic striving, see Jung, *Symbols of Transformation*, pp. 113, 430–32.

too difficult, the task he ought to perform by following in the footsteps of humanity before him. The fabric of the archetypal canon which used to support the average man has given way, and real heroes capable of taking up the struggle for new values are naturally few and far between.[55]

In the conclusion of *Man and Technology*, Ballard maintains that what is needed are new world-symbols that will make possible the "effective integration of the nonobjective dialectic into technological culture. We live, a philosopher has remarked, in a time of twilight, when the old gods have departed and the new ones are not yet come."[56] The nonobjective dialectic refers to the activity that occurs in the life of any person who attempts to remain true to the primary human obligation: to remain a question for oneself, to pursue self-knowledge.

The life of the person who is true to this obligation takes on a tragic form. First, one attempts to identify oneself with some particular role—for example, as a specialist in a technical field. If one is open to the truth, one eventually sees that one's potentialities are not exhausted by that particular role. One is then required to find a more adequate role for oneself. This process of continuing self-evaluation leads one to recognize the limits of one's self-understanding and to see that the good life lies in accepting those limits. So long, however, as the great majority of persons are taken in by the prevailing idea that one can become master of fate (limitations) by transforming the external world, or by training oneself to become a specialist in some technical field, there will be little place for the practice of the tragic pattern that is a necessary condition for genuine human life.

As long as we think that our problems are external, not internal, and moreover as long as we think our problems are "solvable," there will be no significant changes in the direction of the modern technological world. If members of a culture do not know how to criticize their own self-understanding, they can hardly criticize their culture. Ballard is convinced that unless we gain a sense of limits and hence a sense of the tragic dimension of life, we shall end by destroying ourselves. For technological man "is guilty of systematically ignoring the primary human obligation. And the inevitable consequence of this self-ignorance is self-destruction."[57]

From this brief survey of Jung, Neumann and Ballard on archetypes, self, art and history, we can conclude that what we require is

54. Ballard, *Philosophy at the Crossroads*, p. 54.
55. *The Origins and History*, pp. 439–40.
56. *Man and Technology*, p. 234.
57. *Man and Technology*, p. 233.

the emergence of heroes to bring forth symbols powerful enough to let us recognize the limitations of the technological understanding of self and world. We need a rebirth of the sense of tragedy. Yet we cannot predict whether or when such a world-historical event will take place. Jung, who seemed to be relatively hopeful about the appearance of such new symbols in time of need, said that humankind is finally governed by the collective unconscious that corrects imbalances in the psychic structure of a culture. Hence the autonomous archetypes

> do not appear in the dreams of individuals or in works of art unless they are activated by a deviation from the middle way. Whenever conscious life becomes one-sided or adopts a false attitude, these images "instinctively" rise to the surface in dreams and in the visions of artists and seers to restore the psychic balance, whether of the individual or of the epoch.[58]

Ballard, too, is not without hope, although he is somewhat more ironic and skeptical. Without a significant change in self-understanding, Western man is drifting toward a breakdown of technological culture, which would lead to starvation for millions, or to its triumph, which would probably lead to totalitarianism. The goal is not to do away with technology but to find a way to remain human within a technological world.

Toward the end of *Man and Technology*, Ballard observes:

> As Plato might have put it: the human race will not see the end of its troubles until those who pursue the truth about themselves are also those who hold authority in disposing of technological power, and until those who design our technological society become by some divine commission seekers after the truth about themselves.[59]

---

58. *The Spirit in Man*, p. 104.
59. *Man and Technology* , *pp. 233*–34.   For Ballard's views on Plato, see his *Socratic Ignorance: An Essay on Platonic Self-Knowledge* (The Hague: Nijhoff, 1965).

PART THREE

Archaic Dimensions of Life:
Philosophical Interpretations

Edward H. Henderson

7/Archaic Experience and Philosophical Anthropology: The "Enuma Elish" and the Exodus

One way of doing philosophical anthropology is to compare the different ways in which persons articulate archaic human experience. Because, as I shall argue, archaic experience and the world-symbols that bring it into being are constitutive of the human mode of being, to study them and their contrasting forms is to do more than intellectual and cultural history; it is to study different manifestations of human nature, and consequently to bring human nature into sharper focus.

In this essay I shall give a comparative interpretation of the ways in which the ancient Babylonians[1] and the ancient Hebrews gave expression to archaic experience and sought to organize life in relation to it. The objective is to show how both cultural forms involve the same experiential elements and yet organize life in significantly different ways. But the interpretations and the claim that to make them is to do philosophical anthropology require that we first consider the ideas of archaic experience and world-symbols.

Archaic Experience and World-Symbols

Professor Ballard has made the notion of archaic experience fundamental in his philosophical investigations. In "The Subject-Matter of Philosophy"[2] he took a historical view of it. Archaic experience was, he said, "the earliest complete . . . interpretation of the human situation" (p. 24) and was given in the form of myths and their ritual practices. As

1. An earlier version of this interpretation of the ancient Babylonian myth and ritual can be found in *Eros and Nihilism: Studies in the Possibility of a Human World*, Charles Bigger and David Cornay, ed. (Dubuque: Kendall/Hunt, 1976), pp. 141–56.
2. Edward G. Ballard, "The Subject-Matter of Philosophy," in *Tulane Studies in Philosophy* 7 (1958) 5–26.

his work developed, however, his view of archaic experience became ontological rather than historical. Archaic experience is not simply the earliest interpretation of the human condition but the experience that belongs to all human beings of all times and places—essential human experience.

In "Toward a Phenomenology of Man"[3] and *Philosophy at the Crossroads*,[4] Ballard describes it as an experience of the movement and development of the self, the former in terms of human birth, life and death, and the latter in terms of the "crossing of boundaries." Continuing these accounts, *Man and Technology*[5] develops the theme more thoroughly, now under the name of "common experience." Ballard distinguishes common experience from particular experiences by saying that the latter are not universal to humans as humans but exist instead only in relation to some particular role or activity, whereas the former is present in all of human life, whatever the role. Thus common experience is to particular experiences as Plato's cardinal virtues are to the virtues of the particular arts (pp. 18–21).

But what is the character of common or archaic experience? It is, Ballard says, the experience of movement from beginning through middle to end, which every human being undergoes as it attempts some actualization of the possibilities for being a self that it senses, selects, interprets and reinterprets (pp. 120–21). The movement is an ongoing "subjective dialectic." I wish now to take this notion of archaic experience and to develop an account of its relation to world-symbols and hence of its constitutive role in human being.

Human existence is mediated by world-symbols. This mediation gives it its own distinctive characteristics and makes it different from all other forms of life.[6] Not that other animals do not use symbols. They do. In the widest possible sense, a symbol is any object or experience taken to represent or mean something other than itself. Nonhumans certainly use symbols in that wide sense of the term. Indeed, it now appears that chimpanzees can learn human language and even teach it to their offspring. Although it remains true that human beings have much greater ability to complicate their natural languages and to develop artificial ones than do other animals, we should not perhaps define human being simply in terms of language use. But we can, I

3. Edward G. Ballard, "Toward a Phenomenology of Man," in *Proceedings of the American Catholic Philosophical Association*, 1968, pp. 168–74.

4. Edward G. Ballard, *Philosophy at the Crossroads* (Baton Rouge: Louisiana State University Press, 1971).

5. Edward G. Ballard, *Man and Technology* (Pittsburgh: Duquesne University Press, 1978).

6. I have defined human being in terms of symbolic mediation and discussed the idea in "Homo Symbolicus," in *Man and World* 4 (1971) 131–50, and in "The Problem of World," in *Eros and Nihilism*, pp. 2–8.

believe, define it as being mediated through or by world-symbols.[7]

World-symbols are complex symbols constructed through language and imagination and taken to represent the fundamental powers, constituents, relationships and events of reality—those powers, constituents, relationships and events in terms of which whatever happens, whatever exists, whatever is experienced must receive its ultimate explanation. Such comprehensive symbols are rightly called *world-symbols* because they represent reality as a world—that is, as a more or less well ordered setting for life, involving certain possibilities, problems and limits for life. Typically, world-symbols will include some representation of nature, humankind, society, individual selves, usually the divine, and the relationships of these to each other. World-symbols would include the predominant religious story or stories of a culture, such as the Babylonian creation story and the Hebrew story of the exodus we shall interpret later. But world-symbols can also be epic poems, dramas, philosophical worldviews, scientific theories, and so on—or some combination of these.[8]

We must be careful not to think that there is ever one clear, unambiguous and pure world-symbol for each culture, each age or each individual. They are always capable of varied interpretation; changing circumstances provoke new interpretations and even drastic modifications, and contacts between different peoples lead to the mixing of elements from one with elements from another.

The mixing and interpreting is not primarily directed by a concern with logical consistency; hence it is usual that at any time and place several more or less consistent (and hence also more or less conflicting) world-symbols will be effective in the lives of a people. Thus many twentieth-century Westerners live by some form of the Christian or Jewish world-symbol and also by the modern view of the world given by the physical and social sciences. Still, it is possible for purposes of understanding to isolate world-symbols and their uses and interpretations in a given culture and period and to imagine them pure and ideal. So long as we realize what we are doing, such idealization should not lead us too far astray.

World-symbols raise experience to what can truly be called the human level. Without world-symbols, experience would be absorbed in particular projects and objects, taken up with particular needs, ends

7. In my usage, "human" does not refer simply to a particular animal species defined wholly in biological terms. If one or more of the so-called nonhuman animal species should develop the ability to enter into and participate fully in the forms of life that exist through world-symbols, then they would have to be regarded as "human" in my sense.

8. My use of the terms "world" and "world-symbol" differs somewhat from Professor Ballard's in *Man and Technology*, although my account of "world" derives directly from a lecture he gave while a Visiting Professor of Philosophy at Louisiana State University in 1969.

and satisfactions, with food when hungry, drink when thirsty, fighting when attacked, sleep when sleepy, and so on. But when particular experiences with food, sex, self-defense, natural tools, and so on are given a world-symbolic meaning by being made with others to represent a total structure of reality and context for life, then fully human experience comes into existence. The exact nature of that experience will depend upon the kind of particular experiences that are raised to world-symbolic meaning. But all the different forms of experience or life that are brought into existence by world-symbols will have certain features in common. These common features are what we mean by *archaic experience*.

Archaic experience, then, is not just experience that happens to be common to all human beings; it is the experience brought into existence by world-symbols. It is not the experience—as the empirical tradition in philosophy might lead us to expect—of particular objects that happen to come into human consciousness universally—for example, sunshine, rain, night, moon, and the like. These are objects in nonhuman as well as human experience. It is, rather, the common experience of life as a struggle to achieve being and worth over nonbeing and worthlessness, and to create and sustain a world or form of life in which being and worth are truly possible. Although each world-symbol brings into existence a different sense of being and worth, and of nonbeing and worthlessness, and organizes the pursuit of these in different ways, it is still true that there is this common structure in all human experience.

The interpretation of the Babylonian and Hebrew world-symbols will show that both do indeed generate a common human experience and yet do so in such different ways that human life under them involves significantly different expectations, values and forms of personal and interpersonal existence. Let us now see why and how world-symbols truly do generate archaic experience—and consequently how world-symbols and archaic experience can rightly be said to constitute the human mode of being.

First, world-symbols make human life into a pursuit of being over nonbeing. To see how this is so, we have but to imagine what experience without world-symbols would be. It would not involve an idea of a world as a more or less well ordered system of things and powers; it would not even involve a clear sense of individuals existing in relation to each other in time and change, and preserving something of their identity throughout, because the idea of such enduring entities involves the idea of a world in which they have their place. But if there is an idea of a world, then it is possible to think that things have been and can be otherwise than they presently are. It is possible to think that we are participants in the ongoing flux of things, to think that as such we can endure and remain the same throughout some period of the world, and finally to think that the outcome of that flux and of our duration within it is uncertain from moment to moment. It is possible to think that the world can go on without us—and even possible to think that the world itself can simply cease to be. Thus we can say that life by world-symbols makes being something to be achieved and nonbeing something to be overcome.

In the human experience of particular objects and activities, there will be present this sense of being as a value to be realized and of nonbeing as a constant threat. For life without world-symbols there is the experience only of particular ends and satisfactions. But for humans the pursuit of particular organic ends will involve at the same time the pursuit of being and the avoidance of nonbeing. In eating, for example, we seek not only to satisfy hunger but also to secure life and avoid death.

Secondly, world-symbols make human life into a pursuit of higher order value, of value that is not simply a matter of filling organic needs and thus of preserving life, but a value that attaches to human beings *as* human beings. For the very reason that humans formulate world-symbols, they are able to think of themselves as a certain kind or mode of being, having an ideal form and therefore capable in the case of each individual, family and community of attaining a value that belongs and is appropriate to and possible for human being as such—a value that is other than successful metabolism. Such value, as the value of being, may be sought along with the satisfaction of natural, organic needs. Thus, for example, the nonhuman engages in sex to satisfy an organic need, whereas the human may do so to secure his or her worth as man or woman. We may speak, then, of *human worth*. It is what makes life worth the trouble. Some have valued human worth so much that they were willing to give up life itself to realize it: Socrates, Jesus, the Jews at Masada, Bonhoeffer, and others.

It goes without saying that the possibility for human worth carries with it the possibility of failure. For just as world-symbols allow us to imagine and pursue human worth, they also allow us to imagine life as falling apart into disunification, chaos, and wretchedness—and to know when it has happened. Human worth is not simply a fact; it must be achieved. The struggle to do so cannot end so long as life goes on.

Indeed,we should emphasize this last idea, that human life is an ongoing struggle to realize being and worth, and to overcome nonbeing and worthlessness. The experience made possible by world-symbols is not experience in some spectatorial mode in which disinterested minds classify and assess possibilities; it is experience in the participatory mode in which humans and communities of humans know the possibilities as possibilities *for themselves*, and are concerned at the heart of their lives to secure the one and avoid the other.

Archaic experience is the experience of this struggle. All particular experiences, if they are distinctively human experiences, will find their place in it. All possibilities, objects, events, situations, actions, and so on, will be to us as they are because they are taken as either aiding or hindering the effort to realize being and worth.

Thirdly, world-symbols not only bring archaic experience into existence, but they also determine its particular form and content. Being and worth by themselves are abstractions, common characteristics of all human experience but never known by themselves. They are, therefore, given their specific form and content by the world-symbol in relation to which they exist. Consequently, different world-symbols will involve different ideas of being and worth.

Fourthly, world-symbols are the means by which humans make the struggle. They determine the form the struggle itself must take; they define patterns of human life. This being the case, different world-symbols will involve different paths to the achievement of being and worth.

Finally, we may say that human life in being a struggle for being and worth is also at the same time a struggle to create and sustain a world. A world and its world-symbol are not the same. A world is a form of life organized by and known through a world-symbol, whereas a world-symbol is the representation of reality and its constituents as organized according to a certain form. An actual world will include the world-symbol that defines it, plus various activities, functions, customs, values, institutions and practices that make it actual. The achievement of being and worth requires the realization of the world in which they are envisaged as real possibilities. If that world should not exist at all, then the pursuit of that kind of being and worth would be frustrated. Yet the world as represented in the symbol is an ideal; it too is something to be achieved and preserved. Consequently, the struggle for being and worth must also be a struggle for the world in which they are truly possible.

Archaic experience, therefore, is not only the experience of striving for being and worth; it is also the experience of striving for a world in which there is some hope for realizing being and worth.

Archaic Experience in the "Enuma Elish"[9]

The "Enuma Elish" is an ancient story indeed, possibly written as

9. I am dependent here on many scholars and can no longer say precisely what comes from whom. The most important are: W. F. Albright, *From the Stone Age to Christianity*,

long ago as 2000 B.C. and possibly older in oral form. With certain changes of names and detail, the myth served several Mesopotamian powers and cultures. The changes in the name of the primary god reflect the changes of imperial power in the region. For Sumerian culture the chief god was Enlil (see Jacobsen), for Babylonian, Marduk (for Marduk was the god who owned Babylon), for Assyrian, Assur, and for Persian, Bel.

"Once upon a time" or "In the beginning" or, in the words of the myth, "When on high," there was no world of differentiated and systematically related powers and things; instead, reality consisted of Apsu (the male and father) and Tiamat (the female and mother). The myth describes Apsu and Tiamat as waters commingled; they were not the waters as they now are, organized. They belonged to what Eliade calls the Great Time before times and the Place beyond places. The image of a vast ocean without land and without heaven and heavenly bodies is an appropriate one for the primordial no-thingness. There is no world, no cosmos, only darkness around the waters.

The aboriginal waters, however, do not constitute nothingness in the sense of impotence. Their undifferentiatedness is a great power pregnant with determinate being. It is of its very nature to include in its unity two distinguishable powers, the father, Apsu, and the mother, Tiamat. Unless such an incipient distinction of forces were present in the primeval unity, there would be no reason for the growth of the determinate cosmos. But the distinction is there, primordial. Tiamat, as a result of her copulation with Apsu, gives birth to other gods who give birth to still others, and so on, so that the determinate cosmos begins to be differentiated within the original indeterminate commingled waters.

The procreation of gods is at once a cosmogony and a theogony. This means that for its believers the gods and the great natural powers and forces are not separated but merged. The gods exist in this world as fundamental natural powers; conversely, the natural powers are divine and purposive beings. The cosmos is a divine-natural cosmos; and the gods are wholly immanent within it rather than transcendent to it.

2nd ed. (Garden City: Doubleday/Anchor, 1957); Mircea Eliade, *Cosmos and History* (New York: Harper & Row, 1959), and *Myths, Dreams, and Mysteries* (New York: Harper & Row, 1960); Henri Frankfort, *Kingship and the Gods* (Chicago University Press, 1948); Theodor Gaster, *Thespis*, rev. ed. (Garden City: Doubleday, 1961); Alexander Heidel, *The Babylonian Genesis*, 2nd ed. (Chicago University Press, 1951); Thorkild Jacobsen, "Enuma Elish—'The Babylonian Genesis,' " in *The Intellectual Adventure of Ancient Man*, Henri Frankfort, et al., ed. (Chicago University Press, 1946), and *The Treasures of Darkness: A History of Mesopotamian Religion* (Yale University Press, 1976); Samuel Noah Kramer, *The Sacred Marriage Rite* (Bloomington: Indiana University Press, 1969); Cornelius Loew, *Myth, Sacred History, and Philosophy* (New York: Harcourt, Brace & World, 1967); Eric Voegelin, *Israel and Revelation* (Baton Rouge: Louisiana State University Press, 1956).

Returning to the story, we find that Tiamat gives birth to Lahma and Lahamu, gods, who, again, are both purposive beings and constituents of the natural environment. They are, in fact, silt or mud, the first land to develop out of the sea. They in their turn give birth to another male-female pair, and the process continues through several such pairs, each giving rise to the next pair until sky and earth are differentiated.

Notice that this generation of sky and earth does not yet correspond with the final shape of the cosmos. They are still within the belly of Tiamat, the deep, and have not yet been separated. The sky is not above, nor the earth floating on the sea. The time and place are still prime-eval, ab-original, beyond all times and places. (But see Jacobsen for a different interpretation.)

The divine-natural family, however, is not perfectly peaceful. The younger gods, constituting as they do a movement away from indeterminateness (and so from nonbeing or no-thingness) toward increasing differentiation and order (life and full being), are restless. They run and dance within Tiamat's belly, disturbing her and Apsu. Although Mother Tiamat at first grieves at the thought of destroying her children, Apsu and Mummu, their advisor, finally persuade her. As Apsu puts it:

> By day I cannot rest, by night I cannot sleep;
> I will destroy them and put an end to their way,
> That *silence* be established, *and then let us sleep!*[10]

Apsu's desire for silence and sleep has an ontological meaning. Silence and sleep would mean a return of the newly born and only partly developed cosmos into the aboriginal undifferentiatedness. Apsu gets his sleep, but not as he intended; for the younger gods win. And they win when Ea casts a spell upon Apsu, putting him, ironically, into a deep sleep whereby Ea is able to kill him and take his crown.

The main lines of the Babylonian representation of reality and expression of archaic experience are now clear. The cosmos has its very being and life through an opposition of divine-natural powers, the power that moves toward differentiation and order, and the power that resists these and moves to resolve what has come to be distinct and ordered into the primordial condition of undifferentiation. But because both of these powers are always present, the cosmos that has been achieved is not stable and secure. It must be reestablished. The world-symbol thus articulates on a grand scale the experience of an ongoing struggle to achieve being and overcome nonbeing. And this is archaic experience. But let us return to the story.

10. Tablet I, 11. In Heidel, 38–40.

After Ea slays Apsu, he sets up his abode upon him. With this the cosmos has been further differentiated. Until now Earth and Sky were only forces within Tiamat trying to break free. Now Earth is established upon Apsu (is floating on the primeval freshwater sea) and Sky is above earth as light and space, a place for the sun and moon and other heavenly bodies. But Earth is not yet the earth as finally established; it is not yet surrounded by the salt sea.

Notice that the imagery has changed from sexual to military and political. Surely the common experience of sexual reproduction is a good natural symbol for the initial generation of cosmos: it takes an actual experience of creation in human and animal life, and uses it world-symbolically to mean the generation of the basic powers of the whole cosmos. Sexual imagery will reenter in the story of Marduk and Ishtar, for sex is a symbol uniquely appropriate for representing certain aspects of reality. But battle and political imagery are especially appropriate for saying that order, even the barest natural order, always requires the exercise of power and authority over the fundamental tendency toward disintegration and decay. Being is always an overcoming of nonbeing.

After Ea's victory over Apsu, another god, Marduk, the god who is to become the hero of the myth, is born within the sacred dwelling (earth) that Ea has established upon Apsu. The other gods recognize him from the beginning as a superior god. Closely associated with the sun, he seems to be primarily a storm god. Sculptural representations show him with lightning in each hand, and the story tells of his control of rain and wind.

But while Marduk is maturing, the older gods plot revenge. They seek to overthrow the upstart gods, to destroy the cosmos that has begun to grow into shape. To this end Tiamat returns, now with a new consort, Kingu, who will serve as her military advisor and chief. These older gods fume and rage, and Tiamat creates all kinds of horrible monsters. She herself is a monster or dragon. Bas-reliefs show her as grotesque, having the body of a lion with taloned feet and long-clawed hands, her body covered with scales, sprouting large wings from her shoulders. She bares her fangs at Marduk, making her nose like that of a braying donkey. From her head grow two sharp horns (or they may be ears), and an odd feelerlike organ (it looks like a snail out of its shell) sticks out from the middle of her forehead. This hideous Tiamat and her monsters cause great fear among the younger ruling gods, and Ea fails in his effort to repeat on Tiamat the spell of sleep he had worked on Apsu. The cosmos again is threatened. The great salt sea and all its monsters lash the established earth and almost engulf it.

This part of the story demonstrates how pervasive was the experience of the opposition of being and nonbeing. The determinate life and order of the cosmos are never secure. The older gods of indeterminate chaos continue to threaten. Nonbeing is never once and for all overcome but must be continually fought off. Being is not a given; it is not once and for all accomplished; it is a condition that must always be won again in a contest.

Furthermore, the myth says that the contest of being and nonbeing is rooted in the ultimate nature of things; it is no matter for humans only or for humans just insofar as they are distinct from the rest of nature. In fact, the contest exists before persons and society exist, before the cosmos has its final shape; it is germinally present from the beginning. For the Babylonians, the human struggle for being and worth must be fit into this natural-divine world and pursued in its terms. The human world has to be integrated into the cosmos as a whole.

After Ea's failure to subdue Tiamat, his father, Anu, the head of the divine assembly, the Annunaki, goes out against her. He returns in shame and asks to be relieved of the task. The failure of still a second god highlights the severity of the threat of nonbeing. The Annunaki take counsel and call upon Marduk to be their champion. He accepts on the condition that he be given supreme power among all the gods. They accept his condition, confer sovereignty upon him, give him a throne, symbols of office, and most importantly, his weapons: bow, arrow, mace, lightning, fire, the four winds, the evil wind, the hurricane, the whirlwind, the sevenfold wind, the cyclone, the matchless wind. He goes out after Tiamat.

Marduk is so fierce in his approach that all the gods ranged on the side of Tiamat are confused and flee. But Tiamat stands her ground. The opposition of the ultimate powers of the cosmos is concentrated in their confrontation: the god of light, growth, order and being versus the goddess of darkness, death, disorder and nonbeing. Marduk wins the battle and destroys her life. He then captures her consort, Kingu, and the other forces she had mustered. He reigns, sovereign over the cosmos.

But the cosmos has not yet been fully delineated. Marduk undertakes now to complete it by means of his authoritative word. And so the generation of the cosmos proceeds under Marduk's direction. He uses as material what is already at hand, especially the conquered gods of destruction. Tiamat he has split in two like an oyster. From the upper half he forms the roof of the sky, the firmament; and since Tiamat is salt water, he makes sure that the way is barred from her pouring her waters down upon the earth in a deluge. The lower half of Tiamat he ranges round the earth according to the Babylonian belief that the earth is surrounded by the salt sea. Next Marduk builds himself a heavenly residence, apparently on top of the vault of heaven.

Next, Marduk assigns the gods their "places." The story of the apportioning of territories to the gods contains the Babylonian astronomical wisdom, the demarcation of the heavens into different regions marked by the paths traveled by the planets and by the constellations of stars in relation to which the sun and planets move. The moon also is set in place and its phases established. These are the movements by which days, months, seasons and years are reckoned. They are integrally related to the life of vegetation, animals and, of course, human society in its dependence upon crops and herds. For the sprouting and maturing of seed is directly dependent upon the seasonal rain and sun. The life of the herds, their reproduction and produce of milk and cheese, are in turn dependent upon the vegetation.

Because the conditions of life are synchronized with the movements of the heavenly bodies, they are seen as the powers that control the life of the cosmos. Here the one common life of the one divine-natural community is seen most clearly. The cosmos is a family of gods living in relation to each other according to the rhythm marked by the sun, moon and planets, and by their earthly manifestations—the seasonal sun, rain storms, floods, droughts and cold.

The cosmos now in order, the time has come for the creation of humankind. This part of the myth is of the utmost importance. After all, the myth is a fabrication of human beings who seek to locate themselves in the cosmos and to clarify for themselves the possibilities for being and worth, nonbeing and worthlessness. Surely the cosmos is described as an ongoing opposition of being and nonbeing: the storytellers experience it as such in relation to themselves. But until human life can be represented in relation to the whole cosmos, the story cannot tell persons what the possibilities are for themselves and cannot direct their efforts to secure being and worth.

We might expect, therefore, that the story of the creation of humankind would be the most prominent part of the larger story, that the story would center around human life, nature and function. It does not. Humankind here seems more an afterthought than the culmination of the divine work. Humankind is created so that the gods who were defeated but who have now surrendered to Marduk will not have to work but can go free. Human beings are created to be the servants of the gods. This means that they have the responsibility of assisting Marduk and the gods of creation in renewing and maintaining control over Tiamat and the gods of destruction.

There is another important element in the myth's account of the creation of humankind. The gods create humans from the blood of Kingu, from the blood of the very god who had stirred up Tiamat to rebel. Thus the story says that human being contains in itself and as part of its essential nature the tendency toward dissolution and nonbeing. Human nature is not originally created good and subsequently fallen; instead it repeats in itself the same ontological structure as the divine-natural cosmos. Through the myth, human life knows itself to be an overcoming of inner tendencies to nonbeing.

After telling of the creation of humankind, the "Enuma Elish" ends with the creation of a temple to Marduk and the recitation of the names of Marduk. There are, however, other stories of the gods. The New Year festival places great emphasis upon one, the story of Marduk and Ishtar. Because it looms large in the ritual celebration, it can rightly be regarded as part of the Babylonian creation story and world-symbol. In effect, it is a second story of creation but united with the "Enuma Elish" rather than proposed as an alternative.

The details of the story are uncertain,[11] but it tells of Marduk's marriage to Ishtar, of his imprisonment in the underworld—the realm of death—and of his liberation and reunion with Ishtar. The marriage of Marduk to Ishtar is an event in the divine-natural cosmos; it is the fertilization of the earth by the life-giving rain. The imprisonment of Marduk under the earth represents the season of drought and death. His liberation and reunion with Ishtar amounts to the return of the rains and the growing season, the refertilization of the earth and the renewal of life.

The "Enuma Elish" itself, as we saw, also gives a role to sexual procreation in the generation of the cosmos, but places it at the beginning of the story and leaves it behind as the story progresses to military and political imagery. The marriage and remarriage of Marduk and Ishtar, therefore, serve to reintroduce the sexual mode of creation and to unite it with the military-political mode. For here both are involved: the gods of differentiation and order (gods of the upper earth and sky) must overcome by battle and cunning the gods of death and dissolution (gods and demons of the underworld) so as to make possible the reunion of Marduk and Ishtar.

Through this synthesis of images the world-symbol represents the cosmos as existing through both an overcoming of destructive forces and the more positive action of sexual intercourse. Both modes express the archaic experience that being is constantly threatened by nonbeing and that the world exists only through an active accomplishment of one over the other. But the two ways of securing being do constitute a significant distinction, for they define different forms of the threat of nonbeing and different ways of overcoming it.

It should be clear by now that the Babylonian world-symbol does give explicit expression to the archaic experience of the opposed pos-

11. No text has been found that gives it clearly. But accounts of the ritual give clues that make sense when put together with stories of the region. See esp. Samuel N. Kramer, *The Sacred Marriage Rite*, and Theodor Gaster, *Thespis* (footnote 9, above).

sibilities of being and nonbeing. Does it also express the sense of the opposed possibilities of worth and worthlessness? Does it represent a value that attaches to human life *as* human? I believe that it does.

Human beings are surely singled out from among the other beings created by Marduk and the gods. And it is they who are created for the special purpose of serving the gods. Granted that serving the gods aims at securing being over nonbeing, it also defines the form of life that human beings are obliged to follow. And in doing so it defines an *ideal* for social and individual life, the kind of life that *should* be lived. To realize the idea is to achieve the only value that is really possible for humans, at least so far as the Babylonian world-symbol makes it possible to see.

The form of life that defines the human ideal is a life of participation in the victory of Marduk over Tiamat and in the marriage of Marduk to Ishtar. But how can human life participate in these divine-natural events? In the first place, it can participate in them because human nature shares the ontological structure of divine nature. The battle with destructive gods and the marriage that renews life can be repeated in human life, both individual and collective. And in the second place, it can participate in them by ritual repetition, by acting out these events at every appropriate time.

The importance of the ritual participation in the divine-natural cosmos can scarcely be overemphasized. Note that the last work of the gods in "Enuma Elish" before turning over all work to their servants —humankind—is the construction of the temple to Marduk. The temple, called Esagila, is the "mountain" of the gods; it is the place where mortals can enter into the life of the gods. Without the ritual enactment of the story, the world-symbol would be but a way of *thinking about* reality. With the ritual it is truly a way of *living in* the world.

The ritual performance is not merely an *ad hoc* magical act lacking intelligible connection with its desired effects—as, for example, the practice (superstitious) of hanging up horseshoes lacks for us now any intelligible connection with good luck. Rather, the ritual demonstrates the form that life should follow. Just as, say, the Jewish celebration of passover and the Christian celebration of communion enact patterns that all of life is supposed to follow for those who practice them— namely, passing over from death and bondage to life and freedom for the one, and crucifixion that there may be resurrection for the other— so the New Year festival, the Akitu, enacts the form that all Babylonian life is supposed to have—namely, participation in the cosmos over- throw of chaos and in the positive revitalization of cosmos.

The ritual reenactment of creation is not only the effort to achieve human being and worth, however; it is the effort to re-create and make secure the very world in which human being and worth are possible. To us today it may seem absurd to think that human beings can have any hand in the aboriginal creative acts that shape the cosmos itself. But for the ancient Babylonians it was not only possible, it was the primary duty and purpose of mortals to share in the creation of the world. The myth with its ritual celebration, therefore, literally brings into existence a form of life in which human beings struggle after being and worth and at the same time after the form of life that creates and re-creates the very world in which being and worth are possible.

It is easy enough to see what being is in the world of "Enuma Elish"; it is the perpetuation of the power of creative order over chaos, which allows the differentiated things and powers in the cosmos to endure. Being for individuals, for the social, the economic and the political order, and for the world itself requires this same conquest of the powers that dissolve and destroy.

But what kind of human *worth* does the Babylonian world make possible? Human worth comes with the dutiful and successful performance of service to the gods, for this is the purpose, according to the story, for which persons have been created. This service is, as we have seen, the ritual reenactment of the mythic events and then the reenactment of them also on all sides of life—social, political, productive, personal. Consequently, the only human worth that the world-symbol brings to light is participation in the aboriginal creative victory of Marduk over Tiamat and in Marduk's sexual union with Ishtar. If society and the individual can harmonize and integrate with the divine-natural drama, then to that extent human worth is realized. But if instead of integration there is conflict, human worth is not realized.

Mircea Eliade has made us aware that the life of the cosmos, as mythically represented, is cyclical. It begins in this case with the creative victory of Marduk over Tiamat. But inasmuch as Tiamat still threatens, the victory is insecure. The ongoing life of the cosmos, then, continues the struggle with the forces of death and destruction. And the story of Marduk and Ishtar, added to "Enuma Elish," shows that after the victory over Tiamat, Marduk suffers a (temporary) defeat and is imprisoned in the realm of the dead. Thus the victory with which the cosmos begins gives way to defeat. Birth leads to death.

But Marduk's death is not final. The story of his release from the underworld and reunion with his bride is the story of a rebirth of the cosmos. The pattern of cosmic life, then, is birth-life-death-rebirth. And the human ritual that reenacts the myth simply continues that movement from rebirth to life to death to rebirth, and so on. In this movement it is always the same divine-natural acts that are repeated. No new ones occur, only the same ones, which belong always to the beginning of the cosmos.

Inasmuch as the ideal in relation to which humans achieve their worth is that of conformation to and integration into the life of the cosmos, and inasmuch as that life is cyclical, human life also aims at the repetition, within human life itself, of the cycle. There is no ideal for setting human life above nature so that the natural world at hand can be put to new purposes invented by humankind. There is no ideal of developing individual life so that it rises above the limits of nature and achieves a value beyond nature. Human beings are made for the divine-natural cosmos, not it for them.

Indeed, to seek worth through a conquest of natural limits would be destructive of both cosmic and human life. Not that the ancient Babylonians could not envisage a movement beyond the limits of the cosmos. *The Epic of Gilgamesh* presents the story of a man who did try to overcome those limits. But he failed, and his return to the city at the end of his search for immortality seems to say that the only meaning that being can truly have for humankind is to share the life of the community that exists within and supports the divine-natural world.

Stable civil order and extensive political power are among the great achievements of the ancient Middle Eastern peoples. *The Eipc of Gilgamesh* makes much of the passage of Enkidu from his savage to his civilized state, and commentators on the "Enuma Elish" have rightly stressed the political meaning and impact of the myth. These peoples, through their world-symbols, had come to know themselves as significantly other than the divine-natural world as a rhythmic conflict between forces of order and disorder. The city was their glory, and they called it an "enclosure"—that is, a place for persons separated from the rest of the world. It was, as we noted before, finally to the city that Gilgamesh returned to find the human worth he sought.

But the emphasis upon civil life does not negate what we have said about the Babylonians' concern to integrate human life into the movements of the divine-natural cosmos. The city, for all its being enclosed from the world, is still the place where the gods are served. The cities contain the temples, and the ritual celebrations take place mainly in the cities. It is as though the Babylonians achieved a sense of human uniqueness and separation from the rest of nature but in the form of a world-symbol that organized human life as an attempt to negate that very separation.

The world the Babylonians sought to secure was a world contained wholly within the relentless movements of the great forces of nature. Although it encouraged the development of political forms, economic diversity and division of labor, of art and literature and architecture and all those creations that set humankind apart, it still focused all expectations upon the aboriginal past. It looked for nothing fundamentally new, and it sought no help from outside the closed divine-natural cosmos.

There is much wisdom in the Babylonian mode of articulating archaic experience and organizing the struggle for a world in which human being and worth can be achieved. We modern Westerners are especially aware today of the need for an orientation of human life that cultivates a harmony with the powers and movements of nature and breeds into society the sense that human life shares the life-form of the natural world.

The Babylonian articulation of archaic experience is not the only one. In order to illustrate this point and to demonstrate the possibility of comparative philosophical anthropology, we shall briefly consider a contrasting articulation of archaic experience, the one given in the ancient Hebrew story of the exodus. Because life by various reinterpretations of this ancient world-symbol continues in our time, we are more familiar with it and will need but a little space to develop the contrast.

The Exodus and the Covenant[12]

I regard the whole story of the exodus of the Hebrews from Egypt, the covenant at Sinai, and the wandering in the wilderness (as given especially in Exodus) as one world-symbol. More than this could be included—for example, the conquest and the establishment of the Davidic kingdom. But the exodus story has in fact functioned as a complete world-symbol, being a relatively well unified story that defines the essential features of reality.

The comparison of "Enuma Elish" with the exodus story could be questioned on the grounds that the stories serve different purposes: one aims at representing the origin of the cosmos, the other the origin of a people. But if, as I claim, they are both world-symbols and serve to express the possibilities for being and worth and to direct life as the pursuit and maintenance of a world in which they are possible, then to that extent they serve the same purpose and admit of comparison. The fact that they accomplish their purpose so differently becomes highly important.

What for the Hebrew story are the basic constituents, powers, events and relationships of reality? The divine power is, of course, Yahweh. And Yahweh is significantly different from the gods of the "Enuma Elish." First, he is different in being differently related to nature. He is not identified with any particular natural phenomenon or power or

12. For my understanding of the Hebrew story of exodus, I am especially indebted to (besides the authors and works cited in footnote 9, above): John Bright, *A History of Israel* (Philadelphia: Westminster, 1972), and *The Kingdom of God* (Nashville: Abingdon, 1953); Harry M. Buck, *People of the Lord: The History, Scriptures, and Faith of Ancient Israel* (New York: Morrow, 1953); R.A.F. MacKenzie, *Faith and History in the Old Testament* (New York: Macmillan, 1963).

range of these. Yet he is related to natural powers. He accosts Moses from a burning bush on the mountain; he reveals himself especially in the mountain thunderstorms; he causes the reed sea to divide; he causes the Nile to run blood, the land to be covered with locusts and frogs, water to spring from a rock, and so on.

The divine and the natural, then, are not a complex of fundamental powers, giving rise to an ordered cosmos by an opposition in which powers that differentiate and create are the ones that control powers that dissolve and destroy.[13] There is rather a god who transcends the various parts of nature by being limited to none and able to use all to accomplish his purposes. The exodus story itself is not concerned with how the cosmos came to be and does not seem concerned that it could cease to be. Rather, it tells a story of events that occur in a cosmos that already exists.

Monotheism is implicit in the story. Although it represents the Hebrews as worshiping gods other than Yahweh (as in the golden calf episode in Exodus 32), the commandment to have "no other gods before me!" moves clearly toward monotheism—not by denying the existence of other gods but by denying them any function. And if they have no function, they are effectively nonexistent.

Yahweh, then, is all important—and so is his relation to the Hebrews. He is a god who singles out a particular people and calls them into a relationship with himself. Thus he appears to Moses and lays upon him the burden of leading the exodus from Egypt. It is a *new* action. The victory of Marduk over Tiamat and his reunion with Ishtar are not new. They are events through which the divine-natural cosmos takes shape; they take place in the Time before times and in the Place beyond places; they are not additional events in an already existing cosmos. If all goes well and with the help of the ritual celebrations, these *same* acts will occur again and again—or better, the world will return again and again to them in the aboriginal Time and Place. But the exodus takes place in a world that already exists; it is an action added to other actions and events in an ongoing world. It raises human life in that world to an altogether new condition and status, and is thus creative, but it is not a return to the aboriginal Time and Place of cosmic creation.

The interaction of Yahweh and the Hebrews manifests Yahweh's *care*. And care means a different kind of interaction between the divine and the human. The gods of "Enuma Elish" are indifferent to human beings; they do not purpose to save them from their troubles. It is up to

---

13. I am aware of the traces in the Old Testament of a Babylonian type of cosmogonic world-symbol that has Yahweh creating the world through a conquest of the sea monster Rahab. But that is irrelevant to the present analysis, for regardless of what some Hebrews may have believed before or after the exodus, the exodus story does not assert a cosmology like the Babylonian.

humans to serve them and to expect no more than the annual renewal of cosmic order and life. But Yahweh is attuned to the condition of humankind, at least to the condition of a portion of it.

The Hebrews in Egypt do not call upon Yahweh to save them; they apparently do not even know of any god by the name of Yahweh; they only groan in their misery. But Yahweh takes the initiative to bring them out of their misery and to establish them in a community with himself, first showing himself to Moses, then demonstrating his power in the miraculous events leading up to, during, and following the escape. Thus he is a god who undertakes to do something new, something that is more than an event in nature, something that in being based on care for humans has the effect of recognizing a value in human being beyond their value as attendants to some divine-natural process. In fact their value is such in the eyes of Yahweh that he wishes to save them *from* their oppression and *for* a life in community with himself.

The world that Yahweh seeks to establish for his people, then, is not primarily a natural cosmos that regularly repeats itself; it is a community of his people with himself and of themselves with each other through obedience to his will. Much in the story emphasizes the interpersonal form of the Hebrew world. The entire story unfolds as an adventure of Yahweh making himself known through Moses and entering into the lives of the slaves in Egypt. He calls them out; he addresses them through Moses; he gives them his law and seals a covenant with them; he is *present with* them in the ark of the covenant and in the tent of the presence; and he leads them by clouds and by fire.

The relation of Yahweh to his people is thus an ongoing, developing, interpersonal relation, a relation whose form is that of care and command with regard to his people. And just as the story presents Yahweh as doing something new for his people, it presents those who recognize him as called, indeed required, to do something new also. This is the case for Moses when he receives the command to lead the exodus, but it is true also of the whole group of slaves he leads to freedom. Yahweh will create a new and higher life for them—but only if they will trust him to provide for them, follow where he leads them, and seal the covenant with him that will create them truly as his people.

So fundamental to the Hebrew world-symbol is the interpersonal form that, when in the years after the exodus the Hebrews tell stories about the creation of the cosmos so as to relate their own story as Yahweh's people to the story of the cosmos, they imagine the original condition of humankind in terms of the covenant—an interpersonal idea. According to the story of Genesis 2 and 3, the original state of man and woman was one of perfect and unbroken community with Yahweh. He walked and talked with them in the garden; and they, in living through obedience to the god with whom they shared life directly, were able as a result to live in perfect community with each other — they were naked before each other and were not ashamed. Furthermore, the story presents the problems characteristic of human life as the result of the human violation of the interpersonal relationship of trust and obedience that bound man and woman to Yahweh and to each other.

The interpersonal form of life presented by the Hebrew world-symbol is vastly different from the form of life presented in "Enuma Elish." The gods of "Enuma Elish" are, it is true, represented anthropomorphically, yet their personal interaction with humans is quite different. The Babylonian gods do not *care* for the well-being of humankind; and, inasmuch as they themselves are whimsical and not wholly dependable, they do not call for *trust* as the primary response of their human servants. They may be said to require obedience, but it is the obedience of ritual reenactment of the cosmic events only, never obedience to commands to do altogether new things and never obedience to an inner, moral will of the gods.

Prayers of humans are for the gods to do what they have always done — enact victory over chaos and dissolution. There can be no thought that the gods might call persons out to a new and higher level of life, especially that they might elevate human life to the status of community with themselves. Thus the interpersonal elements of the Babylonian story are significantly different from those of the Hebrew story.

The moral dimension of the Hebrew divine-human relationship is also important. The primary service of humankind to Yahweh is obedience, not ritual repetition of events in nature. This does not mean that the Babylonians did not recignize many of the same moral principles as the Hebrews of the Sinai covenant. We know from Hammurabi's code, promulgated centuries before the Mosaic law, that they did. The difference lies in the relation of the law to divine reality. For the Hebrews, the law was an expression of the divine will and purpose, the condition for life as the people of Yahweh. For the Babylonians, there might be divine sanctions to encourage keeping the law, but the law was not significant of the inner will and purpose of the gods.

The exodus story articulates archaic experience by representing the life of the Hebrews as a movement from oppression and bondage to freedom. This is a movement from nonbeing to being, figuratively but also literally, because prior to the exodus they do not exist as the people of Yahweh and because as slaves they have only the lowest existence as humans. It is also a movement from relative worthlessness and unworthiness to human worth, because it is a movement into community with Yahweh. The highest value possible for humankind is to live in that community relationship established by the covenant. Not to belong to the people of Yahweh is to fall short of this highest possible value.

The story also represents being and worth as achievements rather than as givens. Yahweh himself acts to secure being and worth for his people, but his action alone is insufficient. There must also be a trusting and obedient response from the people. Not to make it is to threaten the being and value Yahweh aims to establish for them. The story of the wilderness sojourn, in fact, includes numerous instances of unfaith; the Hebrews fear to live life as a relation of dependence upon Yahweh and do not trust him to preserve and establish them. Thus the story represents human failure as not only possible but actual. It is only because Yahweh persists in his purpose that human failures of faith and obedience are overcome.

We said before that archaic experience is not only the experience of a struggle for being and worth but at the same time an effort to secure a world in which they are truly possible. This is no less true for the ancient Hebrews than for any other people. Consequently, the Hebrew story is not only a way of *thinking*. It organizes life in the form of a personal relation between Yahweh and his people. It is life under the form of the covenant, life under Yahweh through worshipful trust and obedience. When life structures itself in that way, it creates a world and allows for being and worth to overcome nonbeing and worthlessness.

The creation and preservation of the world of the covenant requires ritual celebrations, just as the divine-natural cosmos of the Babylonians did. And many of the Hebrew rites resemble (and even derive from) those of their ancient Middle East neighbors, such as the Babylonians. Yet the exodus story transforms those rites. They cease to be simply repetitions of events in divine nature and efforts to recreate the cosmos; they become interactions with a god who transcends the cosmic powers. The Hebrew celebrations of passover, pentecost and ingathering are reenactments of the events of the exodus, the Sinai covenant, and the wilderness sojourn. But because the events celebrated are not (at least primarily or exclusively) seasonal natural events but acts of Yahweh and responses of his people, they are of a different order from the New Year celebrations of the Babylonians. Consequently, they constitute a different life pattern.

Because the life that secures the Hebrew world of being as the people of Yahweh is not a repetition of natural-cosmic events but faithful, trusting interaction with Yahweh, it focuses upon reality in a dramatically different way than does the Babylonian. It is not concerned with returning everything to the aboriginal Time and Place of cosmic creation, but with bringing all life into an attitude of trust in, dependence upon and submission to the will of Yahweh. For this reason, the world created by the exodus story is open to the future, even expectant of significant new events in which Yahweh will not only preserve cosmic order but establish a more meaningful existence for his people. And because the basic form of life in this world is one of obedient, worshipful interaction with Yahweh, it is one in which new manifestations of Yahweh are possible.

The Hebrew world-symbol, therefore, not only recognizes that humankind stands apart from nature in a unique relation to it through the relation with Yahweh, but it affirms and promotes this difference rather than trying to overcome it. There is still a concern that the life of the community be responsible for the life of nature—the herds and crops. But there is for the ancient Hebrew the sense of having been created for a special and unique value, a value imparted through the elevation of life into community with God.

As in the Babylonian world-symbol, there is much wisdom in this ancient form of life. It has been developed in ways that continue to inspire and direct human life. But our purpose here has been not to prove the truth or superiority of one world-symbol over another—and there are many others besides these—but rather to exhibit the different articulations of archaic experience that they give and the different forms of life that go with them.

Through our discussion we hope to have added sense and depth to the claim that human life is a struggle for being and worth, and for a world that makes these truly possible. And we hope to have shown the usefulness of the notions of "world," "world-symbol," "archaic experience," "being and nonbeing," "worth and worthlessness" in the comparative study of human culture as philosophical anthropology.

Charles P. Bigger

Cynthia A. H. Bigger

8/*Recognition in Biological Systems*

Edward Ballard has suggested that metaphor can affect many of the results achieved by Husserl's *epoche* and phenomenological reduction. Metaphor enables us to free ourselves from certain naturalistic presuppositions and, through the manner in which each of its terms interprets the other, constitutes a horizon through which things show themselves in the manner determined by the metaphor. Metaphor can constitute a model-theoretic way of seeing beings, a way of interpreting them through the dialectical tension created between its terms.

We propose to show that what to the naturalist would be a reductive statement — "life is chemical activity" — is a metaphor opening a categorial horizon within which the teleological characteristics, such as action and intentionality, pertaining to our naive understanding of a living being and those nomological necessities characterizing its chemical processes mutually interpret one another. We can then "see" organisms of the lowest grade of complexity as agents meaningfully responding to their environment and whose being — life — is a function of metabolic activity, which they in turn control and direct according to biological time.

Living things instance the archaic sense of *physis*, for they arise from a process that sustains them in being, and they in turn act as controls (through recognition — which is interpretive — and decision) on this becoming. Not only do organisms organize internal processes through interpretation and appropriate rule-governed action, but they also order themselves to the external world through recognition, to the end of preserving their integrity. Recognition is then the means whereby the organism meaningfully relates to the external environment through its own intrinsic principles of valuation and decision. These systems have Aristotelian intentionality inasmuch as the "moving cause" lies within. Through recognition, mere spatial externality is interpreted as environment, and thus is converted into a field of meanings germain to life, so that these agents can cope with its contingencies. Failure can result in injury or death.

In this paper we shall show how metaphor enables us to construct scientific models. We begin with two allegories; first, with Aristotle who interprets all change through a teleological model, and then with Hobbes who inteprets all life through the model of mechanism. We shall then put these together in a model of living systems through a proper use of metaphor.

Because a meaningful relation with the environment is established with recognition—which contrary to Kant does not always involve concepts—we shall then show through biological examples how recognition is explicable through the model, which, in Whitehead's phrase, lets us see living beings as "organic mechanisms." In constructing the model we draw from Professor Ballard's two great teachers, A.N. Whitehead and Scott Buchanan. Its phenomenological and ontological dimension is intended to reflect Dr. Ballard's interest in Husserl and Heidegger.

Metaphor and Allegory

Husserl does not admit that "life" defines a regional ontology. Had he been a fifth-century Greek, the basic meaning of being he would have thematized in most, if not all, his regional ontologies would have been that of "life." The judgmental sense of "to be" expressed through the copula would have been replaced by the vital sense of *einai* (Greek, "to be"). It is only after Descartes and Galileo denature *physis* that intentionality, in the sense of action and meaning, are attributed to consciousness.

Husserl's own regional ontologies seem to have a naturalistic and subjectivistic basis, but this is not the way to read the "facts" if life itself is understood through agents involved in those intentional performances that he seems to have restricted to consciousness. Thus Husserl seems to follow the positivists in placing animal bodies among the "physical realities" in the "closed nexus of relationships of physical nature," a nexus subject to the reductive explanations of physical laws.[1] Intentionality thus belongs to subjectivity and has no natural analogues.

1. "Phenomenology," article in *Encyclopedia Britannica* (1927), reprinted in Richard M. Zaner and Don Idhe, *Phenomenology and Existentialism* (New York: Putnam, 1973), p. 49. For the role of Cartesianism in Husserl's failure to include plants in a regional ontology, see Robert Sokolowski, *Husserlian Meditations* (Evanston: Northwestern University Press, 1974), p. 75.

Hans Jonas has rather convincingly demonstrated that life is an irreducible parameter for most archaic peoples.[2] Except for the atomists and those modifications effected by Gnostic and Christian metaphysics, Western civilization thematized itself around the concept of a living nature, until the time of Galileo and Descartes, when the metaphysics of death replaced that of life. Now life became the anomality in a nature whose explanation pattern was given through nomological necessities. We wish to retrace this history in terms of certain founding allegories and to develop on this basis a concept of metaphor as a model-theoretic mode of seeing.

In the following discussion, we intend to employ "allegory" to designate a form of analogy—$a:b::c:d$—such that the relation between a and b is articulated by an expansion of the domain signified by the relation between c and d. Thus the relation between love and rhetoric is articulated by Dante in the first ode in the *Convivo* by an account of Venus, its roles and relations. In this sense the second ratio interprets the first by providing images and analogies through which the relation between the first terms can be "seen." Allegory asserts of the first relation—that between a and b—that it is and that it is to be understood through what is shown in the second relation—that between c and d.

In allegory the subject term tends to be taken up into or absorbed by the predicate expression. Where the predicate is a concrete story, as with Edmund Spenser's discussion of a virtue in the *Faery Queen*, and not a theory in the ordinary sense of that term, allegory preserves the integrity of the subject. When, however, I assert "all things are numbers" as an allegory (not a metaphor), I am apt to assume that everything that can be truly said of things can be said in the language of number.[3] It is then a "theory" that envelopes the subject term, as if this were what things really were.

As a counter to these reductive tendencies, we should remember that a painting or an emblem can be allegorical. Through the images and metaphors in the expansion of the "predicative" ratio, we come to see the subject in a certain manner. When the *is* of the allegory is understood as asserting something other than a partial isomorphism between the two ratios and taken instead as a theoretical identification between two terms, then the allegory is transformed into a reductive statement and the predicates (which are now those of a theory whose terms are univocally defined) determine what it is to be an instance of what is identified by the subject.

2. Hans Jonas's *The Phenomenon of Life* (New York, 1966) is an important and pervasive source of our account.

3. Strictly speaking, this is a metaphor. Things and numbers mutually interpret one another through the metaphor of measurement, as we can see by the way in which the physical sciences and mathematics develop together.

For example, I might identify organisms as living; but when I say in the reductive sense that they are chemical processes, I presume that everything that can be said about living things can and should be translated into the language of chemical theory. Because this theory is supposed to be reducible to physics, life becomes a mechanism. The self-selective decisiveness of living systems, whereby they interpret themselves in goal-directed action, then becomes a fiction, and all behavior becomes explicable in and through the interrelation of non-teleological natural necessities.[4]

But theory, as a way of thinking beings, is first of all *theoria*, a way of *seeing* them. A *theoria* is one present at a sacred spectacle wherein a meaning of being is made present through myth and ritual. By participating in the ritual, one experiences through the presented sacred images an ontophany, the capacity to encounter oneself and other beings in a world in a powerful, effective and durative manner. Understanding is what we are in the disclosure of beings through *theoria*.

Theory has its origin and truth conditions in the manner in which it lets us "see" beings through images and models. Consider the allegory that governed Newton's optics, "light is sound." Because we had a particle theory of sound, one was led to think light in similar terms—its reflections, defraction, and the like—and on this basis nomological connections in our modern sense of theory were read off the model and then experimentally established.[5]

Analogies and disanalogies with sound are discerned by exploring the relations suggested in the model. A model that has been established through *theoria* remains a likeness, perhaps even an essential representation; but this does not mean that we have a formal equivalence such that everything really true about the subject domain is expressible in the language of the mechanistic model. Other interpretations may be equally "true" or essential in context. Although we can understand and appreciate Dante, his allegories and metaphors no longer satisfy truth conditions as we understand astronomy and physics. Images fade, and a surfeit can be irresponsible, dulling intelligence.

In metaphor we complete the work of allegory. Then and only then does the formal aspect of each term (ratio) come into view. Here the structures that are referred to in the proper sense by the subject and

4. Given the cybernetic model, it is easy to reduce its components to process explained by the hypothetical-deductive covering-law theory. For a good example, see Ernst Nigel, *The Structure of Science* (London, 1971), pp. 398–446.

5. These relations are developed by Mary Hesse in her model-theoretic approach to science in *Models and Analogies in Science* (University of Notre Dame Press, 1966). Our discussion of metaphor owes much to her discussion, just as what we have said about allegory has its origin in Scott Buchanan's *Poetry and Mathematics*. We would say that we employ metaphor in the Platonic, not the more familiar Aristotelian, sense.

predicate term are seen as mutually interpreting one another. Each articulates, as if the predicate, the other; and in this tension of sameness and otherness we come to see beings in a new and relatively novel manner. Were I to assert, as if for the first time, with the authority of poetry or wide experience, "man is a wolf," then men would be seen as wolflike and wolves would take on certain undesirable human features, perhaps to be hunted as if they were fiends. The Parmenidean sense of *einai* ("to be") as identity that always threatens the "is" of allegory is finally overcome, and now the truth relation becomes that partial or perspectival isomorphism between the two mutually interpreting structures.[6]

Through metaphor, world is revealed as a complex of paired structures, each offering an interpretation of the other. Language is itself a metaphor, asserting of the world an interpretive propositional structure that the propositional structure of the world interprets for us—for example, in experimental procedures, in our search for truth.

These purported mappings can be only partial. Because, as Quine has remarked, everything is in some sense isomorphic with everything else, we are saying little unless there is a criterion of relevance, analogous to Plato's Good or the *we* of Hegel's phenomenology. To avoid the nihilism of mere perspectivalism, we have to understand that as nature gathers itself and as we gather it into language (the noble theme of the *logos*), there is an intentional focus, a grading of relevance so that some relations can be ignored. These ignored relations can be shown in a variety of ways—experimental, historical, philosophical—to be false or irrelevant. Process determines what is given for emphasis, and culture determines how it is to be taken in language.

Being and Life

If *theoria* is the way we understandingly are in relation to beings through models and images, we must also acknowledge Heidegger's point that ontic interpretations presume a deeper, prethematic understanding of Being that determines all interpretation. Heidegger himself returned to the archaic Greek understanding of *physis* (nature) in order to find in it an alternative to the manner in which, on his reading, we have thematized our experience as "presence." We must

6. This definition of the truth relation and of mutual interpretation in the chapter on "Truth" in A. N. Whitehead's *Adventures in Ideas* p. 310, (New York, 1933), was brought to my attention by Dr. Ballard. I think this can be shown to provide an alternative to Heidegger's sometimes improvident critique of the metaphysics of presence and logico-centricism within the metaphysical tradition. Whitehead's metaphysical description of his cosmology as "organic mechanism" is the classical basis of our own metaphor "life is chemical activity."

briefly recapitulate this Heideggerean analysis in this interest of establishing both our sense of *epoche* and our model. The history of the problem of Being will inform the history of the problem of life.

When Aristotle throws out metaphor to satisfy the univocity required in his logic, he invokes the rigidity of the Parmenidean ideal and a set of invidious distinctions recurring in our history as essence/accident, appearance/reality, phenomenal/noumenal, and the like, which are in the end a function of the nominalization of *einai*, "to be." *Einai* has only a present, durative stem and means locative or durative presence, a state that lasts or unfolds in time, as well as a strong veridical sense, "to be so," "to be the case." As stable, enduring Being, it is strongly contrasted by Parmenides with its borrowed aorist *gignesthai* ("come to be," "arise," "take place"). As a participle—a term borrowed from Plato's "participation"—"Being" partakes in a nominal and a verbal sense. *Einai* is nominalizing; *gignesthai* supplies its verbal aspect.

The interrelation of these concepts can be seen in *ousia*, translated as "substance" in most Aristotelian texts. *Ousia* is the abstractive feminine singular participle of *einai*. *Ousia* comes to have the sense of *physis* (nature), that which emergingly, self-gatheringly (*legein* or *logos*) comes forth into un-concealment (*a-letheia*, truth) or presence (*on*, *ousia*, Being in its nominal sense). The nominal sense (what is present, essence, beingness) of the participle dominates its verbal sense (presencing, *genesis*, *gignesthai*). In Plato, the what of the visible radiance of *ousia* is *eidos*, and this move frees *gignesthai* for an even more radical meaning of "presencing" than it enjoys in Heraclitus.

A feature of *einai* is its veridical sense, which we are likely to think of as the certainty of a Cartesian *inspectio*, if not of propositions. The Latin *certitudo* derives from *cernere* (Greek, *krinein*) and has the sense of passing through a sieve, the separation found in de-cide, dis-cern, and the like. In *Timaeus* the receptacle is characterized as the durative nurse of *genesis*, which, through an act like that of a winnowing basket, is decisive, self-selective. Thus the veridicative sense of *einai* lies not so much in the *is* of predication and the way it posits existence in modern logical theory, as it does in a sense of presencing through a self-selective gathering (*logos*).

We can understand Plato's move as designed to restore *peras* (limit) to Being. The idea that Being could be infinite (*apeiron*) would have been anathema to a fifth-century Greek. To be is to be definite, to be bounded, to lie within limits. Now Parmenides certainly intended his *on* (Being) to be bounded, for like a sphere, "it is present within the bounds equally" (Frag. 8.49). But it should be noted that this is one of the signs on the *hodos* to *aletheia*, a denial of incompleteness, which together with ungeneratedness, immobility and indivisibility involve those negative predications that are the mark of non-Being. "It is not in need of anything" (8.32) reminds us, with Spinoza, that we approach Being by the negative way, which entails that Being is infinite, a conclusion that Melissus, if not Parmenides, quickly drew.

Plato is attempting to restore the archaic sense of *physis*. Neo-platonism apparently did not learn this important lesson. When finitude recurs in Christian metaphysics, it is hardly a matter of self-limitation: finite being is posited as such through the act of an infinite God; and thus the emphasis is on the nominal aspect of *ousia* whose contingent presencing is through God, permanent self-presencing.

In Plato *eidos* is not imposed or posited. Nor is it, as in Aristotle, the expression of the potential of *ousia* to be something specifically definite. In *Timaeus*, *psyche* is the fundamental instance of *ousia*; and the self-definition of Becoming, an *apeiron*like notion, as a Being is achieved in self-selection from among the separated ideas through the regulative idea of the Good. These are the constitutive verbal and nominal aspects of *psyche*. Students of Whitehead will recognize herein that decisiveness of the concrescing actual entity with respect to eternal objects that characterizes its conceptual pole.

Truth or unconcealedness is primarily an ontological matter, for what is seen is a presence (*on, ousia*), the visible *eidos* of a self-gathering (*logos*) presencing. On the noetic side, the *logos* is the self-gathering of the knower through dialectic into the radiant light of *eidos*, the Good being the condition for both knowing and Being. In both Plato and pre-Platonic thought, *physis* is a mystery; it either conceals being as it makes present (Heraclitus, Heidegger), or it is a spontaneously self-creative principle (receptacle) that cannot be circumscribed or domesticated by *eidos* (Plato, Whitehead). Though verbal aspects continue to play an important role in Aristotle, *ousia* has an even more nominal aspect than in Plato; *eidos* has the sense of immanent *entelechia*, the *logos* that controls genesis. In his account of *physis*, we lose the mystery of the dynamic *apeiron* (energy in the thermodynamic sense) as the self-gathering presencing common to Heraclitus and Plato. However that may be, we have seen how certainly, definiteness, is achieved through self-gathering, decisive, selective presencing and how our intuitive and discursive apprehension of *eidos* through *logos* is in virtue of that *logos* by which all things collect and steer (or are steered by) themselves (Heraclitus, Frag. 41).

Post-Cartesian philosophy will detach itself from this universal ontological-noetic sense of *logos* whereby all becoming collects and orders itself in presencing itself. Rather than grounding itself in *ousia* or *physis*, it will achieve certainty in the nonrepresentational presence of the self to itself, the "I think . . . " of Kant's transcendental self-consciousness. In this subjective sense of certitude, the *ego cogito* will use logic, the last vestige of the *logos*, to achieve clarity of re-presentation, the manner in which beings are present to consciousness. The mystery will no longer lie in *physis*; rather, that there is a nature to be represented will be the mystery.[7] This tradition, whose epistemology dominates the philosophy of science, is brought into question by life.

Metaphor and the History of Biology

We now wish to examine certain allegories that have played a fateful role in the history of biology. With the exception of the atomists, the Greeks thematized their world through their understanding of the nominal and verbal aspects of *physis*. The dominant allegory, "motion is life," was taken over by Aristotle, the first among biologists, and his mechanics became a chapter in the general teleology of the universe.

In Homeric Greek, certain functions that later became identified with *psyche* were separated. On death, the cause of movement, *thymos*, left the body; the head or dream soul, *psyche*, wandered off to live a shadowy life in Hades. Pythagoras and Heraclitus, emphasizing the nominal and verbal aspects of *physis*, respectively, presided together in the integration of these "functions," together with *noos*, into *psyche*. What we can say about *psyche* will largely have to do with self-motion and the way it is effected by the living agent.

In Aristotle this is largely the function of the animal soul, the paradigm case of a self-changing being—one whose being is through the changes it effects. Through this model all change or motion is understood as either teleologically directed by an act or the immanent fulfillment of an act. Necessity is itself understood under a teleological rubric. Matter (*hyle*) is and has meaning only within the parameters of form, the principle of act; and act does not change in so far as it changes (except incidentally, as the physician can heal himself) some material potentiality into an actuality. Matter itself is the principle of the unintended consequences of act (such as mutations) and is therefore a principle of contingency.

But what is important to note is that Aristotle has no place in his philosophy for those nomological necessities that provide us with grounds for the explanation of natural changes. Necessity is for Aristotle contingent on act, and is thus a hypothetically necessary means to an end. If one is to saw wood, then it is necessary that the means have a certain form. There is no independent identification of

7. We are especially grateful to Dr. David Cornay for the patient help and advice he gave us on this section.

these processes apart from act or form. Aristotle has transformed an allegory, "motion is life," into a reductive statement. Biology is the primary science in a world wherein everything instances life.

In Aristotle act or form bears the sense of Parmenides' permanent presence, both in the sense that it governs changes in the individual and is in the species sempi-eternal. The verbal sense of Being, presencing, is preserved in such changes as nutrition, growth, reproduction and repair; and these are not identifiable or specifiable except through the form (*psyche*) or presence that directs and controls them. There is the sense that presence (Being) is through presencing (Becoming); without nutrition the organism will die; without exercise and good diet there would be ill health. In general, immanent ends are through the becoming they in turn reflexively make possible; but then God establishes the continuity of change and the everlastingness of the kind. Presencing is dependent on presence. This is something that materialism also claims, substituting matter for God as eternal presence.

Aristotle gave the vocabulary of the agent and its acts to philosophy, but he did not provide for the necessities. Though not explored, that possibility was built into the concept of *psyche* by Plato in *Timaeus*. *Eidos*, the work of reason, is through *psyche* a suasive principle with regard to the dynamic, independently identifiable chthonic necessities of the receptacle, and this was the image that we rather disingenuously built into our account of the archaic understanding of *physis*. Act (*psyche*) is like opening a window in order to let thermodynamic laws operate in cooling a room. We need to turn to the way in which Galileo established the role of the necessities and thus laid the foundations for a metaphysics of death.

With Galileo and his successors in the development of mechanics, the verbal sense of Being is lost. The form unique to the species becomes the always present, universal and necessary structure of natural law. Matter also becomes eternal; the impositional and reversible structure of the law determines the nature of matter, its impenetrability, mass and the like. Materialists and idealists will exploit the two sides of this picture. Its epistemological loading can be seen in the way permanent presence is preserved in LaPlace's "superhuman intelligence"; such a being could presence the past, present and future of the entire universe to itself if it could grasp the position at any given time of every particle and the forces acting upon it.

Galileo stripped *psyche* from the science of mechanics. The behavior of an isolated system is a conservative function of its previous behavior; for if at rest so it will remain, or in motion so it will continue uniformly ever and anon. Thus the typical explanation pattern in Galileo will be in terms, not of purpose and intention, but in terms of the nomological necessities. We do not explain change through striving; we subsume initial conditions under a nomological law and deduce what is to be explained therefrom by the *modus ponens*.[8] Though Galileo ignores the counterentropic image suggested in the relation of the *apeiron* receptacle to *eidos*, the hint that there are necessities independent of agency or form in Plato's account of the receptacle is fulfilled. But this now means that for Galileo form, rather than being the condition for change, is the epiphenomenal effect of change. The perfect form of the circle that governed the movement of the spiritualized heavenly bodies in Aristotle's account now became the elliptical orbits that were mere resultants of the centripetal and gravitational forces acting on material planets in Newton's cosmology.

The issue for life was evident; its more or less constant form is the mere eject, rather than agent, of motion.[9] When Hobbes asked the rhetorical question, "What is life but motion, the beginnings whereof are in some principal part within?" he was asserting the converse of Aristotle's allegory and proposing that life be understood through the nomological necessities of mechanics. Descartes managed to find in consciousness a temporary home for act and its teleology; animal life, including that of the human body, was delivered over to mechanism. In reducing *psyche* to consciousness, we have denied to the living organism those functions of remembering, judging, recognizing and deciding that we believe essential to life itself.

In the historical context, Hobbes' allegory was out of season; pumps, levers, pulleys and heat convection do not shed much light on life. Its real promise was recognized only through Comte's positivistic program. Comte proposed that physics play the role previously assigned to religion and metaphysics, and on this basis erected the reductive hierarchy of chemistry, physiology (including psychology) and social physics. With the development of biochemistry it was now appropriate to redefine life in terms of the parameters of mechanism.

Darwin's theory of natural selection seemed to eliminate the role of form and purpose in biology, and the development of genetics from Mendel to the Crick-Watson double-helix model for DNA seemed to provide a mechanism for heredity and material kinds that was reductively chemical. The stereometric nature of this chemistry and the thermodynamic characteristics of these reactions do seem to have an uncanny resemblance to Plato's geometrical chemistry and the role he assigned to the *apeiron*-receptacle in becoming. Could it be that this so-called reduction harbored the seeds for a restoration of the classical sense of *psyche*? What was now required was the concept of an agent

8. The loss in explanatory power in the switch from Aristotelian dynamics to Galilean kinematics is discussed in Paul Feyerabend, *Against Method* (London, 1975), pp. 99–101.

9. Jonas, *Phenomenon of Life*, pp. 62–98.

that, like Plato's reason, would persuade and order these necessities. This restoration hinges on the nature and function of enzymes as agents in the regulation of metabolism. Pasteur, who was the first to recognize the unique role of living systems as agents, was the major nineteenth-century opponent of positivism. Through his work we can begin to see how the metaphor "life is chemical activity" combines the agent model of Plato and Aristotle with the mechanistic model of Galileo and Hobbes in a nonreductive model of living systems.

The early career of Pasteur was devoted to the study of chemical crystals. There are certain chemical structures called optical isomers —molecules that differ from one another as a mirror image differs from that of which it is the image. One should recall at this point that Kant's recognition of this problem of incongruent counterparts led him to claim that space must be understood through sense and its interpretive structures, and not pure mathematics. Pasteur was visually separating these isomers of tartaric acid as left- and right-handed crystals under a microscope. He was surprised to discover that a microorganism growing in an unseparated solution of paratartaric acid could recognize and "consume" the right-handed isomer, leaving the left-handed isomer behind and thus purifying the solution for him. This led him to recognize the unique chemical role of living agents and to his lifelong protest against the stultifying effects of positivistic reductionism: "Positivism, offering me no new idea, leaves me reserved and suspicious."[10]

The role of bacterial agency was first recognized by Pasteur in fermentation. The prevailing theory, advanced by Justus Liebig, explained fermentation in terms of chemical reactions, yeast playing only a secondary role. Liebig reductively explained this reaction as the breakdown of sugar molecules into carbonic acid and alcohol, brought about by the contact of the sugar with unstable organic substances released by dying yeast. A released albuminoid or nitrogeneous material imparted a mechanical vibration to the sugar and produced its breakdown.

Because of his experience with microbes in the paratartrate solution, Pasteur became convinced that microorganisms were vital to fermentation. Through a series of elegant experiments he demonstrated that fermentation depends on living organisms. He showed that different microorganisms were responsible for different ferments, which he was then able to characterize and control. He recognized that animal cells and microorganisms had a similar chemistry and "was the first to

10. The quotation, from Pasteur's Académie Française lecture, and further examples of his attitude to positivism, may be found in René J. Dubos, *Louis Pasteur* (New York: Scribner's, 1950), pp. 385–88.

express in clear chemical terms the analogy between the working of muscle and the metabolism of yeast."[11]

As Tillich remarked, "all symbols have their season." Until the development of physiological chemistry, Hobbes's allegory probably inhibited research. Perhaps only now can we exploit "life is chemical activity" as a model-theoretic way of seeing phenomena. Intentionality and teleology are once again respectable concepts.[12] Philosophy has even found a way of talking about *things*, rather than its own concepts or its own talk, largely through the influence of *de re* modal logic. It is now possible to speak in a more or less respectable manner about *de re* teleological explanation.[13] But it seems to us that these approaches lack a model showing how action and intentionality, usually described in psychic predicates, are related to the mechanics of life. The more linguistic attempts reinforce a Cartesian prejudice that life is mere mechanism. We have a model for mechanism, and we have a fair grasp of the conceptual networks that are entailed in action descriptions; we have to put these together in a manner so as to preserve that interiority associated with consciousness and that exteriority associated with the space of mechanics. Perhaps we are now ready for the metaphor "life is chemical activity."

Now the agent theory, associated by Aristotle with life, will interpret the lawlike structure of chemical change; and these same structures will interpret act. This will enable us to see inwardness, hitherto understood in dualistic Cartesian terms, as a phenomenon within nature explicable through nonvitalistic processes. Moreover we see life, which Aristotle says is the being of living things, as a presence that arises through the energy it utilizes in controlling natural processes, those having to do with repair, reproduction, and the like.[14] This is the *aletheia* uncovered by the model.

Thus we deny the primacy of the role of presence, giving it a coordinate meaning with presencing, and effectively reinstate the ontic Platonic model. This should give us a nondualistic and nonvitalistic model of living systems. We combine the metaphysics of life and death, of agents that can perish and natural processes that preserve a meaning of presence.[15] The model is intended to restore the concept of soul (*psyche*) to *physis*.

11. *Louis Pasteur*, p. 197.

12. Elizabeth Anscombe's *Intention* (Oxford University Press, 1957) made action-theory respectable in analytic circles, while at least a sort of *de dicto* teleology (under a teleological description) received a powerful sanction from Charles Taylor's *The Explanation of Behaviour* (London, 1964).

13. Andrew Woodfield, *Teleology* (Cambridge University Press, 1976).

14. *De Anima*, 415 b 13.

15. For the purpose of this argument, we assume that the chemistry within the organism is nonunique, that it could occur elsewhere within nature. This may be false

As long as we found our ontology on presence or a steady-state variety thereof, it will be difficult to account for the incompleteness characteristic of life. Life is in the making and being made and is characteristically appetitive. Although it is difficult to introduce those desires and feelings, which are among the reasons and causes for human action, into organisms of the lowest grade, an event or process ontology can make this formal accommodation. Agents can control, direct and initiate or terminate processes, however the need that initiates action be physiologically or psychologically specified and understood.

Motivation is a difficult concept at the level of human behavior; but insofar as it is involved in the general teleological aim to sustain and enhance Being through Becoming, it has an ontological root that it shares with the conatus of all living systems. Being is the always unfinished issue of life; failure is non-Being, death. Life belongs to the poetics of Being. Although we cannot confidently say that all organisms feel or desire, we can say that their acts have an analogous motivational structure.

We have elsewhere shown that the integrity or for-itselfness of life is preserved through such self-recognitions as that whereby DNA, the primary meaning of being in microorganisms, is sustained and repaired.[16] We have tried to show that our model must be understood in terms of the creative capacity of living agents, not through those vestiges of permanent presence that permeate the homostatic thesis of cybernetics. We shall now address the problem of recognition at the bacterial and molecular levels to the end of giving further content to this model.

Recognition

We shall be using the concept "environment" to signify that range of worldly phenomena that is effective and meaningful within the parameters of a given recognition function(s), where that function is to be understood under the rubric of acts that through recognition can modify either the agent organism or the phenomena.

Environment is what matters or can matter to a given kind of living being, and is thus a scale and selection, an interpretation, of world (the

---

inasmuch as components of living systems usually provide templates and parts in the laboratory synthesis of these compounds. The notion of death raises doubts about the transcendental ego, central to idealistic versions of *epoche*.

16. Cynthia A. and Charles P. Bigger, "The Non-Reductive Molecular Basis of Life," in *Proceedings of the 16th World Congress of Philosophy* (Düsseldorf, 1978), pp. 91–93. This is intended to correct Jonas's thesis that DNA is a continuent (*The Phenomenon of Life*, pp. 97–98).

given totality) proportioned to the organic kind. A shark and a bacterium can inhabit the same sea, but each dwells within a different environment. There are innumerable ways of giving an inventory of a world, which is like a well-stocked store; to a child it is mostly candy and toys, but to its mother there is a different phenomenal range. Even where these environments overlap, they have different senses. The acts appropriate to a given kind of organism or a subsystem thereof determine the environmental correlate, inasmuch as the acts involved in carrying out and effecting its protointentions determine, within worldly limits, how environment is structured. Both the scope of acts and the environment can change, for better or worse.

We may think of environment in phenomenological terms as a horizon that has a contextually *a priori* categorial structure through which the given kind of organism encounters in recognition those entities that are meaningful for its being and well-being. These categories are molecular interpretive systems.[17] Thus environment is the "outer," "nonself" region that is the correlate of the "inner" structure of act and its material conditions, which involves choice, deliberation, intention, and the like; the (sometimes automatic)[18] functions associated with recognition link this inner ("self") to the outer ("nonself"). Recognition—perceiving something as something—is always a matter of meaning.

Finally, we shall understand "behavior" as the manner in which this linkage is given to an observer in the larger context of world. Our model is intended to enable us to see the complex dialectic of agent, organism, environment and world. It presumes that "recognition" is a fundamental biological category.[19]

Recognition always entails a receptor mechanism through which the

17. In defining the environment through the organism, we respect the Mendelean principle that the form of the organism's act, given through DNA, has relative, if not absolute, priority. Many evolutionary biologists have come to suspect the rigidity of this interpretation; but if characteristics of the environment are acquired and inherited, it is not evident what this mechanism may be. In this sense genetic endowment preserves a meaning of presence that does not admit that it is an interpretation of the environment. On the other hand Professor Stent has argued that the genetic information in the germ cell does not at the present time account for its full expression in the phenotype. There is also evidence in certain DNA repair mechanisms that indicates what was thought to be a mutation by external causes may be a self-induced repair to this damage and that the mutation is the response of the agent to a potentially lethal contingency. We can assume a mutual interpretation, within these limits, between organism and environment even if we do not know the full mechanism involved. "The environment is the organism" is, at the present stage of knowledge, closer to an allegory than a metaphor. There is, however, nothing in our account that precludes the full metaphoric extension of this assertion.

18. Edward G. Ballard, "The Nature of the Object as Experienced."

19. Because we have, since Kant, been led to believe that recognition takes place only in concepts, this thesis is offered as a direct challenge to all forms of transcendental idealism. This also raises questions about Strawson's *m* and *p* predicates.

organism can effectively factor its environment. "Receptor" designates an analogy of function, rather than a material similarity. A receptor protein can play the same role in a cell within the body or in a microorganism that is fulfilled for us by eyes and ears. Formal analogy is involved in all biological discourse, roughly corresponding to what St. Thomas called "analogy of inequality." For example, the role played by the central nervous system in higher vertebrates will be played by various specialized protein molecules in bacteria.

The selection of edible substances and their transport to our mouth by our hands may involve in bacteria receptor molecules and transport systems through the cell membrane. Our pleasure-pain responses may be mirrored in bacterial chemotaxis, a device that enables them to flee noxious conditions and pursue favorable ones.

The Mechanisms of Biochemical Recognition

The basic cellular discriminators, what might be loosely called the nerves of the cell, are specialized protein macromolecules that, by virtue of their unique physical conformation, are able to recognize other smaller molecules, their substrates or ligands, and act upon this recognition in some specific way. The proteins fall into several groups according to function. They may have a catalytic, regulatory, receptor or transport function. More and more frequently one protein molecule is found to perform more than one of these functions, so that a strict division by function is inadequate. This conflicts with the concept of univocal cause central to mechanism. However, the mechanism involved in performing all these functions—that is, the mechanism enabling recognition by the protein of the ligand—is the same. This ability is built into the molecule through its primary chemical structure that determines the protein's three-dimensional configuration.

In order to understand this mechanism, it is necessary to look more closely at the biochemistry of proteins. They are polymers built of repeating subunits called amino acids. The simplest proteins contain around fifty amino acid subunits, whereas the most complex contain several thousand. All amino acids contain a carboxyl group and an amino group, and it is through the linkage of the carboxyl group of one amino acid with the amino group of another to form peptide bonds that the polymer backbone of the protein molecule is formed.

In addition, each amino acid contains a sidechain or functional group. It is through these groups that the twenty different amino acids commonly found in proteins are distinguished. The sidechain gives each type of amino acid a distinct chemical character. As a result, the amino acids can be generally divided into three classes: nonpolar, uncharged polar and charged polar. The nonpolar amino acids (glycine, alanine, leucine, isoleucine, valine, phenylalanine, proline and methionine) possess sidechains related to compounds that have little solubility in water. They are hydrophobic and tend to exclude water by clustering together. In contrast, uncharged polar amino acids (serine, tyrosine, threonine, tryptophan, asparagine, glutamine and cysteine) are hydrophilic and interact with water molecules through the formation of hydrogen bonds. The charged amino acids (aspartic acid, glutamic acid, histidine, lysine and arginine) can participate in electrostatic interations in addition to hydrogen bonding.

Within these three general classes, individual amino acids have additional specialized chemical characteristics. For example, the sulfur atom of the nonpolar amino acid methionine allows interaction with metal ions, and the sulfhydryl group of the uncharged polar amino acid cysteine allows formation of disulfide bonds. It is these sidechains and the chemical diversity they provide that enable proteins to perform a variety of functions.

A protein is synthesized in the cell by addition of specific amino acids end to end in a genetically predetermined order to form polypetide chains. The linear order of amino acids in turn determines the three-dimensional, or tertiary, structure of the protein. The chain folds back on itself in an irregular manner to give a globule-shaped particle. However, the folding is far from random and depends upon the position of the various types of amino acids in the polypeptide chain. Each sidechain will seek its position of lowest chemical potential and, as a consequence, the chain folds in a manner that achieves thermodynamic stability. In general, polar amino acid sidechains are at the surface and hydrophobic groups in the interior. In this way, the sidechains of amino acids that are not adjacent in the linear order of the polymer can come together to create microchemical environments within the protein molecule.

It is at this point in the description of protein biochemistry that we can begin to understand the mechanism of recognition that requires that the protein be able to select and bind the correct ligand. Through the folding of the polypetide chains a site(s) is created in the molecule that spatially and chemically fits the ligand and to which the ligand will bind with great affinity. These sites enable the protein to discriminate between very similar molecules and to bind the correct one. For example, the protein may select one and only one monosaccharide from a group of monosaccharides. Or, it may exhibit stereospecificity; only one optical or geometrical isomer will serve as ligand, even though the only difference in the isomers will be the rotation of one of the functional groups around the axis. It was this sort of selectivity that convinced Pasteur of the role of bacterial agency in fermentation. Life determines an oriented, meaningful spatiality, not mere meaningless coexistence, and can reach out into it to achieve itself.

Recognition and binding of the ligand are followed by a transformation, either catalytic or allosteric, of protein or ligand depending on the function (enzymatic, receptor, regulatory, etc.) of the protein. The "sensory" horizons of agents of the lowest grade are tactile-motile in a strain space.

Recognition and the Control of Biochemical Processes

In the Aristotelian model of the agent, the potential (matter) that is immanently actualized is not specifiable apart from that agent. As the Scholastic philosophers said, form is apportioned to matter. But in our model, the substrate of the act is independently specifiable, for the change could occur apart from the direction of the agent. Thus recognition is now a primary relation between the agent and what the agent directs, even if that agent is more or less specific or on need produced by another agency for a specific substrate. We will now discuss some of the mechanisms involved in metabolism, repair and defense that maintain the sense of "inner" through or against the "outer," of self and nonself.

Enzymes are proteins that exhibit a catalytic function and binding of the appropriate ligand, in this case called the substrate, results in immediate chemical transformation of the ligand. In the substrate binding site, amino acid sidechains are delicately oriented so that the catalytic reaction is facilitated. Specific amino acid sidechains participate in the reaction. As soon as the reaction is complete, the product(s) of the reaction is released from the enzyme. As a catalyst, neither the enzyme as a whole nor the catalytic sidechains are altered by the reaction and the enzyme is able to process a considerable number of substrate molecules very rapidly. The turnover number (number of substrate molecules metabolized per enzyme molecule per minute) for most enzymes is around a thousand but may go as high as a million. The enzymatic reaction is chemically identical to the nonenzymatic one; the difference in the two being that the enzymatic reaction proceeds 10^8 to 10^{11} times faster than the nonenzymatic one! The enzyme *qua* agent gives to the mechanism of chemical change the meaning of biological time; the issue is life and its rhythms, or the crisis of threatened death. The organism must have available the energy or the products of these natural changes if it is to sustain itself. In regulating these changes it plays the role of the chemist in a laboratory, except that time within which a living agent can decide and act has a different meaning than it does for the chemist, for whom the change is hardly life-threatening.

For proteins or sites that are not catalytic, binding of a ligand will result in a change in the shape of the protein, an allosteric transformation. This transformation alters another binding site in the protein so that the molecule is activated or inactivated with respect to a second ligand or the substrate in the case of an enzyme. This type of action is frequently involved in a chain of reactions where binding of the first ligand creates either a negative or positive cascade effect.

The theory of the structure-activity relationship of recognition of ligands by proteins was derived initially from kinetic studies of enzyme activity and binding specificity. Very few of these proteins have been completely defined chemically; but for those which have, the structure has confirmed the theory. A good example, and one of the first of these proteins to be completely characterized, is ribonuclease, an enzyme that catalyzes the cleavage of phosphodiester bonds in ribonucleic acid polymers. This enzyme is a small one with a molecular weight of 13, 680. It contains 124 amino acid residues. In its active conformation it is folded irregularly into a globular shape. Eight cysteines in positions 26, 40, 58, 65, 72, 84, 95 and 110 in the linear chain form four disulfide linkages that stabilize the three-dimensional structure. If the enzyme is denatured—that is, if the chain is unfolded chemically—it will spontaneously refold into the active conformation if returned to normal conditions.

Ribonuclease has a well-defined binding site for the substrate. It contains the sidechains of lysine-7, lysine-41, lysine-66, histidine-12, histidine-119, serine-123 and thereonine-45 (numbers refer to the position of the amino acid in the linear chain). Serine-123 and threonine-45 form hydrogen bonds with the substrate. This binding makes the reaction specific and excludes some very similar molecules. The histidines are involved in the catalytic reaction and act as general acid-base catalysts by donating and receiving protons. The lysines are believed to stabilize the chemical intermediate that the substrate goes through during catalysis. Once the reaction is complete, the transformed substrate is released and the two catalytic histidines are restored to their original chemical state. These two actions—enzymatic and allosteric, stemming from one mechanism for recognition of ligand by protein—are used over and over again in the cell to accomplish a great variety of vital tasks.

In order to maintain the life of the individual and of the species, the bacteria must be able to transform foodstuffs into useful energy and synthesize all the constituents of the cell that are not available in the environment. This involves monitoring material available in the environment and modulating the apparatus of metabolism so that no unnecessary energy is expended on synthesis of preformed materials already available or on the production of the synthetic apparatus itself. In addition, the cell must faithfully reproduce the deoxyribonucleic acid (DNA) molecules, which contain all the genetic information of the species and repair any damage incurred by the DNA. In this paper we shall show how recognition of ligand by protein is vital to all of these activities.

We will first consider how the bacteria protect the integrity of the DNA molecule and its genetic information for transfer to the next generation. DNA is a polymer consisting of four different types of subunits whose linear order forms a code specifying the structures of all proteins synthesized in the cell. Fidelity in replication of the DNA molecule, as well as repair of damage inflicted by external agents (e.g., UV irradiation, X-rays and alkylating chemicals) is essential. To accomplish these ends, the cell employs enzymes.

The DNA molecule consists of two paired, complementary polymer strands; during replication each strand serves as the template for replication of the other. The synthesizing enzymes, DNA polymerases, have a built in proofreading ability, so that if a subunit not specified by the template is inserted into the growing DNA polymer, the enzyme will excise it. It will continue to excise subunits until the correct one is added.

In periods when DNA is not replicating, repair enzymes monitor the DNA polymer searching for damaged subunits. When a damaged area is detected, it is excised and replaced by undamaged subunits. There are a number of different repair enzymes now known and each is specific for a particular type of damage.

It is also possible for bacterial viruses to inject their DNA into a bacterial cell for the purpose of taking over the host cell's machinery for virus replication. The bacterial cell has means for detecting foreign DNA and destroying it before damage is done. Again enzymes called restriction and modification enzymes are involved. These enzymes are capable of recognizing specific sequences of subunits in DNA. The restriction enzymes cleave the DNA molecule when they bind to these sequences. The modification enzymes chemically tag the host DNA at these sequences. This tagging inhibits the action of the restriction enzymes, thus protecting host DNA from destruction by its own enzymes. Tagging serves as a means of distinguishing self from not-self.

Life must discriminate through recognition those things that serve its being from those things that threaten its non-being. The polymerases, repair, restriction and modification enzymes are extremely sophisticated enzymes but the basis for their activities is still the basic protein-ligand recognition mechanism. In this case, the ligand is a small segment of another polymer.[20]

The genetic information encoded in the DNA molecule is primarily information for the structures of all the proteins capable of synthesis by the cell. Some of these are structural proteins but most are the proteins, enzymes, regulators and receptors whose recognition mechanism we have been discussing. To understand why this and not some other information is transmitted from generation to generation, one needs to know that practically all reactions occurring in the cell are mediated by enzymes. Enzymes are the primary agents in the self-synthesis of life. As we shall describe below, this gives the cell, working in conjunction with regulator and receptor proteins, the power to control and manipulate those reactions. Here again the model of a human agent controlling a process is in order. Agents can cope with the random and unexpected and order it to their own ends.

These are two types of reactions that are vital to the life of the individual cell: (1) Breakdown of foodstuffs for capture of energy and as a source of carbon atoms and other elements that are in turn used for (2) synthesis and assembly of cell building blocks. These reactions occur through a series of complex metabolic pathways. Transformation of any particular substrate from x to y is through a series of small intermediate chemical steps, and it is this series that constitutes the metabolic pathway. Each step is catalyzed by a different enzyme and, depending on the type of transformation, this may involve a large number of enzymes. For example, at least twenty enzymes are involved in conversion of glucose to carbon dioxide.

Metabolic pathways only proceed in one direction (synthetic or degradative) and because enzyme reactions are theoretically reversible, energy barriers are set up at different points in a pathway to ensure that the thermodynamic equilibria will favor production of the end products(s) of the pathway. Agents give directionality to processes, inform them with their intentions. For example, if a synthetic pathway converts compound x to y with an input of energy, it will not be possible for the pathway to reverse itself and degrade y to x. Life, as against most natural change, is directed and directional. This is immanent theology.

An enormous expenditure of energy is required to synthesize cell building blocks and much of that energy is used to synthesize the enzymes catalyzing synthesis of other cell constituents. Being is through controlled becoming, agents through the creation of energy that sustains them. In order to conserve energy, the cell operates as

20. Our essay "The Non-Reductive Molecular Basis of Life" covers these processes in more detail (see note 16, above).

efficiently as possible. It economizes by assessing its synthetic needs in light of substrates available in the environment. Many of its pathways can be turned on and off, either at the level of the pathway or at the level of synthesis of enzymes for the pathway. We shall discuss the role played by protein-ligand recognition at each of these levels of control, giving causal process a meaning for life.

First we must consider how the cell assesses conditions in the external environment. It is defined and separated from its external environment by the plasma membrane. This membrane, composed of protein and lipid, is semipermeable and does not merely divide physical space. The membrane provides the environment for vital processes, not a resultant of forces, and gives a meaningful outer environment. It is highly ordered and contains discriminating and selective mechanisms that govern transactions over the boundary and allow the cell to maintain a high concentration of internal molecules.

Cell membranes contain transport systems that promote the passage of solute molecules across the membranes, like the hands that carry food to our mouths that would also select the food by touch. These systems consist of carrier proteins (translocases) that can recognize specific solute molecules, form ligand-protein complexes and, with an input of energy, shunt the ligand to the other side of the membrane where the ligand is released. In some cases the ligand is enzymatically modified during transport; in other cases, it is not. In this manner, sugars, amino acids and inorganic ions are selectively moved in and out of the cell.

The exact details of these transport systems—for example, how many individual proteins make up a system—are not known, because so far only a few transport proteins have been purified. However, it is clear from the experimental evidence that protein-ligand recognition is the basic mechanism in selective transport of solute molecules across the membrane. Sense recognition is essential to an environment; it is a condition for objects to be meaningful, for the intentional directedness of life.

By binding and transporting its ligand, the carrier protein provides a signal to the cell that compound x is now available in the external environment. What happens next depends on whether this is a compound that can be broken down for energy or carbon atoms, or whether it is itself a cell building block that the cell is currently expending energy to synthesize.

If the latter is the case, the cell has two options. It may employ feedback inhibition and turn off synthesis at the level of the pathway or it may stop synthesis of the enzymes for the pathway. In feedback inhibition, the end product of the pathway combines with the first enzyme of the pathway and inhibits its ability to catalyze the first reaction, thus shutting down the pathway temporarily. This is an example of an allosteric transformation. The end product binds to a site on the enzyme other than the enzymatic substrate binding site and alters the shape of the protein so that it can no longer catalyze the reaction with its substrate.

This is the sense in which we stop doing something for a reason given through sensation. Thus when the bacterium is supplied environmentally with, for example, the amino acid isoleucine, transport of isoleucine by carrier proteins into the cell causes an increase in the internal level of the amino acid. At a certain level of concentration, isoleucine inhibits the first enzyme in the pathway for its own synthesis. This sort of control has been referred to as *fine* control over biosynthesis because it can immediately adjust the level of synthesis to a steady-state level of the end product.

The second type of control—repression of enzyme synthesis—is considered *coarse* control but exerts maximum economy by preventing unnecessary protein synthesis. The sequence of events leading to final production of a protein is complex and involves a number of diverse elements. The information for an individual protein is contained in a specific segment of the DNA molecule and is called a gene. In protein synthesis, this information is first transcribed from the gene into ribonucleic (RNA) molecules. The actual assembly of the protein takes place elsewhere on the surface of special particles called ribosomes.

RNA molecules are very similar to DNA molecules; they are polymers and consist of four subunits capable of complementary pairing with the subunits of DNA. RNA is synthesized off the DNA template through the action of enzymes called RNA polymerases. These enzymes recognize and bind to a promoter region at the beginning of the gene. After binding, they move along the template adding one subunit at a time to the growing RNA molecule. However, for repressible genes, this process can be stopped by the binding of a repressor molecule to the operator of the gene.

The operator is a segment of the gene that overlaps the promoter region. If the repressor is binding to its operator, RNA polymerase is physically prevented from binding to its promoter and thus RNA transcription cannot be initiated. Often more than one gene specifying enzymes involved in the same pathway is under the control of a single operator-promoter region and in this way synthesis of the enzymes for the whole pathway can be blocked simultaneously. (When several genes are controlled by one operator, the segment of DNA containing them is called an operon.)

Repressors are regulatory proteins. In the case of repressible protein synthesis, the repressor is inactive until it binds a specific external molecule, the corepressor. Binding of the corepressor to its site in the repressor protein causes an allosteric transformation of the repressor that enables it to recognize and bind to its specific operator segment on the DNA molecule. Thus when the amino acid histidine, which is being synthesized by the cell, appears in the external environment, it acts as a corepressor and activates the histidine operon repressor. The activated repressor binds to its operator and shuts down synthesis of the ten biosynthetic enzymes in the histidine pathway. Every action presupposes a mechanism through which its end is achieved.

If an external molecule, which is not a cell constituent but which could be degraded for energy production or used as a source of carbon or other elements, appears, the type of control is reversed. Pathways are induced instead of being repressed. In this case the repressor is active until it binds the external molecule, the inducer. It is capable of binding the operator and blocking RNA transcription until it is inactivated by binding its specific inducer.

For example, suppose *E. coli* bacteria have been growing on the sugar glucose but are suddenly switched to an environment that contains lactose but no glucose. Lactose cannot be metabolized by the cells. β-galactosidase enzyme, which can split lactose to glucose and galactose, will be immediately synthesized until it reaches a level of about 3,000 molecules per cell. Two other enzymes involved in lactose transport and conversion to a usable form are simultaneously induced. Synthesis of these enzymes was repressed by the active β-galactosidase repressor until lactose appeared and inactivated the repressor.

The binding between an active repressor molecule and the DNA of its operator is strong and, once attached, the repressor will stay put until it is inactivated. However, the bonds between the repressor and the corepressor or inducer are weak ones. They can be rapidly made and broken, and allow the repressor state to adjust rapidly to physiological needs. In addition, the life of the transcribed RNA molecules involved in protein synthesis is brief, approximately three minutes in bacteria. Thus the bacteria can modify the types of proteins being synthesized rapidly in response to environmental changes and insure that specific proteins are produced in appropriate amounts.

Life has its own necessities, and it acts to effect these, to bring about favorable results by controlling itself by selecting means to bring about its ends. Enzymes, themselves chemicals, are seen as formal principles, principles of act, and thus as controlling changes. This is what the metaphor "life is chemical activity" would lead us to expect.

Our description of repressible and inducible systems of regulation in bacteria has purposely been an oversimplified one in order to illustrate the operation of the basic protein-ligand recognition mechanism in this type of regulation. Recent studies have suggested that in the cell various combinations of simple regulatory mechanisms produce complex regulatory systems. For example, in addition to repressors, there are also positive control proteins. When activated, these proteins speed up initiation of RNA transcription by facilitating RNA polymerase binding to its promoter. One operon may be under both positive and negative control.

Goldberger has described a phenomenon—autogenous regulation—that is another example of this. In this mechanism, the product of one of the genes in the operon regulates expression of the operon. In most cases, the regulatory protein has several functions, because it will act as an enzyme or structural protein in addition to acting as a regulatory protein. This protein is frequently the enzyme that catalyzes the first step of a metabolic pathway and is also subject to feedback inhibition. Thus two important mechanisms for control are linked together through the same regulatory protein.

Autogenous regulation gives the cell a buffered control system. The bacterium can respond to changes in the environment by increasing the rate of synthesis of appropriate enzymes, but at the same time it increases synthesis of the regulatory protein that opposes this change. This allows the organism to avoid extreme changes in gene expression. It is likely that even more intricate systems for regulation will be discovered as research in this field continues.

Even an organism as "simple" as a bacterium seems to leave as little as possible to chance in its internal response to external change. This is how it creates its specific environment *a priori*.

Recognition and Motility

If internal recognition is essentially the introduction of temporality into nature and the base of the *physis* model, external recognition further articulates the spatiality that, as the form of coexistence, is the condition for choice and freedom, for evaluation over a continous differential field. Mentality *per se* would seem to require a differential field of others—Derrida's "difference" and "deferral."[21]

In animal and in human life this theme of recognition is played out in motility and the role of recognition in giving us a way of monitoring our actions as we play out our purposes. We shall find analogues of these forms and formal acts at the bacterial level. Here again the primary meaning of spatiality is tactile—kineasothetic, the space of grasping rather than pointing, which differentiates environment from

21. It is as if bacteria were sensitive to "color," but not "red," "brown," etc., or to sound, but not to tones. The field permits ordering by degree, but there is no datum specific to each degree. This is another way of saying that sense is not distanced from its object, but is rather drawn and grasped by it, the way we are grasped by an object of desire when we give ourselves over to it.

those higher spiritual formations that determine world. It is in this connection that the biological agent takes on characteristics Aristotle associated with action that have since Descartes been sublimed to language and mind.

So far, we have discussed how the protein-ligand recognition mechanism is used for control of internal processes in the bacterial cell. In this final example, we shall describe the role it plays in allowing bacteria to respond with physical movement to changes in their environment. Bacterial chemotaxis — the ability of certain bacteria to move toward nutrients and away from noxious chemicals — has been known since the 1880s but only recently have researchers begun to decipher the mechanisms involved. Here we approach the role of sense in motile living agents.

E. coli and *Salmonella typhimurium*, the most studied of the chemotactic bacteria, respond to approximately twenty different chemicals either as attractants or repellents. They also respond to changes in oxygen supply, temperature and pH deviations. They move by means of organelles called flagella, thin helical filaments that extend through the external cell membranes into the medium. They act as rotating propellers. The direction of rotation is reversible and this allows the bacterium to respond appropriately to the presence of a gradient. In the presence of an attractant gradient, the rotation is counterclockwise and the flagella wrap together behind the bacterium. This motion propels the organism forward in the direction of increased concentration of the attractant. If the flagella are rotating clockwise, they rotate individually and this causes the bacterium to tumble. When bacteria are in a "no gradient" situation, they tumble at low frequencies. However, when they are exposed to a repellent gradient, tumbling frequently increases, allowing the organism to move away from the repellent.

Bacteria can "swim" in the appropriate direction at a rate of about twenty micrometers per second, which is twenty to forty body-lengths per second. This is a measure of "short-term memory" involved in gradient recognition. The response is meaningful, varying as conditions vary, and requiring the expenditure of different levels of energy.

We are just beginning to understand the biochemical mechanisms operating in chemotaxis. The first step in chemotaxis is exercise of the basic protein-ligand recognition mechanism. Attractant or repellent molecules bind to receptor proteins at the cell surface. Most of these receptors appear to have a dual function and are, in fact, the carrier proteins (translocases) involved in active transport of ligands across the membrane that we discussed earlier. Binding of the ligand to its specific receptor serves to initiate two different branches of activity — transport and chemotaxis.

The signal sent to the chemotactic pathway when the receptor binds a stimulant molecule results in a change in flagellar rotation and movement up or down the gradient. It is known from genetic studies that at least nine proteins are involved in the signal transfer from receptor to flagellar response. There are also two more membrane proteins that act in conjunction with the receptor. So far, the function of only one of the nine proteins is known. The protein is an enzyme that catalyzes the chemical modification of one of the membrane proteins.

Whatever the details of the mechanism involved, bacteria are able to detect a difference in concentration over time. They do not, as one might expect, measure the change between one end of the cell and the other with two sets of receptors but, as Koshland has shown, one set takes a measurement over several body-lengths. This means that the bacteria possess a "memory." This memory reduces the bacterium's analytical problem from detecting one part in 10^4 to one part in 10^2 to 10^3.

As pointed out by Koshland, the events of chemotaxis lead one to discuss bacteria in terms usually reserved for language-users and identified with higher neutral processes. Bacteria choose to go up or down a chemical gradient. They discriminate between very similar chemical stimuli and have a memory. They learn to respond to new environmental nutrients by inducing the appropriate internal apparatus and appropriate means of sensing them. This is an example of the creativity of life.

Though these terms (choose, discriminate, memory, learn, respond) are used in a different way when applied to higher species, they are descriptive of analogous functions, playing the same role in the life of each kind. They give a meaning of "inwardness" lacking to a mechanical system. It would, however, be wrong to conclude that there are no underlying mechanisms common to both higher and lower forms. The principle that cell behavior can be influenced by the binding of a molecule by a receptor at the cell surface is well known in higher systems—for example, receptor binding of insulin or acetylcholine.

MacNab suggests that the existence of this phenomenon in bacteria indicates its development at a much earlier evolutionary stage than formerly believed. Thus memory and adaptation to environmental changes appear to have emerged early in evolutionary history. Bacterial mechanisms, forming rudimentary sensory systems, may give us the basic underlying molecular model for all sensory systems.

Teleological ends can be achieved by a variety of means. The fact that organisms can achieve the same end in various ways, whether in metabolism and in the internal environment or in motility and the external environment, shows that, at every level, life and freedom are irreducible parameters of living systems.

Recognition is the means whereby agents take up what they bring about, give chemical mechanism a sense, an intentionality, that hitherto phenomenologists have tended to associate with mind and analytic philosophers with language. Recognition is the means whereby life, the being of the organism, is sustained as its own immanent end by a protoreflexivity, a protoself-knowledge, that harbors within it a natural valuation.

Discrimination of self from nonself, of the favorable from the unfavorable, introduces into life the theme of the good. Merleau-Ponty has taught that the body plays a richer role in consciousness that we post-Cartesians are wont to recognize. We find that same role being played out in the dynamic and creative mechanisms of life, even at the lowest grade. Without detracting from the creations of the human soul and spirit, is it not right that we should find their roots in an evolutionary nature?

Conclusion

In this paper we have advanced the thesis that what appears to be a reductive statement—"life is chemical activity"—is a metaphor. We have tried to show that, contrary to Heidegger, our metaphysical tradition contains a meaning of Being that is the dialectic of presence and presencing, and we have, with aid from Plato, found a way to interpret the metaphor "life is chemical activity" that is neither materialistic nor idealistic, neither reductively mechanistic nor vitalistic. We have an *epoche* that is a model-theoretic way of encountering within the ontic horizon it opens the phenomena of life in its *aletheia*.

In our choice of recognition, we have taken a function, which is usually given a linguistic or conceptualistic loading, to show that life at all levels encounters a meaningful environment. In identifying intentional activity (purpose and meaning) with what would normally be considered mechanistic systems, we have tried to see that those problems, which since Descartes have had their focus in consciousness, are coextensive with life.

But life is not a chemical soup: it cannot be understood apart from those agents that, through recognition, guide and control chemical processes that sustain life, the being of the organism. These energetic, metabolic processes that, *qua* becoming, recripocally sustain being, are controlled through recognition. Recognition gives us that dimension of inwardness that is altogether lacking in a purely extensional chemistry. We then attempt through bacterial motion to demonstrate that all living systems must be understood through "psychic" predicates hithertofore reserved for mind.

A scientific metaphor should provide routes for research. Recognition offers many such routes, some of which are being currently investigated. Inasmuch as it functions both within cells and between cells in a multicellular organism, recognition seems to be a basis for organic unity. A cell is a community (com-unity) of agents. Its unity is a function of communication, not just in the sense that a moving object communicates motion to another, but in the sense that meaning is shared-with in the common task of getting on with life. Through communication agents share tasks.

How cells communicate within the body so as to give a common focus to this great society is generally unknown. Failure, as in cancer, is evident. Obviously both senses of communication are involved in complex and simple organisms, the nomological laws of physics and the meaning dimensions first clearly brought into prominence by phenomenology. This would help us to further understand how agents control metabolism and vital processes. How a code that is context-free can take on the contextual sense of agent meaning is certainly the initial problem. This involves a new understanding of DNA.[22]

Bibliographic References

Koshland, D.E., "A Response-Regulator Model in a Simple Sensory System," in *Science* 196 (1978) 1055–63.

Lehninger, A.L., *Biochemistry* (New York: Worth, 1975).

McNab, R.M., "Bacterial Motility and Chemotaxis: The Molecular Biology of a Behavioral System," in *CRC Critical Reviews in Biochemistry*, (1978), pp. 291–341.

Mahler, H.R., and Cordes, E.H., *Biological Chemistry* (New York: Harper & Row, 1971).

Watson, J.D., *Molecular Biology of the Gene* (Menlo Park: Benjamin-Cummings, 1970).

22. This problem was suggested by remarks by Professor Stent at the 16th International Congress for Philosophy, Düsseldorf, September 1978.

Harold Alderman

9/The Text of Memory

For the most part, philosophical discussions of memory have been mixed endeavors. That is, they combine, with differing emphases, descriptive and normative goals insofar as they seek to show what memory or memory claims *are* and insofar as they also argue for a version of what we *ought* to call *good* memory. It seems to me that joining these two endeavors is appropriate, for with memory, as with any other sort of thing, it is in no wise possible to say what makes one of its type superlative without first specifying its type.

It seems to me also, however, that the discussions of memory with which I am acquainted have failed descriptively in the following sorts of ways. They err by treating memory as a species of perception; they err by eliminating important kinds of memorial activity in order to develop consistent descriptions; or, most perniciously, they err by simply ignoring memory itself in order to describe, out of context, the logic of memory claims.[1]

Obviously, if one has ignored the problem of description or gotten it wrong, then so also will one get one's epistemological specifications wrong. With these sorts of issues in mind, I hope in this paper to develop a relatively adequate description of memory, and thus also to suggest what a good memory *really does*.

1. For example, Richard Taylor, "Justification of Memory and the Analogy of Vision," in *Philosophical Review* 65 (1956) 192. Richard Brandt's "Memory Beliefs," in *Philosophical Review* 64 (1955) 78, considers only "retrospective memories," explicitly eliminating skill memory from the class of memories. John O. Nelson's "The Validation of Memory and Our Conception of the Past," in *Philosophical Review* 72 (1963) 65, deals only with the logic of memory claims and the relation between memory claims and "past-tense ground statements." E.M. Zemach's "A Definition of Memory," in *Mind* 77 (1968) 526, is emphatic in separating the problem of justifying memory claims from descriptions of memory. Zemach argues that descriptions of "the *mere* [my emphasis] experience of remembering" cannot shed light on the epistemological problems of memory claims.

When I first began to be puzzled about memory, it occurred to me that total amnesia and total recall might be similar in that they are both deficient forms of memory, and it is this apparently implausible hypothesis that guides this description of what I think persons do when they remember something.

Succinctly, my paper argues against the picture or copy theory of memory that Plato, Aristotle, Hume, Russell, and various contemporary philosophers have adopted.[2] Memory is not, as I shall show, primarily a matter of making copies of past events.[3] It *is* primarily a matter of making sense of things; recalling pictures (or making copies) *may* under some conditions help us do that. But then again sometimes it may not, and therein lies the rub. In what follows I shall clarify my position by arguing that memory is an analog of what Husserl called imaginative or eidetic variation and by appealing to certain memory paradigms.

Content and Sense

Edmund Husserl originally proposed the technique of imaginative variation *(frei variation in Fantasie)* as the key to the problem of specifying the *essential* properties of any object. The technique is thus an ontological one; it is also one of the most straightforward procedures recommended in Husserl's often cryptic work.

Basically the technique goes something like this. Suppose we want to decide, for example, what this piece of paper essentially is. We proceed to find out, according to the technique, by imaginatively varying the properties of the piece of paper until we reach the point at which we find either that we *remove* an essential property of the paper or until we *add* a property that renders the paper no longer paper. Thus, for example, we imagine coloring the paper, reducing its size, removing the type, burning it, and so forth. When we know which of these imaginative changes alters the paperly characteristics of the paper, then we know what paper is. The point, for Husserl, is that paper *qua* paper has a certain objective *sense* that defines it as paper, and through some such imaginative exercise we can find out *what* that objective sense is.

2. In addition to Richard Taylor's defense of this position (see footnote 1, above), see also the following versions of the defense: H. H. Price, "Memory Knowledge," in *Proceedings of the Aristotelian Society*, suppl., 15 (1936) 16; B. Smith, *Memory* (London: Allen & Unwin, 1966).

3. Cf. Charles Landesman, "Philosophical Problems of Memory," in *Journal of Philosophy* 59 (1961) 57. See also R.F. Holland, "The Empiricist Theory of Memory," in *Mind* 63 (1954) 464. Holland argues that the memory-perception analogy leaves out the context and intention of memory and thus leads to the bogus search for Hume's "memory indicator" in terms of which one is supposed to be able to distinguish memorial and imaginative images. Images, in Holland's view, are not *necessary* features of memories.

Memory, in my view, is an analog of this Husserlian procedure in which we vary the objects of past experience in an effort to discover what those objects really are. Memory is an imaginative, eidetic variation of memorial objects: it is a repeatedly renewed search for the appropriate objectivity of its contents. Put another way, memory is a search for the *sense* of things, and *thereby* also a search for the objects of memory.

Given this, it would follow that the most important arguments about memory have to do not with putatively neutral memorial *content* (there is really no such thing) but with the *sense* (i.e., meaning) of that content. To the extent, therefore, that philosophers think that disputes over the veridical character of memorial objects are *primary*, they are missing the fact that this kind of disagreement is vital only because it has to do with more basic disagreements about sense.

Consider, for example, two painters who argue heatedly over their respective memories of, say, Joan Miro's *Composition 1963*. Their argument about line, color, design, and the like, is about *spatial sense*, about the spatial sense of the painting. For painters, things achieve sense in two-dimensional pictorial space, and it would be surprising if their memories were not primarily pictorial. But the painter's pictorial memory is about pictures only because that is how things achieve sense for painters. Such pictorial memory is not, however—for reasons I shall show—an adequate memory paridigm.

With these remarks, I do not mean to suggest that a good memory is one that consists only of a general, free-floating memorial sense devoid of objective content. Such a situation is, indeed, impossible, precisely because having a sense of things means having constituted remembered objects (though not necessarily pictorial ones). A main point of my argument, then, is that we derive recollected objects from the eidetic variation of past experience rather than deriving the sense of things from pictorial recollections.[4] Established sense presents as memorially objective and adequate exactly those objects that give content to that sense.

Remembered and Imagined

From what I have said so far, it would seem that it might be difficult to distinguish remembered and merely imagined objects. First, let me say that the remembered object *is* quite like the imagined object; in fact, therein lies the source of its power. So rather than approach the remembered object, as did Hume, with the fear that I might not be able

4. The difference between memory and recollection is somewhat like the difference between history and chronicle.

to distinguish it from the imagined—and therefore dubiously objective —object, I want to emphasize that the remembered object is *almost* only imaginary.

There is, however, no need for despair. Memory does provide a sort of objective foundation whose adequacy can be contextually and strategically determined. That is, a memory is good (i.e., objective) if it leads to a coherence of experience that both unifies and distinguishes the temporal ecstasies. The test of such objectivity must, to some extent, be a public one: a memory is warranted as "good" if it can be nurtured—and if it is nurturing—throughout its dialogical encounter with the memorial projects of other human beings.

From this line of argument it follows that the idea of an "objective past" is only a regulative ideal synthesized from the very personal dialectic of memorial projects, for which the ideal provides the limiting sense, *objective past*. Although this is so, we do not, of course, thereby get idiosyncratic warranties for asserting that any memorial object that fits *our* projects is thereby veridically recollected. Watergate and the paranoid prove the inadequacy of such arbitrary memorial projects.

Given this portrayal of memory as personal, historical project, the question of the status of memorial pictures is raised anew. It seems to me that an adequate demonstration of the priority of sense-making over picturing lies in the fact that it is normally easier to remember something that makes sense than it is to remember something that does not; if recalling pictures were primary, this would not be so. Nonetheless, we do often picture things when we remember, and I want now to discuss the secondary role of memorial pictures.

In the first place, we observe that although philosophers as divergent in their philosophical commitments as Hume and Husserl have searched for some imagerial feature that would guarantee the veridicalness of perceptual images, the search has proved futile. Images accompanying present experience carry no special epistemological warranty. More importantly, there are many situations in which we recognize or cope with objects without being able, or needing, to form images of them.

Consider, for example, the case of a man congenitally blind who is able to successfully maneuver in a room he, in principle, will never see and who has a very good sense of the utter objectivity of that room. Or consider that many persons can neither envision nor publicly produce clear images of things they very easily recognize. Both of these cases indicate that the recognition of present objects is not tied to the formation of mental images.

Memorial recognition, then, is like present recognition in the following ways. I recognize, for example, my red Volkswagen without being able to form a mental picture that distinguishes it from all the other ones like it in the parking lot, and I can do so because I have a sense that *this* is where I left it in the parking lot and, more decisively, because the key fits and the seat and mirror are adjusted to my size. Given all of this, I may of course be wrong, nonetheless; the general sense of fittingness that enables me to identify my car is fallible.

To emphasize the limited character of "veridical" memorial pictures, it is only necessary to point out that such pictures may make it impossible for us to place ourselves functionally within the matrix of past-present-future. Thus, it may be that under some conditions the best memory is one that does radical violence to "veridical" pictures of the past through selection of detail, emphasis, and the like. Such *good* memories are precisely those—for example, of a concentration camp survivor—that can overthrow the tyranny of a past through acts of imaginative variation.

Memory is not Jack Webb confronting the past and demanding "just the facts, ma'am." Rather it is a tentative archeology that tries to establish the sense of our origins so that we may encounter ourselves as temporal beings who are always beginning and ending, the past itself being both these things. Memorial knowledge is the origin of temporal sense; it is a committed, strategic construction of the sense of one's past.

Thus it seems it is impossible to establish some memory as "objective" by summing up memorial perspectives in order to get the *real* memory; all one would get from such a procedure is a sum of biases, each of which, because it is taken from its worldly matrix, becomes both less interesting and more obscure. Further, having the disparate memories agree that a given summary is the real memory would simply mean that agreement had been reached on some common worldly matrix within which the summary counted as *the* memory.

The Achievement of Forgetting

Given this view of memory, we are in a position to see that forgetting—generally considered a memorial failure—becomes a positive achievement. An unedited memory is like an unedited book: sprawling and awkward, and having no *sense* against which completeness, interestingness, and so forth, might be measured. As Kierkegaard observed in *Either/Or*: "If a man cannot forget, he will never amount to much"—and this for the sorts of reasons that an unedited book will never amount to much. Forgetting, then, is a negative eidetic variation that establishes the essential sense of a remembered event by deleting from it the properties inessential to it. Of course, because remembering does not take place *sub specie eternitatis*, what counts as an *appropriate* forgetting can be determined only in the context of a specific life project. When we criticize someone's forgetfulness as a failure, we most often judge it from a context other than that in which the forgetting originates and counts as an accomplishment.

Thus, for example, a student who forgets material from a lecture may be eliminating material deemed inessential to more pressing and current projects (e.g., a failed marriage); his memory judged by the lecturer *is* bad, but judged from the student's perspective the forgetfulness may be a hard-won accomplishment. The dialectic between the student's and the lecturer's perspectives is what will determine if the particular forgetfulness is strategically successful, and the issue will not always be resolved in favor of the lecturer.

The creative character of forgetting becomes more evident when we understand that specialists have a right—better, an obligation—to forget the nonsense written in their field; only thereby can they make sense of the field and show appropriate respect for it.

This account of forgetfulness helps clarify what goes on in some apparently vicious forms of neurotic memory when persons remember only those aspects of their experience that add to their negative self-images. The construction of such negative self-images is also a kind of accomplishment—however undesirable such accomplishment may seem from the therapeutic perspective. It seems to me, then, that we cannot say of neurotics that they *only* forget those aspects of their experience that would yield a more coherent and pregnant historical encounter (though we can, of course, say this); more importantly, we must say that neurotics remember and forget what they *need* to remember and forget in the construction of a particular life project. If we see neurotic memory, not in terms of a failure to remember but rather as the achievement of a certain style of remembering, we are at least in a position to understand what is being done. Inasmuch as this sort of neurotic memory is moderately pervasive, any adequate description of memory must be able to account for it.

Nothing I have said about neurotic memory, however, may be taken as advocacy. The problem with neurotic memory is that neurotics fixate on a past sense of themselves and let that fixated sense determine present and future senses of themselves; thus they abandon the obligation to eidetically vary their experience in a free search for a self-image or life project. Neurotic memory is the loss of the ability to reconstitute memorial objects in the face of present experience, and it is this inflexibility—manifest also in fanatic memory—that lets neurotics *identify* themselves with some past self-image. In neurotic memory the past moment of the temporal matrix overwhelms the present and future moments as the neurotic takes a monumentalist view of past experience. Nonetheless, despite its failings, neurotic memory is not simply a failure. On the contrary, it is a peculiar sort of memorial achievement that can be understood as such when viewed in the context within which it counts as a memory.

It seems to me, then, that although Freud was correct in showing that memory is a function of a life project, he was wrong in assuming that neurotic memory was *only* a kind of failure. Neurotics forget what they think they need to forget, and it is surely an open question as to whether the neurotic ought to change the life project in terms of which that forgetfulness is an achievement of sorts. Thus Freud's assumption about the healing power of the clear vision that one is supposed to get in depth analysis seems only a theoretical bias: it is not necessarily the case that the more one knows about oneself, the "healthier" one will be. To be able to recall the details of one's past does not necessarily set one free: the case of Oedipus proves this true.

There is, of course, a difference between forgetting and lying, and I do not wish to create grounds for confusing the two. Forgetting, as I have argued, is part of the memorial search for adequate sense. Lying, by contrast, is the explicit denial of some constituted sense, and it holds both the denial and the sense in memory. Thus lying provides two divergent memorial foundations, both of which one must live through in the act of lying. Lying creates a dissonance at the heart of one's memorial project and leads therefore to a dissonant present and future. Forgetting is an essential activity of memory. Lying is the activity of not reporting what is remembered.

The Deficiency of Total Recall

The case of Funes in Borge's story "Funes the Memorious" emphasizes the positive character of forgetting and it also leads us to the apparently implausible conclusion that total recall is *necessarily* a deficient memorial form. Borge's story describes the pathological—though *very* interesting—case of a man who literally recalls everything he has read and experienced. Funes' recall is so total that he does not, for example, count; rather he *remembers* the sums of all number combinations. The affect of Borge's story is to reduce the epistemological ideal of an objective, neutral and total recall to the absurd. The story establishes that the ideal is distinctly odd: Funes is utterly incapable of *doing* anything, so dominated is he by his total recall.

Dysfunctional pathologies are scarcely appropriate knowledge paradigms. The ideal of memorial neutrality thus simply assumes that a spectatorial stance is the appropriate one for forming and evaluating memory claims. Memory claims, however, like all knowledge claims, are rooted in and responsible to some field of action and no stance that deracinates those claims can hope to make sense of them. The case of Funes, the most inactive and memorious of persons, shows that forgetting is the grace that makes history possible. Funes cannot make sense of his life because he cannot forget.

Philosophers, who have never been chary about making odd claims, will, I trust, not be unduly put off by my remarks on total recall. In any event, I wish to make further defense of my position by simply calling attention to two other putative cases of total recall. The first of these is the computer, which is utterly incapable of making sense of its data. The second case is that of the legendary idiot savant who is supposedly able to recall without understanding any text that he or she "reads." Each of these cases stresses that there is no correlation between total recall and the primary sense-making function of memory. The computer, Funes and the idiot savant are *incapable* of making sense of what they "remember." This range of examples thus shows that total recall substitutes the recollected content of memory for its essential sense-making function, and thus it also clarifies the way in which total recall is deficient. This last point can be emphasized by noting the many cases of scholarly secondary sources that show great versatility in recalling the content of a work but seem incapable of making sense of it.

Total recall—and I take "Funes" as the paradigm—thus presumes to place all objects in an apparently neutral space and develops for itself the pretense to memorial perfection exactly because of this neutrality. In this pretense of neutrality, total recall denies the perspectival character of memory and thus it ignores the context from within which it "totally recalls" what it recalls. Given all of this, total recall, like neurotic memory, must be viewed as another form of monumentalism: the neurotic memory fixates on a particular memorial object and derives memorial sense through that fixation. Total recall fixates without discrimination on the whole range of past experience and is incapable of making sense. I am thus in the somewhat odd position of suggesting that neurotic memory, as I have described it, is better memory than total recall—at least it makes some sense.

The indictment of total recall that has been drawn depends on the argument that total recall *cannot* make memorial sense because it disrupts the temporal matrix. This is the strong version of my indictment. The weaker version of the indictment would be that, even if total recall does not necessarily serve this disruptive function, it is still neither a necessary nor a sufficient condition of good memory. The weaker form of the indictment derives from the fact that apparently a great many persons can make sense of past experience without total recall. If there can be good memorial sense-making without total recall, then it stands to reason that total recall is not a necessary condition of good memory.

However, in the light of the range of examples I adduced, it seems to me that my stronger indictment does hold. But even if it could be shown that total recall is, under some conditions, associated with good memorial sense-making, it would still be the case that sense-making is prior. Total recall *may* be the product of memorial sense; it is never its cause. Having even a "total" picture of the past does not necessarily make sense of it. It seems to me, then, that even in imaginable provincial contexts where total recall might be associated with good memory—for example, in art history—the recalled pictures only *help* make sense of the past. Total recall, however, is never part of good memory in the most important kind of remembering: the memorial project of making autobiographical sense of one's own life.[5]

Finally, even if total recall is not always a form of memorial pathology, it is still not what has been claimed for it: a neutral, computerlike recall of the past. Rather, it is a recall of the past from some particular perspective. Thus the pictures of total recall are themselves context-bound and if seen from a different perspective would be recalled in a different fashion. At best, total recall, like all memorial projects, is bound to a context in terms of which its recall is judged "total."

My discussion of total recall clearly depends upon the separation of the picturing and sense-making functions, and perhaps the argument for this separation needs further support. It seems to me that the best way to further establish that this separation is a real one is to call attention to the activity of remembering a skill.

Remembering a skill (i.e., remembering how to do something) is clearly a matter of *sense* measured in present performance and not at all a matter of *picturing* something to be the case. We do not say that one remembers a set of skills if one can recite the training manual through which it was learned. Remembering a skill means knowing how to do something—for example, remembering how to box means being able to box. Thus "I remember how to box" and "I know how to box" are equivalent claims. One may of course also claim "I used to know how to box," in which case one does not also claim to be able to enact a skill.

Remembering a physical skill entails being able to embody the skill, being able to perform it. Such memory thus becomes a paradigm of memory insofar as it—of all memory claims—emphasizes that having a good memory is tied to certain present and future performances. Skill memory is particularly important in emphasizing the place of memorial projects in the temporal matrix, exactly because physical skills are so much more difficult to fake than are merely intellectual ones. That is, in skill memory what counts as a present or future test of the memory claim is always reasonably clear. So also is the tie between memorial claims and such present and future tests.

---

5. A total recall that is not disruptive would presuppose total presence to both future and present experience—that is, it would presuppose a kind of experiential perfection—divinity. By contrast, total amnesia would be utterly diabolical. Here perhaps we have the making of a new theology.

Politicians and college teachers, by contrast, often make intellectual memory claims that can only be shoddily or not at all tested in present experience. When a student mentions a book a teacher has not read in a long time, it is easy for the teacher to respond "yes, I remember that," and then proceed to discuss the book, all the while trying desperately to get a *sense* of the book that would satisfy his or her own memorial needs. The teacher's "faked" memory is like that of the ex-boxer who claims to remember how to box but cannot box. The case of the boxer makes clear *how* the teacher's memory fails, inasmuch as the boxer's poor memory leads to a more readily observable (and more disastrous) present performance.

For these sorts of reasons, skill memory is a paradigm that emphasizes the past-present-future matrix in memorial claims. Thus skill memory makes clear that the question about the soundness of memory is *not* impeded by the fact that we have direct access only to present experience. It is exactly in that experience that the strategic adequacy of memory is tested and, because that strategic test is the only appropriate one, the ontological dilemma about the relation between present images and their past objects is *entirely* irrelevant: it is a game played by epistemologists for their own amusement.

Memory, then, like explanation is context-bound, and what constitutes a "good" memory can be determined only in respect to the general temporal project, of which some memory is the first act. At the personal, autobiographical level — the source of all memorial projects — knowing if someone's memory is "good" entails knowing something about the life in which that memory counts as a memory: the survivor of Dachau and the Fulbright Fellow have different memorial needs.

A final example will illuminate the strategic criterion of good memory being developed here and will also further clarify my argument with the picture or copy theory of memory. The example is nonfiction. Several years ago, my wife and I were sitting in a café in Freiburg, Germany, when she indicated a man sitting at a table beside us and said, "I know that man." She thought for several moments and added, "That's the flashy Spaniard we knew five years ago in Ebersberg, who used to laugh a lot."

I turned and looked, and said, "No, that's not him."

Then the man we had looked at said, "Don't I know you?"

I said, "No, my wife thought you were someone else."

He said, "No! No! I knew you in Ebersberg."

Still not recognizing him, and with a *very clear* picture of the Spaniard in mind, I was forced to remember him. I spoke to my wife and said, "I still don't believe that's him."

She naturally said, "Of course it is!"

With a *still* very clear picture of the Spaniard in mind, I asked the man a few questions:

"Are you Spanish?"

"No. I'm Greek."

"Are you in the tourist business?"

"No. I work for Siemens."

With these questions it became clear that he was not the man my wife thought she remembered. He was, however, another man who was with us at the same time we were acquainted with the Spaniard.

My question is, whose memory was better? Mine or my wife's? My wife misidentified the man but *remembered* him. I did not make the misidentification and did not remember him. It seems clear to me that in this matter my wife's memory was superior to mine, for she had established a memorial project that brought together an experience from five years earlier with the then present one of eating dinner; thus her memory enriched a present moment. My wife had sense; I had only a picture.[6]

The Ethics of Memory

In this paper I have tried to clarify what it means to remember things. Through imaginative variation of my own experience I trust I am warranted in extending this description, at least as a fruitful hunch, to a general description of memory. Philosophers, of course, have always used their personal experience as the basis for more general arguments. In making this confession, I mean to follow Husserl's good example, thereby calling attention not only to a possible provincialism of my paper—but to one of philosophy itself.

A key theme underlying my argument is that philosophy has generally paid attention to memory only insofar as it raises technical problems about the ontological status of memorial pictures. Having done this, philosophy has forgotten that memory's first and primary place is personal and autobiographical. By making these matters explicit I hope to have opened up for more adequate philosophical description the primary locus of memorial claims.

Memory is first and foremost a lived perspective on one's own past, and we must deal with it as such before we can deal adequately with the epistemological normativism that sets up a standard of neutral memorial objectivity. Such epistemological normativism does not tell us what good memory *is*, it tells us what it *ought* to be, and its injunction can be

6. The fact that this event may be read as a conflict between two memories that are only partial or are incomplete for different reasons does not touch my point. My wife's memory *was*, in context, the better memory.

understood only after we have made clear the character of the scientistic world to which it belongs.

The key difficulty of my argument, with its emphasis on the present (and futural) orientation of memory, is that it reduces the objectivity of the past to a kind of regulative ideal. Indeed, I am content that it does so, for with this reduction my paper also suggests how *appropriate* respect may be paid to the past, as we, in memory, make the first creative move to establish for ourselves the temporal matrix within which we must live, thereby recognizing the past as both limit and touchstone, as restraint and ground of all our acts.

Thus it seems to me that a *vividly imagined past* can never pass the strategic test of memory that my account proposes. The past is exactly what cannot be merely imagined; it is, as Nietzsche wrote, "the stone that cannot be moved." A *good* memory thus can never ignore this *sense* of the utter objectivity of something that is past, of *something* that is simply there.

What is it, then, out of which we constitute memorial objects — that is, what do we first eidetically vary in our sense-assigning activity? With this question we are led to try to objectify the hyletic data that precede sense giving. This question thus yields our best mode of getting a sense of the *stuff* out of which we make the human objects of memory.

We cannot, of course, quite succeed in making sense of that stuff, because to do so is to objectify it. Benjy in William Faulkner's *The Sound and the Fury* shows us what this memorial *hyle* is like; so also does Roquentin in Sartre's *Nausea* when he reaches out and touches something that is not quite a doorknob. The *stuff* of memory is *not quite the objects of memory*. I suspect that everyone, in straining to remember some forgotten name or face, encounters, however fleetingly, the *hyle* of memory. I appeal to such experience as confirmation of what I am talking about.

Having thus emphatically rejected the activity of envisioning scenes as the paradigm of memorial activity, I want to say rather that one *reads* one's past the way one reads a book. One searches not for a picture of a set of sentences but for the senses of the text. Memory, then, is like reading in the following two ways: (1) it is possible to understand the sense of a text without picturing sentences, and (2) it is possible to picture all the sentences of a book without understanding the sense of the text. In neither reading nor memory is the possession of mental pictures either a necessary or a sufficient condition of making sense of things.

By way of a final remark, I must admit that I do not know if my account of memory describes what goes on in all instances of memory — though I think it does — but I am sure that it does describe some important sorts of memorial activity that, to the best of my knowledge, have been neglected in philosophical discussions of memory. If my more general claim is false, I am in any event content with the truth of the less general one. If they are both false, perhaps I have at least raised some interesting issues. If I have failed even in this most modest matter, then the responsible reader is professionally obliged to forget my argument.

Lester Embree

10/*Phenomenological Speculations on Lived Marriageability*

Introduction

To make clear to others (and themselves) how they got to where they have seen matters from, phenomenologists look back over the approach they have taken and seek to describe it. Unfortunately, such "methodology" is not always well appreciated. Too often the discussion of constitutive phenomenology never gets beyond the differences between mundane and transcendental and between factual and eidetic procedures. Outsiders are in the odd position of examining and then accepting or rejecting maps of ways they have never taken. Contrariwise, insiders too often assume that the value of a doctrine is obvious and that its ground in seeing (*Evidenz*) is then of the primary importance for the outsider that it is for the insider. Such concerns with method and verification can lead one to believe that a phenomenologist never speculates, will not simply follow out ideas without great attention to procedures and step-by-step seeing.

The present essay is, however, speculative; it is about how some matters *might* look. It contains a minimum in overt methodology and upon examination could perhaps prove false. But how phenomenologists might see some matters and the sort of account they would hope to produce should be evident.

There are several tendencies within phenomenology today. Without discussing them, let me merely identify myself with *constitutive* phenomenology as the tendency that begins with Husserl's *Ideen* (1913), is continued in his later works, and carried further in North America through the work of Cairns, Gurwitsch, Schutz and several of their students and friends. It is an illusion to see oneself as arising without a background—an illusion that prevents one from investigating that background and being able thus to transcend it. Rather than clutter up this essay with detailed discussions of how I agree and disagree with my background and try to go beyond it, let me only say that I follow the spirit more than the letter of this tendency. I will mention names on occasion, but certain expressions are responsibly mine.

The Problem of Lived Marriageability

In *Tristes tropiques*[1] Claude Lévi-Strauss discusses the life of the Bororo Indians of South America, some aspects of which I shall speculate about here. I naturally assume that his ethnography is reliable and hope that I do not distort it.

This group lived in a village laid out in a way that reflected their social and religious system. Twenty-six huts formed a circle around the men's house. The village had a population of about 150 persons. Before the coming of Europeans and their diseases, technology, and so forth, the villages of this people had been much larger, including perhaps 1,000 individuals, and had been arranged in several concentric circles. In most other villages of this people, the Salesian fathers had accomplished a "systematic obliteration of nature culture" through causing the huts to be rearranged in parallel rows:

> Once they had been deprived of their bearings and were without the plan which acted as a confirmation of their native lore, the Indians soon lost any feeling for tradition; it was as if their social and religious systems . . . were too complex to exist without the pattern which was embodied in the plan of the village and of which their awareness was constantly being refreshed by their everyday activities (p. 240).

With his chief informant, Lévi-Strauss went "from house to house, taking a census of the inhabitants, determining their position in the community, and marking out on the ground by means of sticks the imaginary lines of demarcation between sectors associated with an intricate network of privileges, traditions, heirarchial grades, rights and obligations" (p. 241). The population proved to be divided on one level into two "moieties" or subgroups, and this can be signified with an imaginary line bisecting the circle of huts. Let me go beyond the words of Lévi-Strauss and speak here of the "northsiders" and "southsiders" of the village.

An individual belonged to the same moiety as his or her mother and one marriage rule requires one to marry someone from the opposite

1. Translated by John and Doreen Weightman (New York: Pocket Books, 1977).

moiety. Females live in and inherit the houses in which they were born. Upon marriage the man moves to his wife's house, but can visit his mother's home or stay in the men's house "when he finds the atmosphere in the conjugal abode too oppressive (for instance, if his brothers-in-law have come for a visit)" (p. 242).

The bisection of the village into northsiders and southsiders also affects other aspects of Bororo life—the treatment of the dead, for example, being described at length—but let us confine ourselves to marriage. Other social divisions are reflected *geographically* and Lévi-Strauss tries to reconstruct them, but let us here confine ourselves to the articulation of clans into what he calls "grades." "These grades appear to have been endogamous: a member of the upper grade could only marry an upper-grade person (belonging to the other moiety); a middle grade a middle-grade person, and a lower-grade a lower-grade person" (p. 244). However, given the demographic collapse of the village, "only the rule concerning the moieties is strictly respected" (p. 244). Indeed, while the ethnographer who reconstructs genealogies may discern that a second marriage rule was being followed, it is not clear that the Indians did or, perhaps, could recognize it. Here our problem begins to appear.

In closing his two-chapter discussion, Lévi-Strauss writes:

> Bororo society offers a lesson to the student of human nature. If he listens to his native informants they will describe to him, as they did for me, this ballet in which two village moieties strive to live and breathe each through and for the other; exchanging women, possessions, and services in fervent reciprocity; intermarrying their children, burying each other's dead, each providing the other with a guarantee that life is eternal, the world full of help, and society just. To provide evidence of these truths wise men have worked out an impressive cosmology and embodied it in the plan of the village and the layout of the dwellings. . . .
>
> . . . .
>
> In this society, which appears to have delighted in complexity, each clan is divided into three groups—upper, middle, and lower—and over all other rules and regulations hangs the obligation for an upper-grade person from one moiety to marry an upper-grade person from the other, a member of the middle grade to marry a middle-grade person, and a member of the lower grade to marry a lower-grade person; in other words, under the disguise of fraternal institutions, the Bororo village can be seen in the last resort as consisting of three groups each of which intermarries within itself. Three societies which, without realizing it, will remain forever separate and isolated, each imprisoned in a kind of pride which is concealed even from itself by

a smokescreen of institutions, so that each is the unconscious victim of devices the purpose of which it can no longer discover (p. 271).

We are even given a map of the village in which the upper-, middle- and lower-grade huts are shown to be systematically distributed so that this "real" structure is submerged in the "apparent" structure of the village (I believe my use of "real" and "apparent" is in the spirit of Lévi-Strauss's account).

In sum, if I understand Lévi-Strauss correctly, the Bororo of the village he visited believe on one level that the village has two *interdependent* subgroups and also articulate a rule by which a person in one subgroup may marry only a person in the other, anyone in the other subgroup being, allegedly, marriageable. By contrast, however, the ethnologist ascertains from genealogies that in marrying as it actually goes on, not only does a person marry across the line bisecting the village geographically, socially and religiously into northsiders and southsiders, but also a person is further restricted to spouses of his or her same grade, so that the separation of the village into three *independent* parts is fundamental. I assume that if asked about this situation the Indians would deny the priority of the second marriage rule and thus the fundamentality of the trifurcation of the society. Lévi-Strauss in effect interprets the system as having then its apparent and real structure, and, I suppose, a (false) consciousness and a (true) *un*consciousness of it. In other words, there is an ideal behavior, which does not correspond to the actual behavior in all respects, the latter being not so much in conflict with the former as being governed by more specific rules than are recognized in the expressed norm.

As a phenomenologist, I am loath to accept either a reality/ appearance or a consciousness/unconsciousness distinction, at least in the ordinary way in which these oppositions are understood. Rather than attempt to examine Lévi-Strauss's general interpretation, however, let me attempt to develop and solve—speculatively—what seems to be the central problem here.

To begin with, some assumptions made for convenience of expression may be stated. Although probably there are differences among individual families, although probably the parents rather than the children decide officially and actually who shall marry whom, although there are probably additional rules about who proposes and who disposes in such a matter, and so forth, let me abstract from such considerations and, in conformity with the still prevailing Western ideology, speak of "boy marrying girl." Moreover, let us say that "A" is a boy of the northside and of middle rank, "B" is a middle-rank southside girl, "C" is a lower-rank southside girl and "D" is a middle-rank northside girl. We might now ask how B, C and D are perceived as marriageable or unmarriageable by A.

In first approximation, I have just written "perceived." This is meant to contrast with "thought" and "said," for I assume that Lévi-Strauss's ethnography is correct and that how A actually behaves is not in fact recognized and discussed by him adequately. This does not mean that A could not, at least in principle, overcome resistances and come to recognize what the ethnographer has ascertained. However, it does mean that somehow others of the suitable age, sex, and so forth, are regularly related to by him in different ways, such that some can be married and others cannot, even when he cannot say that this is the case or why.

Already the word "perceived" is stretched excessively, for marrying is plainly far more than looking at or grasping emphatically, and yet "behaved," at another extreme, would also be stretched excessively if taken to include the *seeing* of B, C and D by A. What is at issue not only has ingredients of perceiving and behaving in their usual significations, but also has emotional ingredients, the consideration of which gives talk of norms in this connection its right. Whether A recognizes it or not, he has different feelings toward the marriageable as opposed to the unmarriageable girls. As I will try to show more thoroughly below, it seems to me that "*lived* marriageability" is preferable to "perceived," "behaved" or even "felt" because it is inclusive of them all.

Our problem may now be formulated. *Why is B lived by A as marriageable, whereas C and D are lived by A as unmarriageable?* It is superficial (as well as elliptical) to answer, *Because, though both B and C dwell on the correct side of the village, D does not and C is of the incorrect grade—or, more briefly, northside middle-rank boys can only marry southside middle-rank girls.* These are the rules the ethnologist establishes, the rules in accordance with which a people lives, whether it knows it or not.

I do not dispute this finding. What I wonder about is how the living and the lived in these cases can be described and, for that matter, explained. To approach this matter in a consciously phenomenological fashion, we need to get some terms of doctrine and method clear.

A Phenomenological Perspective

In phenomenology the distinction between descriptive accounts and explanatory accounts is fundamental. One must have an answer to the question, *What is it?* before one can answer *Why is it?* adequately. All explanations incorporate descriptions, and bad explanations are often bad because the descriptions are bad. Furthermore, the less useful descriptive accounts proceed from the particular and do not reach the general.

By contrast, let me expound, first, some terms of a general descriptive account and, second, some of a general explanatory account, including some method among the matters accounted for. In the subsequent section I shall return to how the Bororo case might fit this descriptive and explanatory model or, equivalently, how the model might be employed to account for that particular matter.

Descriptive Considerations

How can we most generally describe the matter that the constitutive phenomenologist investigates? To begin with, what is this matter to be called? In rather broad significations, Descartes spoke of "thinking," Hume spoke of "perception" and Husserl spoke of "consciousness." Others have tried "existence," "behavior" and (again) "perception." There is something positive to be said about each of these terms, but they are also "partial" in the sense of emphasizing one aspect over others, such that it is difficult to employ them to express the broad technical signification in question.

If there were no alternatives, one might use all of these words interchangeably and thus attempt to convey a general concept that does not have its own expression, but experience has shown that this strategy does not work very well. If, however, we can avoid the biological and vitalistic connotations, "life" might do the job. In the broadest ordinary signification in English, "life" includes but is not restricted to the cogitative, the perceptual and the conscious. It readily covers as well affective and conative phenomena, and leaves "existence" and "behavior" free for other important employments. In a broad (but not the broadest) signification, it can be opposed to thinking. This is how I usually use it.

To proceed toward a general determination, it seems plain that "life" rather obviously goes on. Conveniently—if at first strangely—we can next recognize a difference between *living*, on the one hand, and the *lived*, on the other. Under French influence we have had a vogue of talk about the "lived world," the "lived body," and the like. I should like not only to keep that fashion but to extend it to the "lived other," the "lived self," and even occasionally to speak of "lived processes of living." To do so I substitute "engaged in" for Husserl's "lived in" where the participation of the ego in his or her life is concerned. Furthermore, I avoid "lived experience"; in my usage, this expression would imply reflection. In my usage "living experience"—if I were to use it—would express what "lived experience" usually expresses. I avoid "experience" wherever possible as simply too polysignificant in ordinary or technical English, being ambiguous, for example, with respect to "experiencing" as contrasted with "the experienced," not to speak of covering "past experience," which is then redundent. With "life," "living" and "lived" (the two last-named employable both as nouns and adjectives), we can start with suitable breadth and familiarity, and then get appropriately technical and specific.

Life (or "living" *and* "the lived") includes but is not restricted to perception (perceiving and the perceived). It also includes other presentational modes of intentiveness, correlative appearances and modes of givenness, as well as various sorts of positional ingredients and components. To distinguish and describe them, one must first of all *reflect*. Indeed, one must reflect in a *theoretical* attitude, but I will not detail that here. Briefly, when one reflects one leaves off straightfor-wardly considering objects *apart from* how they appear, are given to, and are accepted by selves. Instead one takes up this appearing to, givenness to, and acceptedness by selves, as well as the presenting and accepting intentiveness in the correlational situation—a situation of the *lived as lived*, on the one hand, and living *as living "of,"* on the other.

Following Cairns (and before him, Husserl, above all in the *Ideen*), I believe one can reflectively discriminate, on the one hand and in the broad sense, the presentive ingredients in living—for example, perceiving—from, on the other hand, the thetic or positing ingre-dients. Positings include but are not restricted to three broad genera, one that Husserl called "doxa" and two others that I have recom-mended calling, analogously, "pathos" and "praxis." Every process and correlate of living has ingredients and components of all three kinds and, depending on which one predominates in the process of living, we may speak of believings, valuings and (with admitted awkwardness) "usings."

Just as believings are positive, negative or neutral, and steady or unsteady ("certain" or "uncertain"), so are valuings (which include likings, dislikings and apathies) and usings (which are resolute or hesitant). "Striving" can be used as an expression alternative to "using," provided one can avoid comprehending it as necessarily ego-engaged, which seems practically impossible with another expression, "willing." With respect to the praxic or using or striving aspect of concrete living, and taking into consideration whether the object is already actual and might continue to be so or is inactual but might become actual, we can further classify positive and negative "usings" as creative, destructive, preventive or preservative. It is at least as difficult to understand destructive striving under the heading of perception as it is to under-stand hearing under the heading of behavior.

Following Schutz (and before him, Scheler), I consider the *present* phase of the life-streams of others more accessible than that of one's own life, although for the *future* and the *past* stretches of one's own and others' lives the contrary is the case. (Since we are concerned with matters more fundamental than what is thought and said, Schutz's main contributions—i.e., his account of individual and collective common-sense and human-scientific thinking in terms of insider construal, outsider construal, etc.,—will not be drawn upon in the present essay.)

To me it further appears, reflectively, that intellectual ("doxic") processes are more readily observed and grasped in self-observation than in other-observation, but regarding emotional and volitional phenomena—that is, for pathic or "aesthetic" and practical life—the opposite is the case. Where the lived rather than the living is concerned, I am not even sure that the lived as lived by a self is always more accurately grasped reflectively-theoretically in the present than the lived as lived by an other. Beyond such questions of relative accessibility, let me emphasize that we can to some degree reflectively observe other lives, and that the goal of investigation is a general account that can be tried against phenomena from the lives of others as well as from one's own (here I am following Merleau-Ponty and, before him, Paul Guillaume).

In processes predominantly of believing, valuing or using, there is something that is *predominantly* either believed or valued or used, and that something is somehow, in a broad sense, "presented." In earnest processes intentive to real objects—that is, objects in time—the objects that appear are in the present, past or future of the intending. If they are in the present, we have a case of perceiving; in the past, remembering; in the future, expecting. There are three corresponding species of quasi-presentive processes where one "imagines" things as if they were in the present, past or future.

If one were to combine merely formally (a) the steady and the unsteady (b) positive, negative and neutral modes of (c) doxic, pathic and praxic positings with the (d) earnest and fictive (e) perceptive, memorial, and expectational species of presenting, there would be 108 combinations (2x3x3x2x3)! Whether, however, all quintideterminant classes have members, I leave to the reader's reflective-observational discernment, wondering only whether there are steady and unsteady degrees of positional neutrality (some doubt that there is praxic neutrality at all) and furthermore whether the praxic can have other than earnest or fictive *expectational* foundations. All in all, I do believe that this classification of terms for describing processes of living is (a) verifiable and indeed largely true, and (b) affords us considerable descriptive capacity—more, for example, than David Hume's eight trideterminate species of "perceptions" (simple and complex, impressional and ideational, reflectional and sensational; 2x2x2).

With this capacity established for the describing of living, what about the lived? Here I follow Gurwitsch as well as Cairns and Husserl, and I do not believe I am particularly original, except terminologically.

When we reflect on our own lives or on those of others, we find the lived as intentively correlative to living. Where positing and presentive ingredients point out at or "intend to" the lived, the lived as lived with respect to its positedness and presentedness points in at or "indicates" the living. Too frequently the living—lived or noetic—noematic opposition is identified with that between immanence and outward transcendence—that is, between mental life and the real surrounding world. However, there is actually a living-lived opposition within immanence between any stretch of life and other stretches in the future and past of this life, to which it is, respectively, "protentive" and "retrotentive"—to mention but one species.

Before classifying the modes of giveness and positional characteristics in correlation to the classification outlined in previous paragraphs, two differences and relations need to be mentioned. In the first place, when reflected upon rather than unreflectively or straightforwardly lived, an object reveals a difference between the object which is lived and the object *as* it is lived. The latter was named "noema" by Husserl and the former I prefer to call "gegenstand." Following Gurwitsch, I understand the relation of the noema to the gegenstand to be one of part to whole, where the whole is an open totality with gestalt organization. For my present purposes, this development within constitutive phenomenology need not be discussed further.

In the second place and more importantly for present purposes, the full and concrete noema, the lived just and precisely as lived, can be seen to be itself differentiated into its nucleus and noematic characters. If the object were a pencil, for example, on the "nuclear" plane it has as lived, on the one hand, its visual, tactual, olfactory, gustatory and auditory qualities—for example, its shape and colors in various lights, its relative smoothness and roughness at different places on its surface, its rigidity or flexibility and hardnesses and softnesses, its lightness and balance as well, its smells and tastes of cedar, graphite and rubber, and the sound it makes when tapping or tapped by other objects of various sorts. On the other hand, it has relations, such as the spatial ones of being between the knife and the eyeglasses on the desk in the corner; the temporal ones of being after the previous pencil which is now gone, before the subsequent pencil I have not yet purchased, and along with my present stock of paper; and the causal relations—for example, the present point on the pencil as effect of particular processes in the sharpener. Such plainly refinable lines of description pertain to what is noematically nuclear in the lived object both with respect to it in its own right and in relation to its circumstances, which in this case are real. A gegenstand—for example, a person—can include psychic as well as somatic-constituents in its gestalt organization on the nuclear level.

Where the noematic "characteristics" are concerned, they are what remains when the nuclear determinations are abstracted from. Positively speaking, they divide into modes of givenness on the one hand and positional components ("thetic characters") on the other hand. With respect to the first division, there are different ways in which a pencil can appear, according to whether it is remembered rather than perceived or expected rather than remembered, and so forth. The second division parallels the taxonomy of positing ingredients discussed previously and thus includes, but is not restricted to, the doxic, pathic and praxic components the lived has with respect to how it is believed, valued and used. Depending on which positional component predominates (and whether that component is positive or negative), the item in question is a being or entity or a nonentity, or an evil or a good, to be created or destroyed, preserved or prevented as a means or an end, and so forth.

Taking up our pencil again, it is originally constituted positively praxothetically in writing as a writing utensil, a means that will be used to express ideas. It has its *use*, which we can reflectively theoretically thematize and describe as its "utility," something strictly analogous to its value and existence, its goodness and being. Not only can a pencil be used as a means in communication but it can be striven toward as an end — say, in a process of purchasing where money functions as means. Although ordinarily we *use* a pencil, we can of course alternatively live it as an aesthetic object and even go on to thematize and describe its pathic character of, say, handsomeness. We can even predominantly believe in it. The steadiness or unsteadiness of posited objects can also be reflectively described.

One final point concerning the exercise of phenomenological description for which the above terms are offered. There seems to be a tendency to believe that a large portion of our lives is engaged in by us as egos; in other words, that we actively or passively perform most of or at least much of our living processes. Correlatively, everything would then be equally thematic or obtrusive within the lived field, the field of life. However, far and away the greater part of living goes on without ego-engagement, just as the vast bulk of the lived is background, not figure or theme. A large part, furthermore, of non-egoical living is automatic or *primarily passive* — an ego could not engage in it even if it wanted to. This is the level where other lives are fundamentally constituted. The other portion of non-egoical living is *secondarily passive* or habitual; here processes that could be ego-performed derive from original ego-performances and could be ego-performed but go on ordinarily by themselves, without ego-engagement. Thus when my telephone rings it is often automatically picked up, put to my ear, and "hello" said into it before I engage in this process and thematize even emptily whoever might be calling. Our lives as they go on are mostly automatic and, for that matter, practical—something intellectuals tend to forget. The objects lived in them are also usually lived unreflectively. The practical characters that such objects have (characters by virtue of which probably most names for things refer to their uses) seem to be rather permanent but nevertheless have their origins. Why practical objects come to have this or that practical character or use, as well as why they also come to have values, can be asked about, but that is an explanatory rather than a descriptive question.

Explanatory Considerations

Phenomenologists often seem leery about discussing causation. Maybe the need to overcome the stimulus-response approach whereby what I see, for example, causes me to see it (something that must be overcome if the intentiveness of seeing to the seen is to be grasped) is exaggerated. Whatever the motive, it is an error to believe either that there are no causal relations in outwardly perceived matters—for example, that fire is not seen to boil water—or that there are no motivational relations among mental processes, or between them and somatic processes. Causal analysis is a child to be kept in its place but certainly not to be thrown out with the bath water. Most importantly, causal and motivational connections are species of the conditioning conditioned relationship and to explain is thus, in general, to state the conditions for something, which plainly contrasts with describing, where the essence of the matter is told.

Let me sketch some terms in which the living of a pencil might be *explained*. Here my position derives chiefly from Gurwitsch's work in the theory of natural-scientific psychology, but is generalized, supplemented and reexpressed. It may be approached through examination of a popular explanation. Where some may believe that the pencil's having its use is a matter of meaning bestowed on a pregivenly useless object of pure perception, I do not find interpretive cogitative processes, even habitual ones, always and necessarily going on along with the usings of pencils I reflect on, and I do not find the pencils as employed or used to be like cupcakes of received sensuous infrastrata and imposed conceptual frosting. Rather, I find that the pencil as practically lived is an integral matter within which appearing nuclear constituents, manners of givenness, and positional characteristics—the practical or praxic, above all—can be abstractively distinguished and described in the terms laid out above.

Rejecting this dualistic description of the practical object as the product of factors internal (interpretation or signification bestowal) and external (sensuous affection) and following Gurwitsch, I am still willing—on the psychological and, generally, the positive-scientific level—to consider phenomena of living and the lived as conditioned by external and internal factors. That there are two kinds of conditioning factors is compatible with a unitary phenomenon conditioned. I assume, on the level of the natural science of psychology (but only on that level), that physics has correctly determined what the stimuli are that impinge upon my sense organs and cause neurological and thereby psychological events. However, I do not believe, philosophically, that such external factors are perceived or, indeed, are anything other than theoretical entities, mental products, which can nevertheless be as fervently believed in and considered "objective," without being observable, as religious entities are. Not only are the stimuli that an experimental psychologist as such rightly accepts not given, but also it is mere prejudice to believe that there must be a one-to-one correspondence between atomic stimuli and not-normally-discernible sensa within percepts, something Gurwitsch following Koehler has systematically challenged.

For the purposes of the present speculations on lived marriageability, one can abide by a naturalistic attitude and simply assume that when B, C and D are perceived by A, he has generically identical stimuli impinging upon his sensory apparatus in each case. Nevertheless, he lives one girl as marriageable and the others as not. To understand *why*, we must consider other sorts of conditions.

Explaining a case of living and especially the lived is only begun when external factors are taken into account. There are also "internal" factors or conditions that are, to begin with, negatively determined by being considered as all the factors other than the external ones. If we understand the external conditions in such a narrow sense, then organismic conditions—for example, the percentage of alcohol in the blood—are internal conditions. However, it would seem best to me to take external factors more broadly, so as to include not only physical but also physiological events. In this direction "external conditions" become coterminous with natural-scientific conditions. The remaining conditions would then be human-scientific. Whether natural-scientific factors have a priority over human-scientific or vice versa—as I would contend—need not be pursued here.

Where "internal" or "human" conditions are concerned, there is first of all one's attitude or mood and habitual outlook. These occur in the present and within the individual and could plainly be classified further. A second category of human conditions includes events in the individual's past life. If one has written with a pencil before or at least seen another do so, then things of the same or similar appearance are automatically lived (not necessarily but possibly also recognized and interpreted) as writing instruments. These past factors are obviously quite important. Factors of a third sort are more social than "historical." Here, for example, it seems to me that a child in the presence of its parents does not live the world as having the same practical possibilities for mischief as when alone or in the presence of either different adults or only other children.

Seeking to classify the "human" kind of conditions, we might consider (a) the present attitude to be "psychological," (b) the personal past (following Schutz) "biographical," and then recognize (c) "social" factors. If the collective past is recognized as conditioning present life, then there should also be (d) "historical" conditions. (Directly or indirectly and individually or collectively expected events are also conditions for our lives, but to consider them would take us too far afield here. Economic, political, geographical, and other human conditions could probably be specifically delineated, and perhaps the aggregate of the human conditions could be called "anthropological," but that also need not be gone into further here. Plainly, I have no hesitations about explanations in human science — provided, that is, the place of description is respected. In contrast to the natural-scientific conditions, the human-scientific factors are in principle directly observable — that is, even events in the distant past are of such a nature that if one had been there, one could have observed them.

In short and in general, to say *why* something is lived as it is lived involves specifying the conditions under which that something occurs, persists, changes or ceases to be. To establish a childhood event, for example, as condition for an adult attitude, does not, however, mean that the past condition survives somehow into the present. This is as unnecessary (and as unobservable) as the sense data alleged by some to be in the percept corresponding to stimuli believed physically to condition it externally. Above all, simply that there is a multiplicity of conditions does not mean that the event conditioned must be correspondingly multiple, or vice versa. One should attempt to describe what is observable as it is observed and, on the human-scientific plane, to explain it with observables.

Being thus able, in principle, not only to describe but also to explain, we can return to the case of lived marriageability among the Bororo. How could this matter appear in the phenomenological perspective we have now established?

A Speculative Application

Although I have considerable confidence in the above-sketched descriptive and explanatory terms, it will make more sense to most readers if they are related to an empirical case. Let me restate the question developed above: *How does A live B, C and D such that the first is marriageable and the second and third are not?* Equivalently, *How is the marriageability of B and the unmarriageability of C and D lived?*

These questions are answerable, I believe, by means of reflective observation. In this case it is reflection on others in a rather different culture and indeed, for us, as fictively perceived (whereas Lévi-Strauss ernestly perceived and remembered his subjects). But even to fit a feigned case to it makes a descriptive and explanatory model clearer and, even if it is less than empirical testing, it is also more than merely logical analysis. Most important, it is reflective because it is an approach to a matter of living as intentive to something, the lived, and, correlatively, to the lived as indicative of something, the living of it. Such reflectiveness is the basic mark of what is, in the broad sense, a phenomenological account, be the reflection on one's own or on an other's life.

Abiding somewhat abstractly and artificially (but at least explicitly) by the standpoint of an individual who is found to have others of one sort as marriageable and yet others of other sorts as unmarriageable, let us attempt speculatively to "describe" the living—lived matter from the noematic nucleus to the praxothetic positing and then speculate about its human conditions.

The noematic nuclei reflectively disclosed in A's living of B, C and D would probably involve being of a certain sex, age (at least between puberty and menopause, in most cultures), physical well-being (e.g., good teeth), and relevant skills for wifely duties, and so forth. We may assume here that B, C and D are all within acceptable limits in such respects; I doubt that the differences we seek pertain to such aspects of the matter.

Implicitly, in the above description, the individuals B, C and D were abstracted from their places in society. Is being regularly found in one position in society with parents and relatives of one grade rather than another, perhaps a grade with which one's own family more or less frequently and warmly interacts, not something which, upon reflection, pertains to the noematically nuclear plane for a human, just as location in space, time and causality does for a merely physical object, say, a tree? People can come to be lived as having "natural places" in social systems, just as inkwells naturally belong on desks and are out of place on sinks. If so, then we are already beginning to find what might be a solution to our problem. Regardless of whether B, C or D are perceived, remembered or expected (or, correspondingly, feigned) by A, A is a middle-grade northsider and to him B is a middle-grade southsider, C is a lower-grade southsider and D is a middle-grade northsider. Girls B, C and D are all of suitable age, health and skill but they differ with respect to their "place" in society, which I take to lie in the noematically nuclear plane of this lived situation.

Turning now to the thetic or positional aspects of the matter, it seems to me that B, C and D can be assumed to exist for A. I would also say that he has no doubt about their sex, age, skill and social position. However, whether these properties all exist for him thematically need not be assumed. The difference at issue is not the difference between B and C on the one hand as southsiders and D on the other as a northsider, but that of B and D being of middle grade in contrast to C as of lower grade. It may be the case that such differences are presented and believed, but that A and indeed all other Bororo are motivated to *disregard* them and hence are unable to conceptualize and verbalize with respect to them. Then perhaps something like Freudian concepts of repression and resistance—defined, however, in terms of observables—might apply. In any case, it does not seem likely that the marriageability differential of B, C and D is peculiarly doxic.

When we come now to the pathic or affective and praxic or conative ingredients in living, we do seem to have differences. B (and any other nice southside middle-grade girl) is lived as at least *preferable* to C and especially, it would seem, to D. Indeed, probably, she is simply good in opposition to the others, who are bad. On that basis, praxically, she is lived as permitted in contrast to forbidden. The value an other has for a self as habitually lived is not only as much "out there" as hair color, for example, is, but also as just about as permanent. It is not a superficial matter of taste, like the initial disagreeableness of a new food, which can be overcome by a little more trying until one likes it. Values, especially in "cold societies," do not change easily.[2] It is the being deeply "conditioned" to *like* only southside middle-grade girls as potential spouses that makes A's behavior normative, "right" or "correct," and any tendency toward marrying a "wrong" girl, such as C or D, "incorrect." Whether the rightness in this case is universal, objective or absolutely justified is of course not the question here; plainly from the outside we can consider it a culturally relative valuing, but from within the Bororo society it would be quite objective, universal, and justified.

What about the praxic aspect of the matter? How might it be

2. Perhaps this is clear in the life in Lévi-Strauss's chief informant: "This man, who was about thirty-five years old, spoke Portuguese fairly well. He said that he had once been able to read and write the language (although he could no longer do so), having been a pupil at the mission. The fathers, proud of their success, had sent him to Rome, where he had been received by the Holy Father. On his return, there had apparently been an attempt to make him go through a Christian marriage ceremony, without regard for the traditional native rules. This had brought on a spiritual crisis during which he was reconverted to the old Bororo ideal: he then settled in Kajara where, for the last ten or fifteen years, he had been living an exemplary savage life" (p. 236).

described? Perceiving and valuing could be understood as almost spectatorial processes, although once one asks about it, one easily recognizes that such a stance is atypical in life, even if striven for as part of the vocational ideal of the intellectual. Even when not doing anything about getting married, A would be described in ordinary language as "willing" or "unwilling" to marry the different girls. Perhaps this signifies sufficiently just how predominantly praxic a matter marrying is. As we are dealing with it, it would be an error to consider marriage an egoical process. It might be that the choice of individual B over other suitable girls—middle-grade southsiders—is like this and that a decision is made, but where the class of middle-grade southside girls as opposed to girls of lower or higher grade or from the north side are concerned, there would be, I believe, a deeply established habitual disposition whereby A is simply unable to marry C or D. Even so, marrying is something done, a matter of "behavior," a practical activity within which the previously discussed elements of perceiving, believing and above all valuing play their supporting roles in relation to its lead. Correlatively, marriageability and unmarriageability are ultimately practical characteristics, "correct" and "incorrect" *uses* to which others of certain sorts may be put by an individual of a sort. Nevertheless, it would seem that the *pathic foundation* for the praxic ingredient is what distinguishes the concrete life process that is to be classified as praxic by virtue of the positing ingredient pre-dominating in it.

If the foregoing at least speculatively shows how the terms explained earlier might be employed to *describe* lived marriageability among the Bororo, how might we now *explain* why A came to live B, C and D the way he does?

B, C and D are quite familiar to A. Not only which side of the society they live on but also who their parents and relatives are, and thus what level of society they belong to, would have been encountered innumerable times in his past. Further, how middle-grade northsiders relate, say, with middle- as opposed to upper- and lower-grade south- and northsiders, would have also been lived many times. One can further imagine that repeatedly when A, our middle-grade northsider boy, was with his family and seemed interested in interacting with another northsider who was female and of a certain age, and so forth, in a way that was relevant to marriage (sex might be relevant, but then again it might not, but sharing food might be), the atmosphere became frosty as the others in the family felt something was wrong, even if they could not say what it was and took no active steps to interfere. One can further imagine that the negative reaction was perhaps not so intense when it was a southsider and that it was rather positive in affective tone when A relevantly interacted with a nice girl of middle rank who was also from the south side. Such childhood events could, in the social perspective, be the main conditions for an adolescent sense of who could and could not be married.

Whether such conditioning takes place could be ethnographically or otherwise human-scientifically ascertained. Perhaps its intensity and frequency could be gauged and the subsequent mate selections correlated into a generalizing nomothetic explanation. Other human factors (assuming the physical ones constant) could be sought in the same manner.

Note that I do not postulate *talking* within the family about whom one can and cannot marry as a necessary condition, although of course it can be a factor and may well be the main one. But in the present case one marriage rule may be verbalized but the other, the one concerning clan rank, would seem not to be. (Considerable confusion might be avoided in many cases if "verbal" and "nonverbal" were substituted for "conscious" and "unconscious.")

In the case of the Bororo, we have at least an hypothesis about how the entire social system was maintained. This appears in an account of how it was obliterated. When the circular arrangement of the huts of other villages was changed to one of parallel rows, the system collapsed. The central place of the men's house seems to have been especially important. This is "where the bachelors slept and where the male members of the population spent their days when they were not busy fishing or hunting, or involved in some public ceremony on the dance area" (p. 239). I mention this to make it plain that marriage behavior was only part of a whole. Regarding the social and religious system in its entirety, Lévi-Strauss believes that by living with huts arranged as they traditionally were the awareness of the system was constantly refreshed in the lives of the Bororo. If so, then here we have a sort of human-geographical explanation for describable patterns of life. It is fairly plain that there is much more to such systems than either I have discussed or Lévi-Strauss has reported. However, perhaps now they can be explained as well as described without resort to unobservables is at least vaguely recognizable through these phenomenological speculations.

Two more aspects of the matter may be speculated about here. Why were the Bororo unable in fact to recognize and describe all the rules that govern their marrying? In case it was not plain above, I reject unobservable "realities" beyond appearances and "unconsciousnesses" of all sorts. I assume that ethnographers can reconstructively establish not only a sort of general model of how marrying has gone on in a group, as Lévi-Strauss has done through taking down genealogies, but also that one could by observation of other lives see the attraction or aversion to the permissible and forbidden others as it occurs and, in similar fashion, how it is inculcated in the young. In principle, a Bororo could come to recognize that is is not only the exagamous moieties but also the clan grades that found the acceptability of spouses. The question is then why both rules are not "conscious." (It may be that Lévi-Strauss's informant was unusual in even having conceived one of th½ rules; in other words, both rules might be unconceived and unverbalized for the typical Bororo.)

In Lévi-Strauss's discussion an immediate cause of self-deception is the way upper-, middle- and lower-grade huts are systematically mixed together in the village layout. In terms of marriage and other activities, there is not one but *three* two-sided societies that, due to some factors or other, came to be and stay together. If the three independent parts were recognized to be independent by these Indians, the alliance would be questionable and might even crumble, perhaps to the detriment of all. Instead, the Bororo *interpreted* themselves as actually one group with two mutually dependent parts. Misinterpretation can sometimes be beneficial, it seems. That some people are conditioned to overlook or to misinterpret data does not mean that the data or the living of them are "real" or "unconscious," or that these "data" are, absurdly, unobservable. Difficulty is not impossibility.

One might wonder, finally, which norm is stronger, that of northsiders only marrying southsiders or that of Bororo only marrying persons of the same grade. If marriage within one's grade is the stronger norm, then as a society disintegrated we might expect it to survive longer than marriage between moieties. Thus if for A there were only two girls of suitable age left, C and D, which one he married would reveal which norm was the stronger. Lévi-Strauss's contention seems to be that what might be called the latent norm is stronger than what might be called the manifest norm. I do not see that this is necessary. I have suggested how the relative strength of the two norms could be tested. If the grade rule proved stronger than the moiety rule, it would be interesting to see how the event would be handled by the Bororo interpretatively.

Nevertheless (and this is central to the present essay), living and the lived have priority over interpretation and, above all, life can be reflectively observed, described and explained. If these speculations have made this position intelligible, strict investigation could confirm, correct and extend what has been advanced here speculatively.

A Personal Remark:

"Dr. Ballard" offered his first course in phenomenology in Fall 1961. (Tulane students talked about his conversion.) I was in my last undergraduate year and fed up with

philosophy, but I decided to give this new variety a chance. Ed let this lowly undergrad into that advanced seminar. What I first remember is how we all (Ed included) were so impressed at his having tried to do some phenomenology. Incredible to remember, that was when it first dawned on me that one could not only stand in awe of the great historical figures, texts, and movements but also philosophize, not just study but actually do philosophy. I had previously become sceptical after realizing that approachs affect results and not seeing how to select an approach. In that seminar the thought also occured to me that in phenomenology we have an approach that can be taken to itself and not merely a self-investigating but also a self-justifying method. Out of the "academic" woods, I got accepted at Tulane with support but instead left New Orleans for New York, Cairns and Gurwitsch, and no support (Andy Reck said I might like it). Probably out of homesickness once there, I proposed to Ballard that we translate some of Ricoeur's essays on Husserl. I don't know why he agreed, but the royalties on the now over 6,000 copies still take me to SPEP each year. I have done some "scholarship" since I came back to America from New School phenomenology training, but the higher goal established for me in Ed's seminar twenty years ago dominates more and more of my effort. We often effect one another in ways we do not recognize at the time. I owe much to Ed, but would consider him one of my three teachers if there were only that seminar.

PART FOUR

Archaic Experience in Phenomenology:
Philosophical Archeology

John Scanlon

11/*Empirio-Criticism, Descriptive Psychology, and the Experiential World*

The transcendental phenomenological approach to the world, while it claims the dignity of asking ultimate philosophical questions with the rigor they warrant, is elusive and fraught with apparent paradox. In Fink's suggestive formulation, Husserlian phenomenology inquires into the origin of the world in such a novel manner that everything said along the way is not merely provisional but false until rectified by the transcendental reduction.[1] The very meanings of "origin" and "world" remain in suspense until the work of transcendental analysis has been successfully begun. This situation understandably generates great concern over the question of ultimate origins and indubitable beginnings, as witnessed by Husserl's several introductions to phenomenology. But if that concern, however pressing and however fundamental, is followed up exclusively, and if the ultimately justifiable beginning continues to recede to an ever deeper and more complex level, phenomenological philosophy runs the risk of becoming or at least of appearing to be an esoteric project in hyperspecialization: a philosopher's philosophy of the highest order, perhaps incapable of saying anything true.

Besides, a foundation should be judged not only in terms of its solidity but also in terms of what it can found. We are interested in principles not only with regard to their conclusiveness but also with regard to what insights they can generate. Hence, it makes sense to elucidate points which may not contribute to an ultimate foundation

1. Eugen Fink, "Die phänomenologische Philosophie Edmund Husserls in der gegenwärtigen Kritik," in *Studien zur Phänomenologie, 1930–1939* (The Hague: Nijhoff, 1966), pp. 79–156; English translation, "The Phenomenological Philosophy of Edmund Husserl and Contemporary Criticism," in *The Phenomenology of Husserl: Selected Critical Readings* (Chicago: Quadrangle, 1970), pp. 73–147.

but which have been disclosed along the way in that rigorous quest and which have their own clarity in their own limited context. Thus, a more modest approach to the world fits within the larger scheme of phenomenological philosophy. In that approach, ultimate questions of transcendental origin are deliberately set aside and the world itself is taken as origin, though not as ultimate or absolute. It is the approach which attempts to discover the experiential world as ground and source of clarity for all sciences of the natural order (i.e., all sciences not construed as transcendental).[2]

Yet, this approach to the world has its own elusive and enigmatic character. To begin with, the move is motivated by the recognition of a deep-seated crisis in the sciences as they have developed historically and, most especially, in psychology. The sciences have become ever more distant from life, from human concerns and from their own original cognitive goals and promise. After Husserl, further profound and sensitive reflection on the historical roots and apparently inevitable direction of the development of science seems only to enhance the suspicion that Husserl attempted to overcome; viz., that science is incapable of providing genuine knowledge of the world and destined to produce only increased efficiency in manipulating the world technologically — that science is not insight at all, but only power. From that perspective, we might seem to be well advised, recognizing the inherent limitations of the scientific enterprise, to turn to the world of common everyday experience in a spirit which carefully avoids being scientific. Husserl, on the contrary, calls for a *science* of the experiential world.[3]

2. This approach is most clearly adopted in Edmund Husserl, *Phänomenologische Psychologie: Vorlesungen, Sommersemester 1925* (*Husserliana* IX) (The Hague: Nijhoff, 1968); *Phenomenological Psychology: Lectures, Summer Semester, 1925*, translated by John Scanlon (The Hague: Nijhoff, 1977).

3. The connection of a science of the experiential world with a general crisis of science is made emphatically in Edmund Husserl, *Die Krisis der europäischen Wissenschaften und die transzendentale Phänomenologie* (*Husserliana* VI) (The Hague: Nijhoff, 1962); *The Crisis of European Sciences and Transcendental Phenomenology*, translated by David Carr (Evanston: Northwestern Univeristy Press, 1970). Since my discussion will center on the theme of the experiential world as developed in Husserl's *Phenomenological Psychology*, I should point to two connections: (1) In the *Crisis* (p. 173), Husserl indicates the theme that he presents in *Phen. Psych.*, "Even without any transcendental interest — that is, within the 'natural attitude' (in the language of transcendental philosophy the naive attitude, prior to the *epoche*) — the life-world could have become the subject matter of a science of its own, an ontology of the life-world purely as experiential world (i.e., as the world which is coherently, consistently, harmoniously indubitable in actual and possible experiencing intuition)"; in *Phen. Psych.*, the theme is also described as "a world of actual living which includes world-experiencing and world-theorizing life"; (2) In *Phen. Psych.*, though the theme of a general crisis of science is not pronounced, Husserl's point of departure is the debate about the fundamental concepts and appropriate method of psychology; but in that context he finds a basic lack of understanding concerning both nature as the subject matter of the natural sciences and mind or spirit as the subject matter of the human

The question of the sense of such a project can be put in the form of a dilemma. If the experiential world already is the sole ground upon which mundane sciences can be based, and if the sciences willy-nilly constantly turn to experience for direct or indirect confirmation of their theories, then what need is there to add yet another science directed toward that same source, viz., the experiential world? On the other hand, if the scientific mentality inevitably creates a distance between itself and our world, of what use to us is yet another science in our attempt to measure that gap?

The crux of the answer lies in the requirement that this new science be different by being a disclosure of the pre-theoretical experiential world.[4] But the response arouses further suspicion: can we, steeped in the sedimented tradition of centuries of scientific theory, ever hope to return to such a pre-theoretical experience except by a flight of fancy whose result would then be merely a dream world?

Yet, the latent promise of the approach, the hope that sciences — especially psychology and the other human sciences — might thereby be understood as genuine sciences, genuine contributions to our understanding of ourselves and the world rather than mere technical exercises, is alluring enough to call for a serious consideration of the sense of the project. That consideration can be made more concrete if we take into account two historical factors that shed light on Husserl's project: a confrontation with Avenarius and a limited parallel with Dilthey.

This indirect approach might seem to run counter to the main thrust of phenomenology. It would not be unreasonable to object impatiently, in the spirit of phenomenology and in the spirit of a turn toward the world itself, "Instead of 'returning' to this or that philosopher, we should simply 'return' to the natural point of departure itself [i.e., to experience], and instead of beginning with books we should begin immediately with the things [an die Sachen]." That the situation is not all that simple may be suggested by the fact that the above remark, which might readily be imagined to be a typical phenomenological complaint, is actually quoted from one of the major works of the empirio-criticist Avenarius.[5] The demand to return to the things or matters themselves, coupled with a concern for an approach to the experience of the world, an approach unrestricted by historically developed prejudices, will not

---

sciences: "thus both — cultural world and nature [geistige Welt und Natur]" — remained equally unintelligible (p. 40). And in Crisis (p. 3), Husserl writes, "After all, the crisis of a science indicates nothing less than that its genuine scientific character, the whole manner in which it has set its task and developed a methodology for it, has become questionable."
4. Phen. Psych., p. 41.
5. Richard Avenarius, Kritik der reinen Erfahrung. Vol. I (Leipzig: Fries, 1888), p. x.

suffice to define a phenomenological approach to the world, since it characterizes empirio-criticism as well.

Concerning other themes, phenomenological work can perhaps proceed with confidence, in a spirit of continuing and developing an ongoing enterprise. But, unfortunately, the theme of a general science of the experiential world, a theme which plays a pivotal role in Husserl's understanding of phenomenological philosophy—as the basis from which regional ontologies might be developed without being disjointed specializations and as an introduction to the transcendental mode of asking about the world[6] — seems to have remained an interesting, provocative, yet obscure suggestion on Husserl's part. Maybe it will remain too obscure to permit clear-cut development and continuation; maybe a reconsideration of its historical context will diminish the obscurity and clear a path for further work.

> My original formulation of the question [was] suggested by Avenarius' positivistic *doctrine of the natural concept of the world*: the scientific description of the world purely as world of experience.[7]

Whether the overall influence of Avenarius on Husserl be eventually judged beneficial, pernicious, or both, the ingenious strategy of turning to the world purely as given to experience in order to escape the influence of speculative theories about the world and thus to safeguard the positive sciences from the attacks of skepticism and subjectivism is definitely the contribution of Avenarius. Husserl mentions him in this connection as early as 1910/11:

> . . . The positivism of the school of Avenarius which sees in the elimination of all "metaphysical" intrusions in the concept of the world, and in the restitution of the "natural" concept of the world of pure experience, the task of a theory and critique of pure experience.[8]

Avenarius and the Natural Concept of the World

For our present purposes, a brief exposition of the salient features of Avenarius' doctrine of the natural concept of the world of pure experi-

6. The latter role is emphasized in the *Crisis* where the first role is also acknowledged. In *Phen. Psych.*, the former role is emphasized, specifically with regard to psychology.

7. Husserl, Ms. A VIII 20, 47a. This section of that manuscript bears the title "Radikale Begründung der positiven Wissenchaften durch eine Wissenschaft der vorgegebenen Welt aus reiner Erfahrung," and is dated c. 1930.

8. "Aus den Vorlesungen, 'Grundprobleme der Phänomenologie,' Wintersemester 1910/11," in *Zur Phänomenologie der Intersubjektivität* (*Husserliana* XIII) (Hague: Nijhoff, 1973), pp. 131–32.

ence should suffice.[9] First of all, the particular philosophical positions which Avenarius is most intent on combatting are skepticism and idealism. In the course of presenting his own views, Avenarius finds it necessary to distinguish an absolute and a relative perspective, both justified on the basis of pure experience, but not to be mixed or confused with each other. From the absolute perspective, experience is seen to give us things and thoughts as there on their own, existing independently of any contribution from experience. Among the things are also other human beings. And Avenarius considers it a justifiable postulate that other human beings are more than merely mechanical entities. In a long and intricate critique of "introjection," Avenarius seeks to show that we exceed the limits of that justifiable postulate and get involved in inextricable confusion when we attempt to interpret other human beings as having impressions, images, ideas of the world within them, when we go still further and posit an internal being as subject of them, and when we finally ascribe also to ourselves such impressions or images of the world and such a subject underlying them. Positively, experience, once purified of the mystifying influence of such introjection, can be seen to present one world, not a double world of things and minds, of external and internal entities. Further, on that same condition, experience can be seen to present *the world* and not merely impressions, images or ideas of the world beyond which it would make sense to posit some being-in-itself of the world. And, on this account, experience is not in any way subjective; it is not in any significant aspect "mine." I am experienced just as is anything else; I am not an experiencing subject. In fact, the latter expression "experiencing subject" has no experiential validity; it is merely the result of the fallacy of introjection.

At the same time, through the relative perspective, Avenarius takes account of the fact that we experience the world around us as our environment and the fact that sometimes individuals disagree when reporting to each other what experience presents as in each case absolute. Without disturbing the absoluteness of experience, Avenarius attempts to give a scientific account of the correlation of self and world. At this crucial point, the standpoint of the psychophysical experimenter or psychiatrist is taken as definitive, so that Avenarius'

9. This exposition is based on two major works, *Kritik der reinen Erfahrung* and *Der Menschliche Weltbegriff* (Leipzig: Reisland, 1891). The first attempts to lay the basis for Avenarius', position in a scientific precision, the second is a less formal discussion and defense of its philosophical implications. See also Leszek Kolokowski, "Richard Avenarius et le suicide apparent de la philosophie," in *Die Welt des Menschen—Die Welt der Philosophie: Festschrift für Jan Patocka*, Walter Biemel, ed. (The Hague: Nijhoff, 1976), pp. 270–84.

complex *Critique of Pure Experience* is an elaborate attempt to formalize as strictly as possible the functional correlation or "principle coordination" between any central nervous organ "C" and its environment "R" (presumably for *Reiz*, "stimulus").

Given that project and those results, it is not surprising that Husserl, while complaining that Avenarius had bogged down after a good beginning,[10] could also see in his project a brilliant move which could, if taken properly, liberate us from inherited prejudices and confusions concerning nothing less than the world and the self-world correlation.

Viewed retrospectively from the orientation opened up by Husserlian phenomenology, how had Avenarius gotten bogged down? First, in reading Avenarius, one finds a thoroughly sustained, cogently argued, and internally consistent defense of the power and inherent direction of natural experience. Thus, Husserl's overriding concern vis-à-vis Avenarius is to show that, in addition to the straightforward natural attitude of experience brilliantly highlighted by Avenarius as the very heart of the natural concept of the world, an entirely new level of experience is also possible and is required for a more radical investigation of issues that make no sense at all within the natural attitude, or within natural experience directed toward the world as pregiven actuality. Husserl criticizes Avenarius for not being sufficiently radical in his procedure and consequently for not distinguishing between two types of experience and intuition, the natural and the transcendental, and between two types of science built upon them—positive (natural, objective) science and transcendental science.[11] In this basic sense, then, Avenarius is so bogged down in natural experience that he cannot recognize the distinctive character of transcendental experience.

Although Husserl has to end up arduously defending the very reverse of Avenarius' basic position—in so far as he has to exhibit the possibility of a senseful and experientially founded science not restricted within the natural concept of the world—the precision, forcefulness and consistency with which Avenarius has already portrayed this natural concept of the world allows Husserl to encompass that concept as a stage in a more penetrating philosophical reflection:

> Whatever position one may take regarding the particular theories of this "empirio-criticism," an ingenious instinct is displayed in its beginning with the natural concept of the world. If the scientific

10. In "Immanente Philosophie—Avenarius" (probably 1915), *Husserliana* XIII, p. 199, Husserl writes, *"Der Anfang ist bei Avenarius gut, aber er bleibt stecken."*
11. Husserl, K III 27, 2a-2b, "Beilage zur Neubearbeitung der Kant-Lektüre" (enclosed in an envelope dated 15 VIII 1924). This manuscript exists only in Husserl's shorthand; the pertinent passage was transcribed for me by G. Van Kerkhoven.

concept of the world, the natural "representation of the world," is a mere moment in the constitution of universal natural life, then we are referred to a great problem.[12]

Further, any attempt to understand Husserl's approach to the transcendental question via the natural attitude or via the natural concept of the world portrayed by Avenarius should bear in mind that Husserl sees therein a legitimate repudiation of any position that would attempt to attribute to experience not the givenness of the world but the mere appearance of something which would itself transcend experience and would be construed as itself unknowable. Thus, Husserl's approach to subjectivity, whether it be ultimately convincing or not, needs to be interpreted from the start as one which has taken into account Avenarius' drastic critique of subjectivism under the rubric of the fallacy of introjection. And any attempt to relate Husserl's transcendental philosophy to the philosophic tradition should avoid abstractly connecting it with Kant or with the broad tradition of philosophy which begins with Descartes, and it should recognize instead that, with regard to the question of relating experience and the world, Husserl's more immediate link is not with that tradition but with Avenarius' acute critique of it.[13]

But we wish here to disregard the entire area of transcendental questioning in order to come to an understanding concerning a less than ultimate or absolute approach to the world. If we shy away from all questions concerning transcendental origin or transcendental experience, can we still find a sense in which Avenarius gets bogged down in elucidating the natural concept of the world? Here the issue becomes more subtle, and decisive differences more difficult to discern. To obtain an adequate perspective from which to elicit them, let us abandon Avenarius temporarily and approach the issue indirectly, by way of discussing a partial parallel of Husserl with Dilthey.

Dilthey and the Sense of Science

That that detour is not arbitrary is suggested by the structure of Husserl's lectures on phenomenological psychology. The very first

---

12. K III 27, 2b
13. For example, Husserl writes, "*Sehen wir zu! Man behaupte, die Welt sei ganz anders, das sei nicht die wirklicke Welt, sie sei blosse Erscheinung einer transzendenten, unerkennbaren. . . . Kann mich etwas nötigen, den natürlichen Weltbegriff zu ändern, zu sagen (Introjektion), diese gegebene Welt sei blosse Erscheinung in mir, Erscheinung des erfahrenden Menschen, sei etwas in seinem Gerhirn. . . . Ich sehe darin eine sehr wertvolle Tendenz*" (*Husserliana* XIII, p. 197). In another passage, "*Das Ergebnis ist also die totale Umkehrung der Lehre von Avenarius, so sehr es richtig ist, dass keine Transzendantalphilosophie das Sein der Erfahrungswelt preisgeben kann, aber wohl, dass sie sie transzendental verständich machen kann*" (Beilage XIII to

theme developed in the systematic part of those lectures is that of the
concretely intuitive unity of the pre-scientific experiential world. But
the systematic part is preceded by a long and interesting historical
introduction. In the introduction, Husserl discusses at some length the
significance of Dilthey's persuasive yet largely unsuccessful attempt to
promote a descriptive and analytic psychology as a foundation for the
human sciences (*Geisteswissenschaften*). In addition, the introduction
contains a retrospective summary of the significance of Husserl's own
Logical Investigations,[14] in the familiar characterization of them as a
breakthrough of phenomenology which was at the same time a thorough development of the concept of intentionality suggested by Brentano. But, in that context, Husserl also mentions as a historical irony
the fact that Brentano had repudiated the emergent doctrine as too
distant from his own idea of psychology while Dilthey, who had not
influenced Husserl's early work at all,[15] was enthusiastic about Husserl's success in independently carrying out with regard to the elements
of knowledge a concrete segment of that descriptive and analytic
psychology which he, Dilthey, had been advocating.[16]

Such an introduction might easily lead the reader to anticipate that
Husserl would immediately show how the phenomenology that had
emerged in the epistemological context of the *Logical Investigations* and
which he had further developed in the ensuing quarter of a century
could contribute directly to the conceptual foundations of psychology
and, through psychology, of the human sciences generally. Instead,
Husserl takes a longer path which eventually leads up to the need for a
phenomenological psychology but first sees in the critique of psychology's exclusive reliance on the methods of the natural sciences in their
adaptation as modern experimental psychology—a critique in which
he aligns himself with Dilthey—evidence for the need of radical investigation of the sense of science which has to begin with a return to the
concretely intuitive unity of the pre-scientific experiential world.[17]

Phänomenologische Psychologie [*Husserliana* IX], p. 474). In the *Crisis* (p. 195), Husserl lists
Avenarius as the developer of a "transcendental philosophy basically determined by
English empiricism," as part of a tradition not derived from Kant.

14. Edmund Husserl, *Logische Untersuchungen*, 3 vols. (Halle: Niemeyer, 1913–1921);
Logical Investigations, translated by J.N. Findlay, 2 vols. (New York: Humanities, 1970).

15. But Husserl was influenced profoundly by Dilthey beginning in 1905. "*Sie wissen
nicht, dass wenige Gespräche 1905 mit Dilthey in Berlin (nicht seine Schriften) einen Impuls
bedeuteten, der von Husserl der L.U. zu dem der Ideen führte, und dass die unvollständig
dargestellte und eigentlich erst von 1913 bis etwa 1925 konkret vollendete Phänom. der Ideen zu
einer innersten Gemeinschaft mit D., bei wesentlich anders gestalteter Methode geführt hat. Das
muss irgendwie herausgeklärt werden. Weiss noch nicht, wo und wie*" (letter from Husserl to
Misch, June 27, 1929, cited in Georg Misch, *Lebensphilosophie und Phänomenologie*
[Darmstadt: Wissenschaftliche Buchgesellschaft, 1967], pp. 327–28.)

16. *Phen. Psych.*, pp. 24–25.

17. *Phen. Pysch.*, pp. 38–40.

Dilthey approaches psychology from the perspective of a practitioner and theoretician of the human sciences,[18] which in his view, need psychology in at least three ways: to clarify the basic concepts of the human sciences, to contribute toward a unified view of the many human sciences, and to help them incorporate with clarity the profound views of poets and reflective thinkers. To single out the first of these needs, the human scientist operates with concepts which have a psychological dimension to them, such as will or freedom in the study of religion, right or norm in jurisprudence, community or dependence in political science. With regard to such concepts, Dilthey sees the human scientist of his day caught in a dilemma: he could either continue to operate with such concepts without any basic clarification or he could turn to scientific psychology for the requisite clarity. If one took the first option, the unclarity, ambiguity and possible bias of everyday language could vitiate the work of the human scientist. If one turned to psychology, one was no better off: because of the dominance of the methods of the natural sciences as adopted by modern experimental psychology, the human scientist who turned there for help would only be led astray from the genuine goals of the human sciences.

Therefore, Dilthey found it necessary to critique the prevailing trend in psychology by proposing a different approach, one that would be beneficial to the human sciences. The crux of Dilthey's critique (apart from his historical considerations which, ironically, show modern experimental psychology to be the latest descendant in a line that goes back to Wolff's rational psychology) centers around a neat contrast between the access of the natural sciences to nature and the access of the human sciences to psychic life:

> The human sciences are distinguished from the sciences of nature first of all in that the latter have for their objects facts which are presented to consciousness as from the outside, as phenomena and given in isolation, while the objects of the former are given *originaliter* from within as real and as a living continuum [*Zusammenhang*].[19]

From this contrast in access to subject matter derives a further contrast. Since the phenomena studied as objects of the natural sci-

18. *Geisteswissenschaften*, among which Dilthey includes, e.g., the study of religion, jurisprudence, history, political science. The following brief exposition is based on Wilhelm Dilthey, *Ideen zu einer deskriptiven und zergliedernden Psychologie (1894)* (*Gesammelte Schriften* V [Stuttgart: Teubner, 1957]; "Ideas Concerning a Descriptive and Analytic Psychology (1894)," translated by R. Zaner, in *Descriptive Psychology and Historical Understanding* [The Hague: Nijhoff, 1977]). This is the work that Husserl paraphrases at length in *Phen. Psych.*, pp. 3–12.

19. *Ideas*, p. 27 (substituting "sciences" for "studies" in the translation of *Geisteswissenschaften*, because the main point of Dilthey's discussion is the different scientific character of the natural sciences and the human sciences).

ences are given as lacking any intrinsic connection, that connection has to be supplied by the employment of the experimental method. This explanatory and constructive procedure, required in the natural sciences, makes no sense at all in the human sciences because psychic life is originally given as a nexus within which single moments can be isolated for special attention only by an abstractive procedure. Thus hypotheses, in Dilthey's view, exercise a fundamental function in the natural sciences but are relegated to a more supplementary role in psychology and the other human sciences. Consequently, in place of the misguided hypothetically constructive procedure of modern experimental psychology, what is required as foundation for the human sciences and what is possible as an approach to psychic life is a descriptive and analytic psychology: descriptive because the original reality of psychic life is already given as lived; analytic because clarity requires analyzing and distinguishing the chief components and structures of psychic life within the already given overall psychic nexus. In natural science, analysis is employed as a means to arrive at elements from which to explain phenomena theoretically, hypothetically. In psychology and the other human sciences, analysis is employed to articulate moments of an already given unity which is to be recognized and preserved, not to construct a lacking connection. Thus, "we explain nature, we understand psychic life."[20]

Dilthey, concerned with psychic life and all its expressions and products, turns his attention to the foundations of the human sciences but is content to leave the study of nature in a rather enigmatic state as, in effect, the imposition of a hypothetically constructed unity on something given as basically isolated, merely phenomenal, and radically unintelligible. Husserl introduces a consideration of the pre-scientific or pre-theoretical experiential world as required at least partly by Dilthey's critique of modern naturalistically oriented psychology. But Husserl remarks in advance that it is required because both nature and mind have become unintelligible and need to be traced back to their sources in the experiential world, even though the main interest of the lectures is directed toward mind or psychic life in all its forms. After explicitly invoking Dilthey in advance, Husserl soon implicitly evokes the spirit of Avenarius by introducing the expression, "natural concept of the world."[21] Without pursuing Husserl's long route to a phenomenological psychology, we need now to see how this triangular relation of Husserl with Dilthey and Avenarius helps us understand the basic sense of a science of the pre-theoretical experiential world.

20. Ideas, p. 27.
21. *Phen. Psych.*, p. 70.

The Triangulation of Husserl, Avenarius and Dilthey

If we return to Avenarius' presentation of the natural concept of the world in terms of our opening questions, we find that for Avenarius there is no dilemma involved in his relationship to science and to experience; nor is there anything enigmatic or paradoxical about his project. Further, Avenarius' theme does not emerge from any sense of a crisis in science. If anything, we might attribute to Avenarius the recognition of a crisis within philosophy. But once the source of that crisis is identified as the fallacy of introjection, from there on science, philosophy and experience are assured of unimpeded progress. Rather than seeing any distance between science and our world, Avenarius is optimistic that, with constant surveillance against any relapse into subjectivistic introjection, actual experience will constantly approximate pure experience.[22]

But here is something to note, lest we confuse Avenarius with Husserl.[23] If pure experience is a goal to be approximated with the further development of humanity, it is clear that Avenarius will not opt for a mere description of what actually presents itself to experience, since at any given time ordinary everyday experience may well contain unnoticed metaphysical intrusions which only scientifically refined experience can extirpate. For this reason, it would be pointless to single out discrepancies between Avenarius' position and our actual experience. As Husserl suggests, though Avenarius begins well, he does not continue on the path of a genuine description of the world of pretheoretical experience. A mere glimpse at that world sufficed to provide him with the absolute perspective as a weapon against subjectivism. But the final word on the relative perspective rests with psychophysical experimentation or psychiatry, itself taken as an absolute perspective.

Thus, for Avenarius, scientific theory is not to be set aside in approaching pure experience; on the contrary, it is the surest access to it. And he clearly advocates no *epoche* with regard to all inherited philosophical theory. Rather, naturalism, mechanism and objectivism are unquestioned platforms to be refined and defended, as empiriocriticism, against all rival theories.

Only by being radically transformed, even within the limits of the natural attitude, can Avenarius' proposal become Husserl's theme.

---

22. "*Die* Kritik *hatte ihre Aufgabe . . . beendet mit der Aufnahme,* dass überhaupt die menschlichen Weltbegriffe *. . . sich einem rein empirischen Weltbegriff annähern*" (Menschliche Weltbegriff, p. xii).

23. It would not be the first time. One of Husserl's manuscripts (M III 7, 6b) contains the following excerpt from Theodore Elsenhans, "Phänomenologie, Psychologie, Erkenntnistheorie," *Kant-Studien* XX (1915), pp. 224–75: "*Wie bei Avenarius so mischen sich in der Phänomenologie der natürliche Standpunkt und ein wissenschaftlicher.*"

The crucial point of that transformation, in terms of which description is taken seriously as a scientific procedure with regard to the world of experience, is suggested by the following quotation:

> Instead of being performed in the phenomenological attitude such an essential description [i.e., of the world purely as world of experience] can be performed also in the natural attitude. Then it becomes the beginning of a "pure internal psychology" (thus already in the lecture of 1910/11) — of a human-scientific psychology of the individual human being and of the human community. Then the world purely as world of experience is called, for instance, the experiential representation of the world.[24]

Dilthey, we recall, saw the basis for different procedures in the natural sciences and in the human sciences in a sharp contrast in the access to their respective objects. What happens if we approach the experiential world with that contrast in mind? Curiously, the experiential world seems to resemble psychic life rather than nature. The experiential world is given to experience as itself actual, and not as a mere phenomenon or mere appearance of something transcending experience. Further, nothing in the experiential world is ever given in isolation. Rather, every entity is experienced as filling part of one continuous experiential space, enduring in one continuous experiential time and interacting in typical patterns of regularity with other entities of its environment. And just as we can observe psychic life only from the always limited perspective of a momentary lived experience from which the whole of psychic life can be discerned as its vast nexus, its broader context, the same relati/nship holds concerning our experience of the world. The world is not an object of experience on its own; but it is the constant context of experience for any and every single entity that can be experienced. Only by explicating the positive significance of the empty horizons of any object or field of objects can we make thematic the sense of the world as the encompassing horizonal context for them.

But now the secret is out. Of course! The very project of the description of the world purely as world for experience is a psychological enterprise. To recognize the experiential world as a psychological theme is not to identify it with psychic life, however. It was not in vain that Husserl, in his introduction to the lectures, emphasized as the essential point of the *Logical Investigations* the establishment of the possibility of correlational research by which objects of all sorts can be related to their corresponding modes of intentional lived experience

---

24. A VII 20, 47a, b (see note 7, above).

without being reduced to psychic entities themselves. Thus, here, the world is not a psychological theme; the correlation of experience with experienced world is.[25]

And we should also be careful to note how it is a psychological theme. In place of Avenarius' objectivistic psychophysical orientation, Husserl takes the theme as one for a human-scientifically oriented psychology. Instead of relegating the "principle coordination" of self and world to the explanatory theory and experimentation of the psychophysicist, this coordination itself becomes the subject matter of description. And that description can be carried out only from the perspective of a participant observer. I observe the world oriented around me as my surrounding world in my ongoing experience, and on the basis of that observation I can understand others' oriented perspectives. Avenarius' absolute perspective is shattered: all that remains of it is the unwavering perceptual belief in the actual existence of the world presented to experience. Experience discloses itself to be subjectively relative rather than absolute. Thus, introjection is not required to posit myself as an experiencing subject, but only reflective attention to such facets of how experience takes place as spatial situatedness, perspectival orientation and the functioning of kinesthetic bodily sense.

Just as Husserl had independently executed a segment of a descriptive and analytic psychology in the *Logical Investigations*, he can be seen to be presenting another segment of it under the title "descriptive science of the experiential world." And though his ingenious development of this theme can be seen as a transformation of Avenarius' project under the human-scientific inspiration of Dilthey, it is not arbitrary or opportunistic. Ultimately, the key to his distinctive position lies in the *Logical Investigations*, in which perception is already taken as presenting an object itself as opposed to a mere image, idea or impression of one and in which perception and all other cognitive processes are taken from the start as lived experience, but above all in the concrete intentional analysis by which intentional experiences and intentional objects can be described in correlation.

The triangulation we have pursued clarifies the sense of the project considered. Clearly, it is not a matter of fleeing all trace of anything scientific. Rather, it is a matter, at this primitive level of questioning, of deferring all hypothetical and constructive theorizing and of developing that sort of descriptive and analytic science that remains close to life and seeks to enhance our understanding of humanity. For, as much as the natural sciences are an integral part of our historical heritage, the human sciences are all the more so.

25. But note that it precedes and sets the stage for an explicitly phenomenological psychology, which comes much later in the lectures.

But if the project is to make sense, we should also frame it with a sense of limit. Dilthey's remarks on the significance of a descriptive and analytic psychology are exemplary in that respect. He emphasizes that, though it is an indispensable approach to psychic life, it captures only what can be brought to consciousness and highlighted by internal experience. What is thus discerned is seen as something influenced by a developed psychic nexus which we can never fully apprehend, so that hypotheses have to be invoked eventually to try to explain what we do not understand even within our own psychic life, and the entire enterprise of descriptive and analytic psychology, though fundamental, is far from exhaustive. It needs to be supplemented by such disciplines as comparative psychology, cultural anthropology, and history. One gets the impression that even the most astute psychological description and analysis amounts, relatively speaking, to a brilliant flash of lightning which illumines momentarily a small segment of a vast landscape shrouded in darkness and extending to unknown depths.

That sense of limit needs to be transposed to Husserl's project if we are to do it justice. The project, it must be borne in mind, is psychological, not transcendental. It tells us nothing about the world. It attempts to discover truths about one limited aspect of our access to the world, viz., experience of the world and the-world-as-correlate-of-experience (*Erfahrungswelt*). As basically psychological, the project is innocent of sociological, historical, cultural dimensions of our concrete way of experiencing; such dimensions would still have to be introduced to make definite the still abstractly psychological scheme of experience disclosed reflectively. But even within the psychological dimension of the question, experience as sheer experience of a world is a mere moment abstracted from the complexly woven fabric of psychic life with its emotive and instinctual depths, which may ultimately resist merely descriptive intentional analysis.

Bernard P. Dauenhauer

12/*Mere Things*

It is a commonplace today to say that there is no perception without interpretation, that interpretation is involved in the perceptual process from its inception. But even if this commonplace is accepted, one is still entitled to ask about the elements involved in the perceptual process. In this paper, I shall develop some leads provided by Edward Ballard in *Man and Technology*[1] concerning this matter.

Specifically, I shall try to clarify the character of that which is interpreted, the given, the mere thing. I shall try to show, through appropriate descriptions, that its character is perceptually grasped as that which allows and sustains a delimited range of actual or motivatedly possible perceptual interpretations. In other words, the character of the mere thing is not grasped in any single perceptual performance, but rather is grasped, though not exhaustively, through the interplay of multiple interpretations and observations or receptions of the mere thing.

Ballard defines perceiving as "interpreting that which one has passively received" (MT, p. 17). We passively receive presentations, and what is presented is the given—what I call the mere thing. Interpretation is "the active going out to meet this given or aspect of it to which one has learned to be sensitive" (MT, p. 17).

The interpretation process, according to Ballard, takes place on two levels. On the one hand, there is involuntary interpretation. This moves along automatic and habitual routes to indicate or identify what is presented, what is passively received. On the other hand, there is reflective interpretation. This is consciously deliberative. It involves a

1. Edward G. Ballard, *Man and Technology* (Pittsburgh: Duquesne University Press, 1978). Hereafter MT.

thoughtful application of principles to the involuntarily interpreted presentation.

Interpretation, whether involuntary or reflective, is not, however, a sheerly gratuitous element in perception. According to Ballard,

> interpretation is in no sense an arbitrary imposition of meanings upon a characterless given. What the character of this given is, however, can be determined only by testing the intitial interpretation against other perceptual interpretations, which in their turn have the *imprimatur* of survival in competition or cooperation with other interpreted possibilities (MT, p. 18).

Perception, Ballard continues, is itself a component of experience. Experience includes self-perception as well as other-perception. Experience is a trial that makes manifest either the object experienced, oneself or, usually, both. There are, Ballard says, experiences common to all persons. Among these he mentions perceived objects, existence amidst nature and with others, the events of birth, living and death (MT, pp. 19–21). Other examples are food and shelter.

Ballard's account is, I think, in the main correct. But to develop it, one might ask, What is this mere thing, this received given, that interpretation goes out to meet? What is it about the perceived object that, even if it is always interpreted, allows it to be the basis of experience common to all persons?

To pursue this issue, let me ask further, What distinction is contained in the following pairs of reports of perceptual experience: "There are pine trees in the yard" and "There are attractive and valuable pine trees in the yard"? "On August 4, 1914, German troops crossed the frontier of Belgium" and "On August 4, 1914, German troops committed aggression against Belgium"? The second member of each pair clearly involves an interpretation of something referred to by the first member, to which it is linked.[2] Even if one admits, as I am prepared to do, that the first members of these pairs report perceptual *interpretations*, one still should ask both what is being interpreted and what distinguishes the "first member" and the "second member" kinds of interpretation.[3] This paper sets forth some elements that must be included in any satisfactory solution to the first of these issues, the issue concerning what is being interpreted.

In order to uncover the character of the perceptually interpreted

2. I am not interested here in the question of whether one of these reports is founded upon the other.

3. This issue is treated, in other terms, by Hannah Arendt. See the essay "Truth and Politics" in her *Between Past and Future* (New York: Viking, 1968), esp. pp. 236–64.

given,[4] I address three interrelated questions: (I) What must any interpretation involve if it is to count as an interpretation? (II) What must the given, the mere thing, be if two or more interpretations can deal with it? (III) What test or tests can be used to determine the worth of an interpretation?

Re I. This question has two sides. It asks: (a) What are the fundamental characteristics of interpretation as such? and (b) What must the given be if perceptual interpretations, and not mere arbitrary inventions, are to be possible?

Among the fundamental or intrinsic characteristics of interpretation are the following: (1) Every interpretation is, in some manner, elicited. It is a response to what might be called a theme or a text. Some interpretations are directly elicited by other interpretations. But if a sufficiently comprehensive sequence of interpretations is examined, it will be seen that at least some interpretations are not primordially responses to other interpretations.

(2) Every interpretation carries with it the sense that its content is not exhaustively dependent upon its author. At least some other persons could have made the same interpretation. No interpretation is, in its sense, radically private.

(3) Every interpretation appeals to something other than itself for confirmation. I will devote more attention to this characteristic when I take up question III posed above.

(4) Every interpretation, as part of an ongoing life, implies that it is associable with some other interpretations performed either by the same author or by other authors. Grounds for the association of the several interpretations are provided by both the noetic and the noematic dimensions of the associable interpretations. Thus, sightings are associable with other sightings and smelled honeysuckle is associable with touched honeysuckle.

(5) Many interpretations have as a characteristic that they can be appropriately performed again. This possible reiterability of the same interpretation is not simply the possible reactivation of the original interpretation in memory nor is it an imaginative version of the same. Rather, at least some perceptual interpretations involve the expectation that on other occasions the same perceptual interpretation will be called for.[5]

---

4. My approach here owes much to Husserl. See his *Formal and Transcendental Logic*, translated by Dorion Cairns (The Hague: Nijhoff, 1969), pp. 313–29, and his *Cartesian Meditations*, translated by Dorion Cairns (The Hague: Nijhoff, 1969), pp. 75–81. Ballard, too, relies on Husserl: see MT, pp. 236–37 fn. 13.

5. I am inclined to think that some perceptual interpretations lack this fifth characteristic. People do say: "No one will ever see *that* again."

Undoubtedly, other intrinsic features of perceptual interpretation could be identified. But there is no need here for a more detailed analysis.

Let me turn now to the secod side of this question and set forth the intrinsic characteristics that must belong to the mere thing if perceptual interpretation is to be possible, if the given is indeed to be *met* by an interpretation: (1) Whatever else it may be, the given is not private. It is in principle available for interpretation by more than one person. It may be available immediately or only through the mediation of another interpretation. But it is available.

(2) The given is that which not only instigates the interpretation but also somehow authenticates it. This characteristic, too, will be developed more fully in my discussion of question III.

(3) The mere thing is given as not all of a piece. It elicits and authenticates interpretations that claim to take note of differences. It is given as not being a seamless whole. In effect, the mere thing is given both as complex and as one of a multiplicity of mere things. The mere thing is given as one of a multitude of things, each of which is endowed with a distinctive character to be acknowledged in the interpretation.

(4) The multiple, differentiated things are given as fitting together. Of course this in no way implies that a kind of Leibnizian principle of plenitude holds. Perhaps it is not even the case that all the givens that in fact are encountered fit together. I need not take up that issue for present purposes. But no mere thing is given as fully isolated from every other given. It is always given as part of a complex totality, as part of some context.[6]

(5) The mere thing is not given as that which will automatically authenticate just any interpretation. It is given as that which makes demands upon the interpreter to interpret well.

(6) At least some mere things are given as lasting a while. They are not evanescent. They call for an interpretation that embodies the expectation that the same interpretation will be called for again.

Though it is likely that additional intrinsic features of the given could be specified, enough material is now on hand to give a satisfactory response to the question concerning what a perceptual interpretation must involve if it is to count as a perceptual interpretation. On the one hand, no perceptual interpretation can either eliminate or stand in isolation from every other motivatedly possible interpretation. To the contrary, every interpretation is associable with some other interpretations, whether these other interpretations are elicited by the "same" or by a "different" given, or whether these other interpretations are

6. See in this connection, Heidegger, *Being and Time*, translated by John Macquarrie and Edward Robinson (New York: Harper and Row, 1962), pp. 114–21. Hereafter BT.

performed by the same author or by other authors. On the other hand, every mere thing is given both as public—as in conjunction with at least some other mere things—and as that which can withhold as well as grant authentications to interpretations.

Re II. The second of my three questions takes up the same topic as the first, but from another vantage point. Specifically, it develops the second side of the first question. It asks: What must the given be if two or more perceptual interpretations can be made of it? This question itself, like the first, has two parts: (a) What must the given be if two or more numerically distinct psychic processes of interpretation having the same noetic and noematic correlates can be effected with reference to it? and (b) What must the given be if two or more interpretations that differ either noetically or noematically or in both ways can be made of it?

Part (a) of this second question is concerned with what there is about the mere thing that makes it possible for a person to see the pine tree twice as the same. Note that the question is not: Why does one *think* or *believe* that one sees the pine tree twice as the same? *This* question can be taken as bearing on the identity of the interpreter. As such, it is of considerable importance but is tangential to the present topic. This question can also be taken, though, as a challenge to some purported actual sequence of identical perceptual interpretations. Taken this way, the question presupposes that some genuine sequence of this kind is both possible and recognizable and in fact sometimes occurs. It presupposes that at least some givens can permit and sustain such sequences. Just as all coins cannot be counterfeit and there still be coins, so all claims of such sequences cannot be spurious and there still be such claims.[7]

For a person genuinely to effect a sequence of identical perceptual interpretations in a sequence of noetic acts of the same kind—for example, in a sequence of visual perceivings—the mere thing must give itself as persisting as it has been and in its difference from other mere things for more than the specific moments of the special interpretive performances. This is not to say that no modifications of any sort have occurred in either the interpreter or the given. The same visually perceived skunk may be smelled differently. But it is to say that, whatever these modifications are, all the interpretations in the sequence are elicited by and seek confirmation from the same source, *interpreted as the same*.

Part (b) of the second question is somewhat more complicated. It asks what the given must be if different interpretations can be made of it.

---

7. See Gilbert Ryle, *Dilemmas* (Cambridge University Press, 1964), pp. 94–95.

When different interpretations are made of the given, these several interpretations may be either compatible with one another or not.

Consider, first, a set of interpretations none of which is reducible without remainder to another and all of which are compatible with one another. What must the given be for such a set to be both possible and possibly authenticable by the given? For such a set to be possible and authenticable, either the given must in principle have a definitive interpretation, an ideal interpretation, which *all* the interpretations in question here either approximate to a greater or lesser degree or in which they are all embraced eminently, or it must be such that it both permits and sustains multiple compatible interpretations without calling for a definitive interpretation.

The first alternative has been held, on one form or another, by many thinkers down through the ages. But is has several substantial weaknesses. First, the "ideal interpretation" could not logically be a member of the set of interpretations under consideration. Second, candidates for the title of "ideal interpretation" are obviously in short supply. But the basic objection to this alternative is that any purported ideal perceptual interpretation would not really be a perceptual interpretation. All perception is perspectival, both noetically and noematically. There is no ideal perspective. As a consequence, there is no phenomenal reason to claim that the mere thing admits of a perfect, ideal interpretation to which all other interpretations should conform.

The second alternative, then, is to be accepted. But to acknowledge that the mere thing both permits and sustains multiple compatible interpretations without calling for a definitive interpretation has a consequence of capital importance. If several compatible but fundamentally irreducible interpretations are both permitted and sustained by a particular given, then the character of the given is not exhaustively a function of any of the interpretations in question. The mere thing is not a bare particular. It is not, prior to interpretation, simply amorphous.

One reaches the same conclusion by considering several perceptual interpretations of the same given that are incompatible with one another *as interpretations of the same given*. Because the issue here is perception—a contingent, empirical affair—the ground of the incompatibility of the several interpretations cannot be exclusively syntactic or formal. How can two perceptual interpretations be found, *on empirical grounds*, to be incompatible? For this to occur, the mere thing must be sufficiently determinate and sufficiently accessible, independently of any specific interpretation, to invalidate some interpretations. That is, the mere thing cannot be given as so characterless that any and all interpretations are authenticated by it. Some perceptual interpretations are misinterpretations.

I conclude, then, that all perceptual interpretations respond to givens that are in some nontrivial sense determinate independently of interpretation. This does not mean, though, that the determinate quality of the mere thing can be definitively captured by some *ideal* interpretation. On the contrary, it belongs to the very character of the determinate mere thing that it be given as that which both sustains multiple interpretations irreducible to one another and that it can invalidate some other proposed interpretations.

These conclusions allow one to make sense of some key dimensions of the phenomena of "perceptual translation," of cultural or individual comparison, and of disagreement. By perceptual translation, I mean the shifting from one perceptual interpretation to another. Thus, one can shift from seeing a tree as a pine and not a spruce, to seeing it as a source of fuel, or as a shelter for birds. But one cannot see it as a thirst quencher for oneself or as an aid for poor eyesight. The given is determinate enough both to rule in some perceptual translations and to rule out others.[8] These excluded translations may indeed be merely formally or emptily possible. But there is no experiential evidence for claiming that anyone performs them.

In a cultural comparison, one examines the ways in which two different cultures deal with the same thing. For example, one can compare how two cultures deal with sexual intercourse. The given, the phenomenon of copulation, is perceptually interpreted in different ways. But one can compare interpretations only if the interpretations respond to the same given. Properly speaking, a perceptual interpretation dealing with copulation is not comparable to one dealing with cooking. That one can recognize which perceptual interpretations can sensefully be compared to one another requires, among other things, that the given in question be qualitatively marked off from other givens. These considerations are confirmed most vividly when the one making the comparison is oneself a practicing member of one of the cultures being compared.

Beyond the phenomena of cultural comparison and perceptual translation, there is the phenomenon of perceptual disagreement. Two persons report seeing the same thing in incompatible ways. The particular facet of this immensely intricate phenomenon that I want to single out here is one that bears upon the resolution of the disagreement. Confronted with disagreement, one can find it worthwhile to

---

8. There may be no limits to the range of translations that can be expressed in pure poetry, poetry playing only with words. But such poetry does not claim to report immediate perceptual interpretations.

"take another look" at the mere thing. Regardless of the outcome of taking this further look, it is both possible and senseful to do so in the interest of resolving the disagreement. This can be the case only if the given itself is already sufficiently determinate to serve as a guide to appropriate interpretation.

The occurrence of misinterpretations and of disagreements, even if they are subsequently resolved, leads to the third of my questions — namely, what test or tests can be used to determine the worth of an interpretation?

Re III. This question focuses upon two characteristics of interpretation that were noted in dealing with question I. There I pointed out that every interpretation appeals to something other than itself for confirmation and that the mere thing is that which not only instigates the interpretation but also somehow authenticates it.

Ballard says the perceptual interpretations are tested against other perceptual interpretations that have survived in competition or cooperation with still other "interpreted possibilities." This is correct as far as it goes. But it is either incomplete or vague.

Ballard, as mentioned above, distinguishes between involuntary and reflective interpretation. Involuntary interpretation, he says,

> embraces ways of locating the presented in space and time which are engrained in the nervous system, as well as identifying objects, their use, and their meaning which are dictated by cultural patterns of response and action and which in virtue of long use have become second nature (MT, p. 17).

What Ballard calls involuntary interpretation in fact involves two distinct elements — namely, the automatic or, as I would prefer to call it, the spontaneous, and the habitual. Both may be prereflective. And they may in fact be *partially* inseparable. But they are two; not one. If the habitual is "second nature," then the automatic is "first nature." What transpires automatically and what transpires habitually transpire in different ways.

It is, of course, permissible to call both of them interpretations. But one must keep the equivocation in mind. To avoid this problem, I prefer not to speak of the automatic response as an interpretation. This in no way prevents me from acknowledging that every given involves a recipient, a dative of manifestation. Mere things are not inaccessible things-in-themselves. They are *perceived* mere things.

The force of my insistence upon the distinction between automatic and habitual responses to perceptual givens becomes clearer when one considers both of these in connection with reflective interpretation. Assume that "There are pines in the yard" reports my habitually registered perception of the state of affairs prevailing in my yard.[9] Then suppose two other persons, one of whom says to me, "I see that there are both white and longleaf pines in the yard," and the other, "I see that there are both pines and oaks in the yard." I now begin to reflect. Part of the reflection consists in determining whether the three reports are logically compatible. But part of the reflection requires that I look again at the yard. This look is a looking past my habitual interpretation toward my "first nature" or automatic reception of the mere thing. This reception may indeed not be a full-fledged response until it is interpreted. But the given is not received as that which is fully fixed in a specific habitual or reflective interpretation.

But let me return to the example. Suppose I find, in looking again, that there is a basis, previously not noted by me, for distinguishing between white and longleaf pines, but that I cannot see anything I am prepared to call an oak. What I find here in reflection is that my habitual interpretation is both confirmed and refined, that one of my partners' interpretation is confirmed as it stands and that the other partner's report is partially confirmed and partially disconfirmed.

Of course this need not be the end of the matter. The "oak-seer" may well press the point. Or the refinement may be regarded as trivial. But what must be noticed here is that another look, another taking in of the mere thing, was intrinsically ingredient to the full assessment of the three perceptual interpretations in question. There is, as I acknowledged earlier, no definitive look, no nonperspectival perceiving. Every habitual and voluntary or reflective interpretation is tested *in part* by being referred to the mere thing.[10]

This means that a perceptual interpretation is tested to determine whether it is true to the given. The test involves a reobserving or receiving of the mere thing to determine whether its character permits and sustains the proposed interpretation. Of course, if this test is to have a chance of being effective, the mere thing looked at again must be recognized as, in relevant respects, the same thing. Ballard himself, following Husserl, has nicely emphasized that to claim to grasp an empirical truth as true is to claim *to see* the correspondence between a concept, image or interpretive principle and the object in question

9. See Robert Sokolowski, *Husserlian Meditations* (Evanston: Northwestern University Press, 1974), pp. 116–23 on reports and registrations.

10. The issue of the kind of testing that goes on between what Ballard calls the habitual and the voluntary interpretations is more complicated than either he or I have suggested. If traditional interpretations are included within the scope of the habitual, then it is the case that new, voluntary interpretations are tested by the traditional ones. The testings, though, are different. This complex matter cannot be tacked here. But for some pertinent considerations, see my "Discourse, Silence, and Tradition," in *The Review of Metaphysics*, Vol. XXXII, No. 3, pp.437-451.

(MT, pp. 90–96). But truth need not require judgment. Perceptual interpretations, too, can be true. They are true when they are seen to be permitted and sustained by the character of the given, by the mere thing that presents itself for interpretation (BT, p. 57).

Notice that even if part of the testing of an interpretation involves looking at the given multiple looks are involved. And there are no absolutely privileged looks. Nonetheless, there is reason to distinguish "initial" sightings from resightings. The character of the given is presented in each of these in a different way. In the initial sighting, the mere thing is met as an occasion for a response or interpretation. In the resightings it is seen as both occasion and criterion for a response. The upshot of the possibility of resighting as distinct from initial sighting is that interpretations cannot be said necessarily to block access to the given. Rather they can intensify and focus the resightings of the given.

Notice, too, that further looks are always in order. There is no "last" look. Through the looking again, the truth of a perceptual interpretation can indeed by ascertained. But it is and is perceptually recognizable as not being the *whole* truth about the character of the mere thing in question. There is no such thing as a perceptual interpretation that is the whole truth.

The responses to the three questions with which I have dealt furnish the warrant for the two connected claims I have made about the character of the mere thing. First, the character of the mere thing is perceptually grasped as that which allows and sustains a delimited range of actual and motivatedly possible true perceptual interpretations. Second, the character of the mere thing is not grasped in a single perceptual performance but is grasped, though not exhaustively, through the interplay of multiple interpretations and viewings or receptions of the mere thing.[11]

There are several nontrivial implications of these claims that also find support in the descriptions I have offered. First, the character of the given can be reported indirectly, but not directly, in words. Each report directly expresses some specific interpretation of the mere thing. To the extent that the interpretation it reports is found to be sustained by the given, the report contributes to marking out the range of the sustainable interpretations of the given. That range is determined by the character of the mere thing.

Second, though the range of interpretations that the given can sustain is finite, there is no way to determine *a priori* the specific limits

11. It should be noted that nothing in my account commits me to claiming that I can determine unequivocally and definitively how many or how many kinds of mere things there are. I also think that my account is, for the most part, compatible with Heidegger's treatment of thing and world in *Being and Time*.

of the range. The range becomes manifest only through the historical interplay of sightings and interpretations. Though some lines of interpretation may be sufficiently disconfirmed to be abandoned, the scope of motivatedly possible confirmable lines of interpretation only appears in the course of proposing and testing interpretations.

The upshot of the position that I have presented here is that even though there is not definitive and exhaustive interpretation of the mere thing, the mere thing is no Kantian thing-in-itself. Its character is accessible to perception but is always perceived in an interpretation. Thus in perceptual experience there is still a firm foundation for raising and settling the question of the correctness of the interpretation. To interpret properly one must be rightly guided by the given.[12] To interpret well is to function well with reference to the mere thing. To do so one must align himself, and remain aligned, with the given. Such aligning without the functioning, the interpreting, is sterile. The functioning without the alignment is reckless.

Though I do not claim to have fully answered the question about the character of the mere thing that is perceptually interpreted, I have, I believe, shown some of the elements that a comprehensive answer must acknowledge and encompass.

12. What I say about the call of the mere thing to which we respond is evidently akin to what Heidegger says about the call of conscience. He says: "Yet what the call discloses is unequivocal, even though it may undergo a different interpretation in the individual *Dasein* in accordance with its own possibilities of understanding. While the content of the call is seemingly indefinite, the *direction it takes* is a sure one and is not to be overlooked" (BT, p. 318). See also what he says about anticipating the indefinite certainty of death (BT, p. 310). If *Dasein* is fundamentally disclosive, then it is not surprising that the kind of call to which it responds in disclosing the world is structurally similar to that to which it responds in disclosing its own kind of Being—namely, a call that gives a sure direction while leaving room for different interpretations.

Alexander von Schoenborn

13/*Heidegger's Articulation of Falling*

Parsing Heidegger has its difficulties. But these pale in the light of a philosopher's task of understanding and assessing both Heidegger's philosophical claims and the concepts fashioned in and for the making of these claims. From among such concepts, that of falling has increasingly struck me as one of the most obscure in Heidegger's arsenal. Such obscurity would not be of major import—no philosopher wholly keeps the promise of his or her work—were not this concept both central to any coherent statement of Heidegger's major claims in *Sein und Zeit*[1] and of independent philosophical importance in its own right.

I shall therefore first exhibit this putative importance of the concept of falling in both of the respects just mentioned, especially the latter. In this connection I shall show that other philosophers, notably Plato and Kant, have sought to determine the same phenomenon that Heidegger seeks to exhibit by means of his concept of falling and that there are reasons for preferring Heidegger's account, if its problematic aspects can be resolved. I shall then discriminate and discuss some of the aporiae that this Heideggerian concept harbors. This aporetic discussion will be guided by a preview of the phenomenon at issue under non-Heideggerian descriptions obtained in the initial part of this paper.

Thus the dual task of the present paper—exhibiting the import of Heidegger's concept of falling and pinpointing some of its difficulties

Edward G. Ballard was once my doctoral mentor. He is my teacher still and my friend as well. I am deeply grateful to him for having given of himself in so many ways. By means of the present essay I would like to thank him for one of these: fostering a sense of patience as a philosophical virtue.

1. I must presuppose in this paper some familiarity on the reader's part with Heidegger's philosophical work and the terminology in which it is couched.

—is a modest one: doing some of the preliminary work required if the concept at issue is subsequently to be clarified adequately.

I have remarked that "falling" plays an important role within Heidegger's philosophy because the concept thus expressed is utilized by him in major claims developed in *Being and Time*. Thus clarity in regard to this concept is essential for a faithful and coherent understanding and appropriating of these claims. This sort of importance can be demonstrated quickly on a verbal and textual level by recalling Heidegger's summation of what he has tried to accomplish in the published portion of *Being and Time*:

> The task in our considerations thus far has been to interpret in an existential-ontological manner the *primordial whole* of factical *Dasein* in regard to the possibilities of authentic and inauthentic existing in terms of *the basis* of this whole. Temporality has manifested itself as this basis and thus as the ontological meaning [*Seinssinn*] of care.[2]

This "primordial whole," *Dasein's* Being as care, has "falling" as one of its essential determinations:

> *Dasein's* Being is care. It comprises in itself facticity (thrownness), existence (projection), and falling (SZ, p. 284).
> These existential determinations do not belong to a composite as pieces, one of which might sometimes be missing. Instead, there is interwoven a primordial connection which makes up that totality of the structural whole which we are seeking (SZ, p. 191).

Moreover—and I here point ahead to one of the problematic aspects of the concept of falling—this concept plays a crucial role at yet another place in Heidegger's summation of what he has tried to accomplish. He has sought to interpret that "primordial whole," which I have discussed thus far, "in regard to the possibilities of authentic and inauthentic existing." When he first subjects the phenomenon he terms "falling" to thematic analysis, Heidegger points out that "what we called the inauthenticity of *Dasein* is now more precisely determined by means of the interpretation of falling" (SZ, pp. 175–76).

In short, even these few textual references suffice to make my point: becoming clear about the concept in question is essential for a faithful and coherent understanding of *Being and Time*. Of course this only

---

2. Martin Heidegger, *Sein und Zeit* (Tübingen: Niemeyer, 1957), p. 436; translated by John Macquarrie and Edward Robinson, *Being and Time* (New York: Harper & Row, 1962). Inasmuch as my translations from Heidegger's *magnum opus* frequently differ from those in the published English version, all subsequent references to this work will be made in terms of the German pagination (referenced in the margins of the English edition). Hereafter SZ.

establishes that the clarification of "falling" is important to anyone seeking to understand Heidegger's work. But because not everyone in the philosophic community seems impelled by this desideratum, I want to suggest that the concept in question is of some independent philosophical importance as well.

The simplest way of exhibiting such independent philosophical importance is to claim that what Heidegger terms "falling" is a phenomenon also seen by other major thinkers, but insufficiently grasped and determined by them in spite of its recognized importance. But given the differences, between philosophers, of terminology, conceptual articulation and interpretive purview, such a claim requires some prior orientation and directions as to where to look. Let me therefore meet this requirement before warranting the claim just made.

In his self-interpretive *Letter on Humanism*, Heidegger states that "the meaning of the term 'falling' in *Being and Time* is the forgetting of the truth of Being in favor of the impact of beings unconsidered in their nature."[3] Inasmuch as Heidegger defines philosophy as an explicit and recollective concern on behalf of that truth of Being,[4] the remark just cited suggests looking to those thinkers who take philosophy to be a departure from the manner and context of ordinary living and who see in this living not just a prephilosophic where-from but a certain animus or resistance toward that departure.

The remark thus suggests looking primarily to diverse forms of transcendental philosophy and to such practitioners as Plato, Kant, Hegel and Husserl. I will therefore turn to the first two of these thinkers—Plato and Kant are not only the most widely known but also, in many respects, the most divergent of these philosophers—in order to warrant the claim that what Heidegger terms "falling" is a phenomenon also seen by other major thinkers, but insufficiently grasped and determined by them in spite of its recognized importance.

Plato: Falling is Forgetting

Perhaps no excerpt from a philosopher's writings is as well known as Plato's "Myth of the Cave" with its depiction of our ordinary lives as imprisonment in a cave, fettered from infancy, and of education as our attempt to emancipate ourselves from our chains. How do we come to be so imprisoned and what constitutes our chains? It is in Plato's partial

---

3. Martin Heidegger, *Über den Humanismus* (Frankfurt: Klostermann, 1947), p. 21: "*Das Vergessen der Wahrheit des Seins zugunsten des Andrangs des im Wesen unbedachten Seienden. . . .*"

4. Martin Heidegger, *Kant und das Problem der Metaphysik* (Frankfurt: Klostermann, 1951), pp. 210–11; cf. SZ, p. 38.

answer to this question that we find an analogue to Heidegger's concept of "falling."

According to Plato, the human being is by nature, in its innermost and ownmost possibility, a light-gazer, a friend of the Forms, an acquaintance with the Ideas—that is, with Being. By this Plato does not merely mean that we more fully become ourselves insofar as we intentionally acquaint ourselves with Being by asking about it, by philosophizing. He means primarily that the human being *qua* human is always already acquainted with Being. But Plato also insists that we begin our lives by forgetting Being and hence by forgetting our nature as a relatedness with Being.

On Plato's view, this forgetting is primarily a function of our embodiment, whereby the "soul" is dragged into the domain of the changing things around us. Moving here wholly within the ordinary understanding of time, Plato construes this embodiment as in each case an occurrence at a determinate point of time. Because the forgetting of Being is said to occur at this point, the familiarity with Being is mythically pushed into a prior existence of the "soul."

Plato clearly recognizes that more is at issue here than such a *fait accompli* that would make us simply the victim of our ontological constitution. For when elsewhere, in the *Phaedo*, he takes up the metaphor of imprisonment in relation to our embodiment, he writes:

> Every seeker after wisdom knows that up to the time when philosophy takes it over, his soul is a helpless prisoner, chained hand and foot in the body, compelled to view reality not directly but only through its prison bars, and wallowing in utter ignorance. And philosophy can see that the imprisonment is ingeniously effected by the prisoner's own active desire, which makes him first accessory to his own confinement.[5]

In the pages immediately preceding the remarks just cited, Plato elaborates on this "active desire." The "soul" that has not "pursued philosophy in the right way and really practiced how to face death easily" becomes too attached to the body. In this process, the "soul" is "so beguiled by the body and its passions and pleasures that nothing seems real to it but those physical things which can be touched and seen. . . ." Concurrently, it is "accustomed to hate and fear and avoid what is invisible and hidden from our eyes, but intelligible and comprehensible by philosophy."[6]

But let me return to the Myth of the Cave and Plato's account of what

---

5. Plato, *Phaedo*, 82d–83a, in Edith Hamilton and Huntington Cairns, ed., *The Collected Dialogues of Plato* (New York: Pantheon, 1961), p. 66.

6. *Phaedo*, 83e–81c; *Collected Dialogues*, p. 64.

the forgetting of Being implies. The most obvious consequence is that we neither are ourselves nor know ourselves. Moreover, because anything else can also only be known insofar as it is apprehended in its Idea, we lack, because of our forgetting, the ultimate standard for what really exists and what can truly be said. That we spontaneously address whatever presents itself—the shadows on our cave's wall—as "what is" and as "the true" indicates that the forgetting of Being is never wholly achieved. But the very fact that it is the shadows that are so addressed indicates that the forgetting is sufficient to make us oblivious to the contrasts between reality and semblance, truth and untruth. When these contrasts perforce do emerge—when, in Plato's myth, the prisoner is made to stand up and turn around—they are misconstrued, the real being taken as the illusory, the illusory as the real.

In short, it is not merely the case, as Plato's remarks in the *Phaedo* might suggest, that Being is forgotten in favor of the impact of beings. Rather, the latter as unconsidered in their nature become indistinguishable from their mere appearances. Hence the distinctions between Being and beings and between truth and untruth relative to each become extinguished. Life in the cave is therefore essentially characterized by ambiguity, hearsay and a lust for novel shadows. Such a life is not only a consequence of the forgetting of Being but in turn furthers and intensifies that forgetting, making the persons living it first accessory to their own confinement.

The main content of the Myth of the Cave is, of course, a model of *paideia*, of the possible way of striving to emancipate ourselves from the condition just described. Let me allude briefly to some of the points Plato makes here insofar as they bear on the account I have just given.

The first attempt at emancipation, occurring wholly within the cave, fails. It fails not only because the need for habituation is not taken into account, but because even in regard to the truth of things the contrasts between the real and the illusory, the true and the untrue, require for their right demarcation the explicit grasp of the Ideas, of Being. Hence emancipation can succeed only by meeting this requirement.

Meeting this requirement takes the form of recollecting Being. This recollection is necessarily violent: it involves changing the habits of a lifetime and, more radically, arresting that "active desire" that makes us responsible for our imprisonment. Though Plato does not say so in the Myth of the Cave, it is wonder that is this arresting factor and thus constitutes the origin of philosophy.[7] To the extent that this violence of arrest and rehabilitation is endured and the recollection of Being succeeds, human beings become themselves—that is, attain their nature.

7. Plato, *Theaetetus*, 155d; *Collected Dialogues*, p. 860.

That Heidegger wishes to capture this same phenomenon of our imprisonment and self-imprisonment is clear from the mere textual fact that his account of falling matches that of Plato point by point. I have already cited him to the effect that "the meaning of the term 'falling' in *Being and Time* is the forgetting of the truth of Being in favor of the impact of beings unconsidered in their nature." This forgetting is *ipso facto* a forgetting of *Dasein's* own Being. For *"Dasein* is ontically distinctive in that it *is* ontological" — that is, "understanding of Being is itself a determination of *Dasein's* Being" (SZ, p. 12).

As this process of forgetting, falling is a "movement" (SZ, p. 180). This movement "manifests the throwing and movement characteristic of the thrownness" of *Dasein* (SZ, p. 179). The throwness of *Dasein* consists in "its being delivered over to itself as an entity"[8] in such a way as "to have to be" that entity (SZ, pp. 134–35). This "being delivered over" is alternately expressed by Heidegger as "being taken in by what-is" in the sense of "gaining a foothold in what-is".[9]

This ongoing process is the "throw" in which *Dasein* remains as long as it exists (SZ, p. 179). Unless "caught" or arrested, however, throw or movement is also a being taken in by what-is in the further sense of being captivated by or absorbed in what-is (SZ, p. 348). Such being absorbed in what-is is falling (SZ, p. 175; cf. p. 139).

> Owing to being absorbed in, losing itself in, what-is — both in itself, in the *Dasein*, as well as in the entities which *Dasein* is not — *Dasein* knows nothing of the fact that it has already understood Being. The factically existing *Dasein* has forgotten this *prius*.[10]

But, as Plato already observed, this forgetting is not just a case of being victimized by one's ontological constitution. By allowing this movement to proceed unchecked, *Dasein* evades confrontation with the negativity pervading its Being.

This evasion is primarily a "flight" in the face of *Dasein's* mortality (SZ, p. 254). In this flight, moreover, *Dasein* seeks to "mask" that which it flees (SZ, p. 256). As the terms "flight" and "mask" already suggest, *Dasein* colludes with the tendency in its Being that I have been discussing.[11] Through this collusion, falling is intensified as "an increasing forgetting" (SZ, p. 347).

8. *Kant und das Problem der Metaphysik*, p. 206.
9. Martin Heidegger, *Vom Wesen des Grundes* (Frankfurt: Klostermann, 1955), p. 45: *"von Seiendem eingenommen," "im Seienden Boden genommen."*
10. Heidegger, *Die Grundprobleme der Phänomenologie* (Frankfurt: Klostermann, 1975), p. 463.
11. For Heidegger's own allusion to these passive and active aspects of falling, see his *Was ist Metaphysik?* (Frankfurt: Klostermann, 1960), p. 36.

"Because *Dasein* is essentially falling, its state of Being is such that it is in 'untruth' " (SZ, p. 222). "Untruth" in this remark has to be taken, I would suggest, as a formalization.[12] When deformalized, the term here means primarily ontological untruth (though not falsehood) and secondarily, as a consequence, ontic untruth. Because *Dasein* forgets Being, lets it be hidden, it lacks the appropriate standard for discerning and explicitly distinguishing the truth and untruth of what-is. The result is not precisely ontic untruth. Rather, the result is that it is "no longer decidable what is disclosed in genuine understanding and what is not" (SZ, p. 173):

> Everything looks as if it were genuinely understood, genuinely appropriated and said, though at bottom it is not; or else it does not look so, and yet at bottom it is (SZ, p. 173).

"This ambiguity is always tossing to curiosity that which it seeks; and it gives hearsay the semblance of deciding everything" (SZ, p. 174):

> Idle talk, curiosity and ambiguity characterize the way in which, in an everyday manner, *Dasein* is its "there" — the disclosedness of Being-in-the-world. As definite existential characteristics, these are not present-at-hand in *Dasein*, but help to make up its Being. In these, and in the way they are interconnected in their Being, there is revealed a basic kind of Being which belongs to everydayness; we call this the *"falling"* of *Dasein* (SZ, p. 176).

This everydayness of *Dasein* — "how it is initially and for the most part" (SZ, p. 16) — is therefore characterized by Heidegger as "that mode of Being of man which essentially aims at holding *Dasein* and its understanding of Being — that is, primordial finitude, in forgottenness"[13]

Given the Platonic account I sketched earlier, it is clear that Heidegger's account of falling corresponds to it point by point. This correspondence continues through the model of *paideia*. Heidegger distinguishes three distinct levels or states — everydayness, positive science, and philosophy — with the ordering principle being the functioning of ontological truth — that is, the relative overtness of the understanding of Being.[14] Explicating this understanding of Being takes the form of recollection,[15] and is necessarily violent in running counter to the interpretive tendencies of everydayness (SZ, pp. 315 and 327). This explicative violence has the ground of its possibility in the deeper,

---

12. For an analog, see SZ, p. 35.
13. *Kant und das Problem*, p. 211.
14. For further detail on this point, see my "Heideggerian Everydayness," in *Southwestern Journal of Philosophy*, vol. 3, no. 3.
15. *Kant und das Problem*, p. 211.

existential violence of a mood—dread—that arrests *Dasein's* falling self-construal (SZ, p. 187).

The recollection of Being is explicit transcendence. Because transcendence is the "basic constitution" of *Dasein*,[16] the latter thus attains to its "nature" in becoming the questioning of Being.

I have now completed establishing the correspondence of Heidegger's account of falling with that of Plato. I have spent what may seem an inordinate amount of time and effort on this mapping. I have done so because an aporetic discussion, to be fruitful, requires some prior familiarity with the phenomenon at issue. Plato's account, both simpler than Heidegger's and familiar to all of us, serves to meet the need for a preview and overview of the phenomenon of falling under a non-Heideggerian description.

Heidegger: The Plenary Openness

This still leaves the crucial question, Given the similarities adduced, why should Heidegger's account be preferred? Various sorts of reasons can here be offered; I will content myself with the following three.

First, Plato's account of falling takes the form largely of either episodic remarks or "likely stories." In contrast, Heidegger's analysis of falling, as already suggested by my initial remarks on the important role of the concept of falling in *Being and Time*, is much more elaborate, extending far beyond the various aspects mentioned thus far in this paper. Falling is subjected to thematic analysis both in Heidegger's *magnum opus* and in others of his works rather than being, so to speak, glimpsed in passing. Heidegger's account is, as he himself remarks in reference to this context, "spoken without the myth of the soul."[17] In short, the first reason is that Heidegger's analysis promises a genuinely philosophical understanding of the phenomenon of falling in a way that Plato's account does not and indeed cannot.

My second and third reasons for preferring Heidegger's account are substantive. Put in critical form, they amount to the charges that Plato's account is flawed by operating within the ordinary understanding of time and by an ontology that, instead of interrogating the meaning of Being, tacitly equates it with constant presence. The issues thus raised—that of the genesis of time and that of the meaning of Being—are broader and deeper than that of an adequate explication of falling but bear directly on this explication.

In summarizing Plato's account of falling or imprisonment, I fo-

16. *Vom Wesen des Grundes*, p. 22.
17. *Grundprobleme der Phänomenologie*, p. 465.

cused primarily on two factors: the ontological constitution of concrete embodied persons and the active desire of most such persons to collude with the dynamic thrust of that constitution. Let me focus on each of these factors in turn, the first in regard to time, the second in regard to the meaning of Being.

Being the brilliant phenomenologist he is, Plato notices that concrete or factic human existence has as its *a priori* a certain "always already": the always already of being embodied and in the midst of things; the always already of familiarity with the Ideas as condition of specifically human embodiment; the always already of the Ideas, together with our being familiar with them, having become hidden; and even the always already of the possibility of having "really practiced how to face death easily."

Plato recognizes further that this "always already" has a temporal sense. But he then interprets this sense in terms of time as ordinarily construed, so that whatever has this character is interpreted as past, as something that was or happened at a determinate point of time now passed. It is clearly this interpretation that forces Plato to have recourse to the myth of the "soul's" preexistence. Such further Platonic doctrines as the entitative status of "soul," the resulting ontological dualism constitutive of persons, facing death as preparing for a future separation of the "soul" from its temporary housing, and the immortality of the "soul," are either consequences of or buttressed by this recourse.

By way of contrast, Heidegger is able both to demonstrate several modes of temporal ordering[18] and to exhibit the genesis of that mode that is time as ordinarily understood from out of time as the temporality of human existence (SZ, pp. 420–27). This allows him to take up that "always already" character discerned by Plato, but to interpret it as the existential temporal meaning of the thrownness of human existence. This in turn makes it possible to see the "always already" as a character not of what and of how *Dasein* was but of how it is—it is as having been—"as long" as it is (SZ, p. 328).

In particular reference now to the problem of falling, this means that Heidegger can give an account "without the myth of the soul." I take this cryptic disclaimer to mean that there is no need for recourse to a preexisting "soul" entity or to the ontological dualism this implies for the Being of persons. This philosophic gain is a compelling reason for preferring Heidegger's account.

There is some reason to think that Plato may in fact have glimpsed time *qua* human temporalizing.[19] But even if this is the case, this

---

18. For the clearest such demonstration, see Heidegger's *Grundprobleme der Phänomenologie*, pp. 324–88.

19. For example, see the tantalizing but cryptic remark in Plato's *Theaetetus*, 186b; *Collected Dialogues*, p. 891.

glimpse remained merely that. The reason for this can be found in Plato's ontology. Let me very briefly turn to the latter in connection with that second key feature—"active desire"—of falling as described by Plato.

Plato's ontology, as indeed Greek thought generally, is dominated by two models: things as paradigmatic for what-is and seeing as paradigmatic for understanding. Both models draw their persuasiveness from a largely tacit understanding of Being as constant presence. Thus the understanding of Being that distinguishes human beings from other things is interpreted as a noncorporeal seeing, *qua* objective having in front of oneself, of Being *qua* constant *idea, eidos* or *morphe*.

This spectator view, when applied to humankind's understanding of its own Being, in which the understanding of all other modes of Being is rooted, precludes an adequate interpretation of human existence as that "to be [*Zu-sein*]" that it is *Dasein's* task not to note but at any moment to accomplish as its ownmost possibility (SZ, p. 42). More specifically, the performative and projective character of man's Being cannot be properly and conceptually articulated. And to the extent that this character is "seen," as it is by Aristotle especially, it is grounded in the ousiological structure of Being characteristic of things.

The point of these general remarks, as they bear on Plato's "active desire," is that the meaning of "active" remains perforce underdeveloped. Plato's account speaks largely in a passive voice: in terms of a being dragged, being captivated or being beguiled. Indeed, it is the dominance of this voice, the thrown rather than the projective aspect of human existence, that accounts for the prominence of that temporal "always already" that I discussed in my previous point.

Further implications can be drawn concerning the contrasting form of life that has managed to still or arrest falling's active desire. But enough! I think I have sufficiently shown why Heidegger's account of falling is to be preferred and thus have partially warranted the importance I have claimed for this account.

Kant: Falling is Trivializing

Such importance can, as I have suggested, also be exhibited through reference to the work of Kant. My recourse to Kant, not having to perform the additional task of providing a preview, will be brief. I simply want to show that this thinker, though not formulating his problematic in terms of Being, nevertheless sees that same phenomenon of falling as have Plato and Heidegger. And by noting the sketchy and unsatisfactory nature of Kant's pertinent account, I point again to the importance of Heidegger's treatment of falling.

For the sake of brevity, I will limit my remarks to the *Critique of Pure*

Reason. Where in this work might one expect Kant's discussion of this phenomenon? Using Plato's Myth of the Cave as a guide, one would expect this discussion where what is at issue is the awakening of philosophy. Because Kant states that he was "awakened from dogmatic slumber" by the "antinomy of pure reason"[20] and that the latter serves to awaken philosophy itself from its dogmatic slumber,[21] let me turn to the section that bears this title in the first *Critique*.

The section entitled "The Antinomy of Pure Reason" is a part of the "Transcendental Dialectic" — that is, a part of that part of the *Critique* in which Kant is concerned with diagnosing the "transcendental illusion" that prompts the erection of transcendent principles.[22] This illusion is a necessary one, in the sense that it "does not cease even after it has been detected and its invalidity clearly revealed by transcendental criticism.[23] It is a natural illusion,

> not one in which a bungler might entangle himself through lack of knowledge, or one which some sophist has artificially invented to confuse thinking people, but one inseparable from human reason, and which, even after its deceptiveness has been exposed, will not cease to play tricks with reason and continually entrap it into momentary aberrations ever and again calling for correction.[24]

What prompts this illusion, inseparable from human reason? To be concrete let me focus on one of the Antinomies. In the Third Antinomy, for example, we watch Reason bring to bear its principle:

> If the conditioned is given, the entire sum of conditions, and consequently the absolutely unconditioned (through which alone the conditioned has been possible) is also given.[25]

It becomes clear that the transcendental illusion stems from failure to distinguish between the analytic logical relation of "conditioned" and "condition," between the empirical relation of a given appearance to the givenness of its cause, and between the transcendental relation of appearance and thing in itself.[26] The resulting deceptiveness of both thesis and antithesis, as precritically stated, is "a quite natural illusion of

---

20. Immanuel Kant, Letter to Garve, September 21, 1798, cited in Heinz Heimsoeth, *Tranzendentale Dialektik* (Berlin: de Gruyter, 1967), vol. 2, p. 199, n. 1.

21. Immanuel Kant, *Prolegomena to Any Future Metaphysics* (Indianapolis: Library of Liberal Arts, 1950), p. 86.

22. Immanuel Kant, *Critique of Pure Reason*, translated by Norman Kemp Smith (New York: St. Martin's, 1961), p. 298.

23. *Critique of Pure Reason*, p. 299.

24. *Critique of Pure Reason*, p. 300.

25. *Critique of Pure Reason*, p. 386.

26. *Critique of Pure Reason*, pp. 443–45.

common sense [*der gemeinen Vernunft*]," which, in particular, finds it "natural to regard appearances as things in themselves."[27] It is because transcendental criticism uncovers the differences between appearances and things in themselves that it is able to resolve the Antinomies, thereby providing an indirect proof of the ideality of space and time[28] and thus constituting itself as transcendental idealism.

What Kant seems to be saying is that human reason has a natural tendency to turn into common sense, thereby making itself common in the sense of vulgarizing itself by uprooting and trivializing itself. This tendency, which can be arrested but not eradicated, consists in an extinction of distinctions implicitly already drawn. The distinctions in question are primarily those of a transcendental character.

It is not necessary to go on and substitute "ontological" for "transcendental"—as Heidegger does on the basis of Kantian suggestions —to recognize that what Kant has in view here is the phenomenon of falling. But it is also hardly necessary to note that Kant's occasional remarks not only do not take us very far toward an understanding of this phenomenon, but lag behind what Plato already accomplished. There is no mention of the already pretheoretic detachment that can be effected by mood and the role of moods generally in both falling and its possible counter is neglected. There is no account of what prompts reason to make itself common. Perhaps it was his confidence in the sufficiency of the discipline of enlightened criticism that made a deeper and fuller account of falling seem unnecessary.

Obstacles to Appropriation

I have now completed the first of the two tasks of this paper. Throughout this discussion, I have presupposed that Heidegger's concept can be coherently understood and genuinely appropriated. But there are obstacles, difficulties, in Heidegger's account that stand in the way of such appropriation. A fruitful discussion of these requires a preview (and overview) of the phenomenon of falling under a non-Heideggerian description. My recourse to Plato's and Kant's accounts was intended to meet this requirement. In particular, I recalled Plato's account in some detail. And I documented the correspondence of this account with that of Heidegger sufficiently to establish the viability of this preview. With this preview before us, let me now turn to the aporiae harbored by Heidegger's concept of falling.

Given the intense scrutiny to which Heidegger's work has been subjected, these difficulties obviously have been noticed either individually or even in their interconnection. And one can point to some

27. *Critique of Pure Reason*, p. 445.
28. *Critique of Pure Reason*, pp. 448–49.

valiant attempts at clarification and resolution, notably by Ernst Tugendhat in his *Der Wahrheitsbegriff bei Husserl und Heidegger*[29] and by Michael E. Zimmerman in his "On Discriminating Everydayness, Unownedness, and Falling in *Being and Time*."[30] But however valiant, these attempts cannot be said to have been successful. Hence the task remains of identifying and discussing the difficulties at issue until they are either resolved or shown to be insolvable.

The difficulties concern the relations between the concept of falling and certain other concepts that seem to be used either synonymously or as partial explications and, as so used, seem to produce incompatible characterizations. Put in the form of key problematic phrases, the difficulties concern the relations between "falling" and "Being-in-untruth," "Being-alongside," "inauthenticity" and "everydayness."

Let me begin with Heidegger's characterization of falling as "the forgetting of the truth of Being." Because this remark is taken from *Über den Humanismus*, it opens the possibility that it represents one of Heidegger's post-*Kehre* reinterpretations of his earlier work in *Sein und Zeit*. To obviate this possibility, I indicated earlier that he already viewed falling in this way at the time of the publication of the latter work.[31] But I know of no secondary work that has successfully managed to integrate this characterization with those others found in Heidegger's *magnum opus*.

The general tendency in the secondary literature is to mention this characterization *qua Seinsvergessenheit*, but then to orient the actual explication of the concept of falling wholly in terms of *Dasein's* irresoluteness—that is, in terms of a privative form of disclosedness.[32] Disclosedness, however, is existentiell truth and thus a form of ontic truth.[33] And though all ontic truth has its preontological dimension, the ontological difference, here in its veridical aspect, must nevertheless by maintained. On the other hand, those who have not followed the general tendency just discussed and, instead, have sought to bring Heidegger's self-interpretive characterization of falling front and center seem to lose hold of the integrity of *Dasein's* care-structure.[34]

Heidegger has urged that all concrete analyses in *Being and Time* be assessed "solely in the direction of the enabling [conditions: *die Ermög-*

---

29. Ernst Tugendhat, *Der Wahrheitsbegriff bei Husserl und Heidegger* (Berlin: de Gruyter, 1967), pp. 310–27.
30. Michael E. Zimmerman, "On Discriminating Everydayness, Unownedness, and Falling in *Being and Time*," in *Research in Phenomenology* 5 (1975) 109–27.
31. It is to be recalled that the lectures comprising *Grundprobleme der Phänomenologie* were given immediately following the publication of *Sein und Zeit*.
32. For example, see the two studies mentioned in notes 29 and 30, above.
33. *Vom Wesen des Grundes*, p. 13.
34. For example, see William J. Richardson, SJ, "Heidegger's Weg durch die Phänomenologie zum Seinsdenken," in *Philosophisches Jahrbuch* (Sonderdruck, 1965), p. 391.

lichung] of the question of Being."[35] It is in terms of this direction that I began this paper, with the surmise that the concept of falling is intended to direct attention to human living insofar as it is non- or even anti-philosophical. Heidegger has drawn attention to the crucial role that the circular structure of existence plays in the movement of the self-constitution of philosophy (SZ, p. 315). And his remarks in this connection have been ably interpreted and developed.[36] But the import of this same circular structure for the constitution of antiphilosophy, for falling as a preeminent *Vollzugsform* of Being-in-the-world,[37] has been relatively ignored.

What would not ignoring this structure mean? Projecting itself primarily upon its Being-alongside, an ontic manifest-making, *Dasein* is enthralled—truth binds *eo ipso*—by entities within the world in such a way as to understand itself in terms of them. This self-entanglement is made possible by *Seinsvergessenheit* or ontological untruth. This is the sole extent—because merely setting out a correlate to Plato's account—to which I earlier deformalized "untruth" in Heidegger's dictum: "Because *Dasein* is essentially falling, its state of Being is such that it is in 'untruth' " (SZ, p. 222). But it is now necessary to recognize that ontological untruth in turn has a foundation.[38]

This foundation is existentiell untruth *qua Dasein's* irresoluteness. *Dasein* masks and flees from the nugatory aspects of its Being, the existence in terms of which it understands itself (SZ, p. 285), by understanding itself in terms of its possibilities of Being-alongside while masking their character as possibilities.

In short, falling as antiphilosophy is a spiral "whirling" (SZ, p. 285) or vortex of ontico-ontological closure, the vanishing point of which would be the extinction of the ontological difference.

This circle is not fully stepped out in the published portion of *Being and Time*, no more than is the countermovement of self-transparency and the task of philosophical inquiry inscribed therein.[39] Once this is recognized, it also becomes possible to grasp why the account of authenticity and inauthenticity in *Being and Time*, as "*Dasein's* basic existentiell possibilities" (SZ, p. 350; cf. pp. 191, 304 and 328), must needs be preliminary and incomplete as well:

> Likewise, the terms "authenticity" and "inauthenticity," which are
> used in a preliminary fashion, do not imply a moral-existentiell or

35. *Vom Wesen des Grundes*, p. 42.
36. See esp. Fridolin Wiplinger, *Wahrheit und Geschichtlichkeit* (Munich: Alber, 1961), pp. 155–67.
37. Martin Heidegger, *Logik* (Frankfurt: Klostermann, 1976), p. 213.
38. Heidegger's post-*Kehre* modifications are not at issue here.
39. *Kant und das Problem*, p. 212.

an "anthropological" distinction, but rather a relation which, because hidden hitherto from philosophy, has yet to be thought for the first time, an "ecstatic" relation of the essence of man to the truth of Being.[40]

Let me now turn to the next two problematic phrases—"Being-alongside" and "inauthenticity"—as related to "falling." I want to discuss these together, because the same fundamental difficulty arises in each case. I already anticipated this common difficulty at the beginning of this paper by noting that, in *Being and Time*, the concept of falling seems to occur on two different levels: as an essential component of *Dasein's* care-structure and as a more precise determination of inauthentic existing, which is one of the two possibilities in respect to which that care-structure is interpreted. Is "falling" an essential component of the care-structure, having, like "project" and "thrownness," authenticity and inauthenticity as its existentiell modalizations? Or is "falling" the inauthentic existentiell modalization of the two other components?

The first of these two possibilities is maintained by Wiplinger:

> If falling constitutes an "essential ontological structure of *Dasein* itself," then this means that *no Dasein* is ever able to exist as not falling. However, this does not mean that the exhibited structures of disclosure are not to be understood as modes of closure. It does not mean that everything is now turned around, that *Dasein's* gaze is inescapably fixed at the ontic, the "world." Rather, *Dasein* can existentielly modify itself as falling into authenticity or inauthenticity.[41]

The second of these possibilities is maintained by Pöggeler and Tugendhat. In the latter's words:

> Heidegger has attempted to combine falling with thrownness and with project into a "structural whole" of disclosiveness under the title, "care." Falling, however, cannot be grasped as on the same level, *qua* formal structural moment, with thrownness and project. Instead, it is, structurally considered, *qua* "inauthenticity," a specific *modality*, though dominating the whole Being of *Dasein*, *of* thrownness and project alongside the other modality of "authenticity," which—as anxiety and resoluteness—likewise is a modality of thrownness as well as of project. But now these fundamental possibilities are not to remain placed merely indifferently next to each other and as mere modification vis-à-vis the formal structural moments, but rather are to be understood in the unity of a

40. *Über den Humanismus*, p. 21.
41. *Wahrheit und Geschichtlichkeit*, p. 220.

whole of movement. Only insofar as "the" disclosiveness is understood not as a "structural whole" but as a nexus of movement,
does it appear meaningful to see disclosiveness as a unity of
thrownness, project *and* falling. Even so, of course, the structural
heterogeneity of these moments cannot be overlooked: thrownness and project modify themselves in this movement, falling
characterizes the movement itself.[42]

Because Heidegger uses "falling" and "Being-alongside" interchangeably (SZ, pp. 192–93) — for the reasons I tried to present in
discussing falling as "Being-in-untruth" — the very same alternatives
have been raised in regard to "Being-alongside" as I have just presented in regard to "falling."[43] Several further permutations are possible here, depending on the understanding of "inauthenticity."
Heidegger states:

> Inauthenticity characterizes a kind of Being into which *Dasein* can
> divert itself and has for the most part always diverted itself; but
> *Dasein* does not necessarily and constantly have to divert itself into
> this kind of Being (SZ, p. 259).

If this claim is taken to mean that inauthenticity is simply a possible
existentiell modalization of the care-structure, then two possibilities
arise. Either falling is assimilated to inauthenticity so construed, in
which case Being-alongside is viewed as a formal, existential and
essential structure "always" constitutive of *Dasein's* existence and hence
sometimes authentic and sometimes fallingly inauthentic. This is
Friedrich Wilhelm von Herrmann's view.[44] Or Being-alongside is
assimilated to inauthenticity so construed, in which case there is an
authentic falling and inauthentic falling. This is the view held by
Michael E. Zimmerman.[45]

Two things can, I think, be confidently maintained in regard to the
possible construals just sketched. First, there is no textual warrant
whatsoever for the distinction between an authentic and inauthentic
falling (or Being-alongside). Heidegger nowhere draws this distinction.

Second, drawing this distinction nevertheless derives its plausibility
from the construal of inauthenticity outlined above. It is this construal
of inauthenticity that emerges as the underlying problem. This

42. *Der Wahrheitsbegriff*, pp. 316–18; see also Otto Pöggeler, *Der Denkweg Martin Heideggers* (Pfullingen: Neske, 1963), p. 210.

43. Wolfgang Müller-Lauter, *Möglichkeit und Wirklichkeit bei Martin Heidegger* (Berlin: de Gruyter, 1960), pp. 68–70.

44. Friedrich Wilhelm von Herrmann, *Die Selbstinterpretation Martin Heideggers* (Meisenheim: Hain, 1964), pp. 158–60.

45. "On Discriminating Everydayness," pp. 124–27.

emerges even more clearly in the light of another Heideggerian remark: "Inauthenticity belongs to the nature of factical *Dasein*. Authenticity is only a modification and not a total obliteration of inauthenticity."[46] This remark seems to elevate inauthenticity from a possible existentiell modalization of the care-structure to an existential structural component of care. Whereas this puts "inauthenticity" on a par with "falling" and "Being-alongside"—indeed makes these terms interchangeable—it clearly makes inauthenticity as an existentiell possibility problematic.[47]

I would suggest that the direction in which to look for a resolution of this complex aporia is found in two other remarks of Heidegger:

> The structures of *Dasein*, temporality itself, are not something like a constantly available frame [*Gerüst*] for a possible present-at-hand entity but rather, in terms of their ownmost [*eigensten*] meaning, possibilities of *Dasein* to be and only that.[48]
> This supposed "frame" participates in [*macht mit*] the mode of Being of *Dasein* (SZ, p. 176).

Although I do not pretend to fathom these two remarks, they clearly point to the need for an elaboration of the possibility character of *Dasein*, of the distinction between existentiell and existential possibility and of the dynamic modalizations that can obtain between them.

There is a further suggestion to be made in terms of the construal of falling I offered earlier. This concerns the dynamic character of falling as a movement. Heidegger's account of the temporalizing of authentic and inauthentic existence suggests that something like Aristotle's interpretation of rest as a limiting case of motion may illuminate modalities of falling pertinent to the preceding discussion (see SZ, pp. 338 and 344).

I have not yet directly discussed the final problematic notion relative to falling—everydayness. But it will be clear to anyone familiar with *Being and Time* that the two aporiae I have developed thus far can equally well be posed in terms of everydayness.[49]

There are of course further problems here, such as Heidegger's characterization of everydayness as a "peculiar indifference" vis-à-vis authenticity and inauthenticity.[50] But inasmuch as these problems are largely a function of the two already delineated, they can wait for another day.

46. *Grundprobleme der Phänomenologie*, p. 243.
47. See John Macquarrie, *An Existentialist Theology* (New York: Harper Torchbooks, 1965), p. 148.
48. *Logik*, p. 414.
49. See SZ, p. 85, on the aporia just developed, and *Kant und das Problem der Metaphysik*, p. 211, for the aporia developed first.
50. *Logik*, pp. 229-30.

Bibliography of Edward G. Ballard

I. BOOKS:

Art and Analysis (The Hague: Nijhoff, 1957), xiv, 220.

Socratic Ignorance, An Essay on Platonic Self-Knowledge (The Hague: Nijhoff, 1960), vi, 190.

Philosophy at the Crossroads (Baton Rouge: Louisiana State University Press, 1971), viii, 305.

Man and Technology: Toward the Measurement of a Culture (Pittsburgh: Duquesne University Press, 1977), x, 251.

Principles of a Descriptive Philosophy. Ohio U.P. Forthcoming.

II. TRANSLATED BOOKS:

The Philosophy of Jules Lachelier (An introduction to and a translation of his 1901 volume), (The Hague: Nijhoff, 1960), xv, 118.

Husserl, An Analysis of his Phenomenology (Foreword by E.G. Ballard, trans. E.G. Ballard and L.E. Embree), (Evanston, Illinois: Northwestern University Press, 1967), xxii, 238.

III. CONTRIBUTIONS TO BOOKS:

"Gabriel Marcel: The Mystery of Being," in *Existential Philosophers,* ed. George A. Schrader, Jr. (New York: McGraw-Hill, 1967), 209-260.

"Jules Lachelier," in *American Encyclopedia of Philosophy,* ed. Paul Edwards (1966), 374-5.

"Heidegger's View and Evaluation of Nature and Natural Science," in *Heidegger and the Path of Thinking,* ed. John Sallis, (Pittsburgh: Duquesne University Press, 1970), 37-64.

"The Visual Perception of Distance," in *Phenomenology in Perspective,* ed. F.J. Smith (The Hague: Nijhoff, 1970), 187-201.

"On the Method of Phenomenological Reduction, its Presuppositions and its Future," in *Life-World and Consciousness, Essays for Aron Gurwitsch,* ed.

Lester E. Embree (Evanston, Illinois: Northwestern University Press, 1972), 101-124.

"World and Culture," in *Essays in Humanity and Technology*, eds. D. Lovekin and D.P. Verene (Dixon, Illinois: Sauk Valley College, 1978), 3-29.

"The Sense of the Comic," in *Dictionary of the History of Ideas*, ed. P.P. Wiener (New York: Charles Scribners' Sons, 1973), Vol. I, pp. 467-470.

"The Sense of the Tragic," *op. cit.*, Vol. IV, pp. 411-417.

"Alms for Oblivion: An Essay on Experienced Time and Objective Time," in *Phenomenological Perspectives: Historical and Systematic Essays in Honor of Herbert Spiegelberg*, ed. Philip J. Bossert (The Hague: Martinus Nijhoff, 1975), pp. 168-187.

"On the Pattern of Phenomenological Method," in *Martin Heidegger in Europe and America* (The Hague: Martinus Nijhoff, 1973), pp. 183-193.

"A Brief Moral Discourse," in *Eros and Nihilism*, eds. Charles Bigger and David Cornay (Dubuque, Iowa: Kendall/Hunt Publishing Co., 1976), pp. 1-2.

"Toward a Phenomenology of Man," *Ibid.*, pp. 160-165.

"On Dialectic, Mechanical and Human," in *Communication Philosophy: The Human Condition in a Technological Age*, ed. Michael J. Hyde. (University of Alabama Press, 1981).

"Man or Technology: Which is to Rule," in *Phenomenology and the Understanding of Human Destiny*, ed. Stephen Skousgaard (Washington, D.C., The Univ. Press of America, 1981), pp. 3-19.

IV. *EDITED BOOK:*

Martin Heidegger: In Europe and America, eds. Edward G. Ballard and Charles E. Scott (The Hague: Martinus Nijhoff, 1973), pp. 200.

V. *ARTICLES*

"Of Poetic Knowledge," *Abstracts of Dissertations*, 1945-47, (Charlottesville, Virginia: University of Virginia Press, 1948), 78-81.

"Metaphysics and Metaphor," *Journal of Philosophy*, XLV, No. 8 (April 1948), 208-214.

"An Augustinian Theory of Signs," *The New Scholasticism*, (April 1949), 207-211.

"A Note for the Philosophy of History," *Journal of Philosophy*, XLVI, No. 2 (April 1949), 270-275.

"A Paradox of Measurement," *Philosophy of Science*, XVI, No. 2 (April 1949), 134-136.

"The Two Republics," *Education*, LXX, No. 10 (June 1950), 1-6.

"A Pattern in Poetry," *Journal of Education*, CXXXIV, No. 2 (Feb. 1951), 54-57.

"Faith and Platonic Philosophy," *Anglican Review of Theology*, XLIII, No. 2 (April 1951), 81-92.

"The Subject of Aristotle's Poetics," *The Personalist*, XXXII, No. 4 (Autumn 1951), 391-397.

"Reason and Convention," *Tulane Studies in Philosophy*, ed. James K. Feibleman I (1952), 21-42.

"Toward a Philosophy for Literature," *Hibbert Journal*, LI, No. 201 (Jan. 1953), 149-155.

"The Routine of Discovery," *Philosophy of Science*, XX, No. 2 (April 1953), 157-163.

"Truth and Insight into Value," *Tulane Studies in Philosophy*, ed. James K. Feibleman II (1953), 5-23.

"Method in Philosophy and Science," *The Personalist*, XXXIV, No. 3 (Summer 1953), 269-278.

"In Defense of Symbolic Aesthetics," *Journal of Aesthetics and Art Criticism*, XII, No. 1 (Sept. 1953) 38-43.

"Operationalism and Theory of Measurement," *Methodos*, V, No. 19 (1953), 233-239.

"Charity and Independence," *Anglican Review of Theology*, XXXVI, No. 2 (April 1954), 123-129.

"Some Reflections on Freedom," *The Southern Philosopher*, XXXVI, No. 2 (June 1954), 1-6.

"The Kantian Solution of the Problem of Man Within Nature," *Tulane Studies in Philosophy*, ed. James K. Feibleman III (1954), 7-40.

"The Unbinding of Prometheus," *Classical Journal*, L, No. 5 (Feb. 1955), 217-220.

"The Idealism of Jules Lachelier," *Review of Metaphysics*, VIII, No. 4 (June 1955), 685-705.

"An Estimate of Dewey's Art as Experience," *Tulane Studies in Philosophy*, IV (1955), 5-18.

"On the Nature and Use of Dialectic," *Philosophy of Science*, XXII, No. 3 (July 1955), 205-213. Japanese translation in *Americana*, II, No. 8 (Aug. 1956) 84-95.

"Literary Truth and Positivistic Criticism," *The Southern Philosopher*, V, No. 2 (April 1956), 1-6.

"Category and Paradox," *Tulane Studies in Philosophy*, V (1956), 5-23.

"Charity and Independence," reprinted in *Faculty Papers*, 4th Series, (1957), 13-21.

"Descartes Revision of the Cartesian Dualism," *Philosophical Quarterly*, VII, No. 4 (June 1957), 249-259.

"Individual and Person," *Philosophy and Phenomenological Research*, XVIII, No. 1 (Sept. 1957), 59-67.

"Plato's Movement from an Ethics of the Person to a Science of Particulars," *Tulane Studies in Philosophy*, VI (1957), 5-41.

"On Kant's Refutation of Metaphysics," *New Scholasticism*, (June 1958), 235-252.

"The Subject Matter of Philosophy," *Tulane Studies in Philosophy*, VII (1958), 5-26.

"On the Nature of Romanticism," *Tulane Studies in Philosophy*, VIII (1959), 61-95.

"On the Uses of Analogy in Philosophy," *Atti Del XII Congresso Internationale di Filosofia*, V (1960), 38-43.

"The Philosophy of Merleau-Ponty," *Tulane Studies in Philosophy,* IX (1960), 165-187.

"On Cognition of the Pre-Cognitive," *Philosophical Quarterly,* (July 1961), 238-244.

"Socrates' Problem," *Ethics,* LXXI, No. 4 (July 1961), 296-300.

"Kant, Whitehead, and the Philosophy of Mathematics," *Tulane Studies in Philosophy,* X (1961), 3-29.

"A Kantian Interpretation of the Special Theory of Relativity," *Kant-studien,* LII (1961), 401-410.

"On Parsing the Parmenides," *Review of Metaphysics,* XV, No. 3 (March 1962), 434-449.

"Husserl's Philosophy of Intersubjectivity in Relation to his Rational Ideal," *Tulane Studies in Philosophy,* XI (1962), 3-38.

"A Use for Atheism in Ethics," *Journal of Religion and Mental Health,* II (Winter 1963), 150-155.

"A Brief Introduction to the Philosophy of Martin Heidegger," *Tulane Studies in Philosophy,* XII (1964), 106-151.

"On Ritual and Persuasion in the Philosophy of Plato," *Southern Journal of Philosophy,* II (1964), 49-55.

"A Demonstration of Being," Acts of XIII International Congress of Philosophy (for 1964), *Memorials Del XIII Congresso Internacional de Filosofia,* de Septiembre de 1963, IX (Mexico, 1964), 45-51.

"Renaissance Space and the Humean Development in Philosophical Psychology," *Tulane Studies in Philosophy,* XIII (1964), 55-80.

"Truth and Subjectivity," *Tulane Studies in Philosophy,* XIV (1965), 3-12.

"On Being and the Meaning of Being," *Southern Journal of Philosophy,* IV, No. 4 (1966), 248-265.

"On Truth, Its Nature, Context, and Source," *Man and World,* I, No. 1 (1968), 113-136.

"Toward a Phenomenology of Man," *Proceedings of the American Catholic Philosophical Association* (Washington, D.C.: The Catholic University of America, 1968), 169-174.

"On Good and Evil in Philosophy of Art and Aesthetic Theory," *Southern Journal of Philosophy,* VII, No. 3 (1969), 273-288.

"Beyond and Aside from Existentialism," *The Southern Review,* VI (NS), No. 3 (1970), 830-842.

"On the Pattern of Phenomenological Method," *Southern Journal of Philosophy,* VIII, No. 4 (1970), 421-432.

"On the Phenomenon of Obligation," *Tulane Studies in Philosophy,* XXI (1972), 139-157.

"Unmasking the Person," *The Southern Journal of Philosophy,* XI, Nos. 1 & 2 (1973), pp. 7-14.

"The Nature of the Object as Experienced," in *Research in Phenomenology,* IV (1976), pp. 105-138.

"The Idea of Being: A Platonic Speculation," *Tulane Studies in Philosophy,* XXVII ed. Robert C. Wittlemore (1978), pp. 13-25.

VI. *CRITICAL REVIEWS:*

"Art and the Universe," (Review of *The World of Art* by Paul Weiss) *The Yale Review,* (Summer 1961), 610-612.

"Heidegger on Bringing Kant to Stand," (Review of *What is a Thing?* by M. Heidegger) *Southern Journal of Philosophy,* VII, No. 1 (1969), 91-103.

"Faith in Athens and in Jerusalem," (Review of *Athens and Jerusalem* by L. Shestov) *Man and World,* II, No. 2 (1969), 302-309.

"What Is Technology?" (Review of *Techniques and Praxis* by Don Ihde) *Journal of Phenomenological Psychology,* 1981. pp. 165-173.

(Also about 25 short reviews in various periodicals.)

About the Contributors

HAROLD ALDERMAN is Professor of Philosophy at Sonoma State University. He is the author of *Nietzsche's Gift* (1979) as well as numerous articles on a variety of philosophical themes. Currently on a grant from the National Endowment for the Humanities, he is writing a book on the nature of philosophy.

C. ANITA H. BIGGER received her Ph.D. in microbiology from Louisiana State University, Baton Rouge, Louisiana, in 1971. She was awarded a National Institute of Health Fellowship for postdoctoral work in molecular biology at the University of Edinburgh, Scotland, in 1972. Since 1976, she has been staff scientist in the Chemical Carcinogenesis Program of the National Cancer Institute Frederick Cancer Research Facility, Frederick Maryland, where she studies interactions of chemical carcinogens with DNA.

CHARLES P. BIGGER is Professor of Philosophy at Louisiana State University. His major interests have been in the area of the history of philosophy. His focus is mainly on Plato, Kant, Whitehead, Husserl, and Heidegger.

BERNARD P. DAUENHAUER (Ph.D. Tulane) is Professor of Philosophy at the University of Georgia. He is the author of *Silence: The Phenomenon and Its Ontological Significance* and of articles published in *Review of Metaphysics, Research in Phenomenology,* and several other philosophical journals.

LESTER EMBREE (Ph.D., New School, 1972) is Professor of Philosophy at Duquesne University. His B.A. is from Tulane University, where he studied with E. G. Ballard, with whom he subsequently translated Paul Ricoeur's *Husserl: An Analysis of His Phenomenology* (Northwestern University Press, 1967). He has published widely in Constitutive Phenomenology, Philosophy of the Human Sciences, and History of Modern Philosophy.

EDWARD HUGH HENDERSON received the Ph.D. in philosophy from Tulane University where, while studying with Professor Ballard, he first became interested in the idea of 'archaic experience.' From 1964-1966 he taught philosophy at Westminster College in Missouri and then came to Louisiana State University in Baton Rouge where he is now associate professor and chairman. Professor Henderson has published on themes in philosophical anthropology and philosophical theology in *Philosophy Today, Man and World, The Anglican Theology Review,* and the *International Journal for Philosophy of Religion.*

CAROL A. KATES is an Associate Professor of Philosophy at Ithaca College. Her research and publications have focused on issues in phenomenology, linguistics, and the philosophy of art, most recently in *Pragmatics and Semantics* (Cornell University Press, 1980).

DAVID FARRELL KRELL is Associate Professor on the Faculty of Languages and Literatures of the University of Mannheim, West Germany. Dr. Krell has edited and co-translated Martin Heidegger's *Basic Writings, Early Greek Thinking,* and *Nietzsche.* He is the author of numerous articles in scholarly journals and of the forthcoming monograph *On the Verge: A Philosophy of Memory and Recollection.*

ANDREW J. RECK is Professor and Chairman of the Department of Philosophy at Tulane University. He is the author of *Recent American Philosophy* (1964), *The New American Philosophers* (1968), and *Speculative Philosophy* (1972). His edition of George Herbert Mead's *Selected Writings* was published by the University of Chicago Press in 1981.

JOHN SALLIS is Chairman of the Philosophy Department at Duquesne University. He studied at Tulane University and at the University of Freiburg. He is the author of *Phenomenology and the Return to Beginnings* (1973), *Being and Logos: The Way of Platonic Dialogue* (1975), and *The Gathering of Reason* (1980) and the founder and editor of *Research in Phenomenology.*

JOHN SCANLON is Professor of Philosophy at Duquesne University. Professor Ballard was director of his Ph.D. dissertation in 1968: "Edmund Husserl's Conception of Philosophy as Rigorous Science." He translated Edmund Husserl's lectures, *Phenomenological Psychology* (Nijhoff, 1977) and is the author of several articles dealing with phenomenological topics. He is presently translating Wilhelm Dilthey's *Der Aufbau der Geschichtlichen Welt in den Geisteswissenschaften* to be published by Princeton University Press.

CHARLES SCOTT is Professor of Philosophy at Vanderbilt University. With Professor Ballard he edited *Martin Heidegger: In Europe and America.* He is also author of *Boundaries in Mind: A Study of Immediate Awareness Based in Psychotherapy* (1982).

DR. ALEXANDER VON SCHOENBORN is Associate Professor of Philosophy at The University of Missouri-Columbia. He has taught at Fordham University and The University of Texas-Austin and has been a Visiting Fellow in Austrilia and Germany. His focal concerns in the history of philosophy have been Kant, Hegel and Heidegger.

MICHAEL E. ZIMMERMAN, Associate Professor of Philosophy at Tulane University, wrote his Ph.D. dissertation under the direction of Edward G. Ballard. In 1979, he was awarded the Mortar Board Award for teaching excellence, presented annually by students of Newcomb College of Tulane University. His book, *Eclipse of the Self,* appeared in the spring of 1981.